Contents

How to Use This Book

This book will help you and your students discover how God's people can celebrate God's gifts to us as they participate in a variety of holiday Bible lessons.

If you are a teacher or small-group leader in any children's program (Sunday School, second hour, mid-week, etc.),

1. Look at the Contents to see a list of the holidays in this book: seasonal and church calendar holidays as well as Hebrew holidays celebrated by God's people in the Old Testament.

2. Skim through one lesson to see the kinds of resources provided: Bible story, object talk, art activity, active game, coloring page, puzzle page.

3. As each holiday approaches, consider which of the resources in the appropriate lesson you can use with your class. You may wish to add an activity or two to your existing curriculum, or you may wish to replace the entire lesson.

If you are the children's pastor,

1. Follow the directions in number one and two above.

2. Several weeks prior to a holiday, photocopy the appropriate lesson and provide it to teachers and small-group leaders so they can become familiar with the lesson content and prepare materials to supplement or replace their existing lesson.

3. Consider planning a special elective class that will help children gain an understanding of the Old Testament holidays God designed to help His provision and gifts (see Bible lessons on pp. 117-237).

AGES 6-12

Gospel Light's

BIG BOOK

OF HOLIDAY AND BIBLE CELEBRATIONS

30 Ready-to-Use Bible Lessons for Ages 6 to 12

- 14 seasonal holiday lessons
- 16 lessons about Bible-times celebrations
- Great time-saving resource

Reproducible!

Gospel Light

How to Make Clean Copies from This Book

Editorial Staff

Founder, Dr. Henrietta Mears • **Publisher Emeritus,** William T. Greig • **Publisher, Children's Curriculum and Resources,** Bill Greig III • **Senior Consulting Publisher,** Dr. Elmer L. Towns • **Product Line Manager,** Cary Maxon • **Senior Managing Editor,** Sheryl Haystead • **Senior Consulting Editor,** Wesley Haystead, M.S.Ed. • **Senior Editor, Biblical and Theological Issues,** Bayard Taylor, M.Div. • **Editorial Team,** Mary Davis, Carol Eide • **Art Directors,** Lenndy McCullough, Christina Renée Sharp, Samantha A. Hsu • **Designer,** Zelle Olson

Thanksgiving
Song of Thankfulness

Bible Verse

The Lord is my strength and my song; he has become my salvation. He is my God, and I will praise him. Exodus 15:2

Bible Story Reference

Exodus 14,15

FOCUS

Give thanks to God for His care for us.

Teacher's Devotional

Americans and Canadians often consider Thanksgiving a holiday linked to their national histories, calling up images of Pilgrims and explorers, of wars ended and feasts made to declare friendship with native peoples. However, at least eight countries worldwide have a declared day of national thanksgiving and most cultures celebrate the bounty of the year's harvest in some way. Certainly God's mandate to ancient Israel to celebrate the Feast of Tabernacles, thanking God for His goodness, lays the pattern for all these celebrations (see Leviticus 23:33-43) and for those examples of thankfulness found throughout the Bible, such as today's story of celebration after the Israelites' deliverance from Egypt.

In the United States, occasional days of thanksgiving were sometimes declared; but in 1863, because of the efforts of Sarah Josepha Hale, President Lincoln finally declared a national holiday of thanksgiving to be kept yearly. In his proclamation, he declared:

No human counsel hath devised nor hath any mortal hand worked out these great things. They are the gracious gifts of the Most High God, who, while dealing with us in anger for our sins, hath nevertheless remembered mercy. It has seemed to me fit and proper that they should be solemnly, reverently and gratefully acknowledged as with one heart and voice by the whole American People. I do therefore invite my fellow citizens in every part of the United States . . . to set apart and observe the last Thursday of November next, as a day of Thanksgiving and Praise to our beneficent Father who dwelleth in the Heavens. And I recommend to them that while offering up the ascriptions justly due to Him for such singular deliverances and blessings, they do also, with humble penitence for our national perverseness and disobedience . . . fervently implore the interposition of the Almighty Hand to heal the wounds of the nation and to restore it as soon as may be consistent with the Divine purposes to the full enjoyment of peace, harmony, tranquillity and Union.

In whatever country we live, these truths remain: God is good and we depend daily on His mercy and grace, which are always far more than we deserve. Because of Him, we always have a great deal to celebrate! Take delight in sharing His goodness!

Story Center

Materials
Bible.

Before the Story
Guide students to briefly practice signs for underlined words.

When has someone told you thank-you?

Today we're going to hear about a time God's people did something special to say thank-you to God.

Tell the Story
As you tell the story, lead students in responding as shown when you say the underlined words.

1. Moses and the Israelites had been slaves in <u>Egypt</u>. But then God set them free! He showed His mighty power and finally Pharaoh, the ruler of <u>Egypt</u>, agreed to let the people leave. The people quickly hurried away from <u>Egypt</u>. They wouldn't have to be slaves any longer! Hundreds and thousands of Israelite people followed Moses away from <u>Egypt</u>. And all the time, God showed them where to go. During the day, God sent a big cloud to move in front of them. At night, God sent a tall pillar of fire to guide them, so they always knew where to go.

2. Late one afternoon the Israelites came to a big sea called the Red Sea, or the Sea of Reeds. Just as everyone was setting up their tents, Moses and the people heard a loud rumbling sound. *Was it thunder?* they wondered. No! It was the sound of horses and chariots and <u>soldiers</u>! Pharaoh, the king of Egypt, and his <u>army</u> were rumbling closer, coming to take the Israelites back to Egypt!

3. The Israelites looked around. They felt like running—but there was nowhere to go! The <u>sea</u> was in front of them and the soldiers were coming right behind them! The people were angry and afraid. "Why did you bring us here to die?" they shouted at Moses. "We can't go forward because of the <u>sea</u>. We can't go back because of the soldiers. What can we do?"

4. "Don't be afraid," Moses said. "God will help us." And Moses was right! Before Pharaoh and his soldiers could reach the Israelites, God moved the big <u>cloud</u> right in front of the Egyptians. The <u>cloud</u> made the sky so dark the Egyptians had to stop. They couldn't see anything!

1. Egypt: Crooked right index finger on forehead.

2. Soldiers, army: Right fist below left shoulder; left fist several inches below right.

3. Sea: Touch lips a few times; move hands forward in wavy motion.

4. Cloud: Curve raised hands; make circular movements to side.

5. Then God told Moses, "Hold your hand over the shore of the sea." As Moses lifted his hand, a big <u>wind</u> began to roar through the night. All night long the <u>wind</u> blew. It blew so hard that the waters of the sea began to separate. The <u>wind</u> made the wet ground dry. Soon there was a big dry path right through the MIDDLE of the sea!

6. The people felt like cheering! Quickly, they lined up and <u>walked</u> after Moses along the dry path. All of the Israelite families and their animals <u>walked</u> across the floor of the sea on dry ground, with a wall of water on their right and a wall of water on their left. And they all <u>walked</u> across safely. No one even got WET!

7. But Pharaoh's <u>army</u> hadn't gone away. They were still right behind them! The horses and chariots and soldiers rushed right after the Israelites down the path through the sea. But once Pharaoh and all the <u>army</u> were in the middle of the path, God showed His power once again. God told Moses to stretch his hand out over the sea. As Moses did, the wind stopped. The walls of water came CRASH-ING down—right over Pharaoh's <u>army</u>!

8. The Israelites looked back over the sea. There were no soldiers, no chariots and no Pharaoh to hurt them or take them back to slavery. God had saved them again! Every-one was VERY happy! And they wanted to show God how thankful they were for their safety. Moses made up a <u>song</u> to praise and thank God for His great power. His sister, Miriam, and all the women joined in, <u>singing</u> and dancing and playing instruments to show their love for God. It was the biggest celebration and the best party they had ever seen. And it was all because of God and His power!

5. Wind: Hold hands in front; move in unison along curved path.

6. Walk: Alternately move hands back and forth.

7. Army: Right fist below left shoulder; left fist several inches below right.

8. Song, singing: Move right hand back and forth in front of left palm.

● ●

Discussion Questions

Who helped the Israelites leave Egypt? (God showed His power to force Pharaoh to let them go.) **How did God help them?** (Kept the Egyptian army away with a cloud. Sent a wind and made a path through the Red Sea.) **How did the Israelites show their thanks and celebrate?** (Sang and danced.)

   It's easy to forget about the good things God gives us or to take them for granted. But when we stop and think about what our lives would be like with-out God's care for us, we want to celebrate and thank Him!

Thanksgiving
Object Talk

Scripture Background
Exodus 14, 15

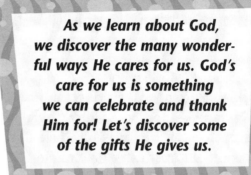

As we learn about God, we discover the many wonderful ways He cares for us. God's care for us is something we can celebrate and thank Him for! Let's discover some of the gifts He gives us.

Materials
Bible with bookmark at Exodus 15:2, cornucopia or large basket, magazine pictures of good things God has given us (food, family, friends, church, parks, school, nature items—one picture for each student, including several examples from each category).

Prepare the Activity
Place pictures in cornucopia or large basket.

Lead the Activity
1. Ask a volunteer to take a picture from the cornucopia or basket, identifying the picture for the entire group. **What is one thing about this picture that makes you want to thank God?** Repeat, using a different volunteer for each picture in the cornucopia or basket.

2. At your signal, students group themselves into categories according to their pictures. Repeat as time allows, having students select new pictures.

3. **What are some of the things people do to show their thankfulness?** (Say "thank you." Write thank-you notes.) **In several countries around the world, such as the United States, Canada, Brazil and Argentina, Thanksgiving Day is celebrated to thank God for the good things He gives.** (Optional: If your students celebrate Thanksgiving, invite volunteers to tell about their family celebrations.)

Conclude
Read Exodus 15:2 aloud. **What are some of the ways we can praise God for the good things He gives us?** (Sing songs that thank God. Read God's Word. Pray to God.) Pray, thanking God for His loving care and the good things He has given us.

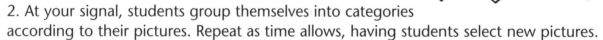

Additional Information for Older Students
The United States and Canada celebrate Thanksgiving Day in similar ways but on different days. In Canada, Thanksgiving Day is celebrated on the second Monday in October. Canada's Parliament, in 1957, decreed it should be "a day of general thanksgiving to almighty God for the bountiful harvest with which Canada has been blessed." In the United States, Thanksgiving Day is celebrated on the last Thursday in November. President Abraham Lincoln issued a proclamation in 1863 to set this day aside "as a day of Thanksgiving and Praise to our beneficent Father."

Thanksgiving

Active Game Center: Pumpkin Praise

Materials

Four to eight pumpkins of any size for every 10 students, black permanent markers.

Prepare the Game

Arrange pumpkins to create an obstacle course in your playing area (see sketch). Create one obstacle course for every 10 students. Place a marker next to the last pumpkin in each course.

> *Thanksgiving time reminds us to give thanks to God for His care for us. Let's play a game to thank God for the great things He has given us.*

Lead the Game

1. Students line up in a single-file line at the beginning of the obstacle course. Demonstrate how to complete the obstacle course (which order and direction to run around each pumpkin, whether to circle around each pumpkin or just pass by it, etc.). **When you reach the last pumpkin in your course, use the marker to write or draw on the pumpkin something for which you are thankful. What is something that you are thankful for?** Print volunteer's response on the pumpkin as an example.

2. At your signal, first student in line begins obstacle course. When student has finished course and written on pumpkin, he or she tags the next student in line who begins obstacle course. Continue until each student has had a turn. Then ask volunteers to tell their responses from the pumpkins.

Options

1. Instead of using real pumpkins, cut pumpkin shapes from orange construction paper or make your own paper-bag pumpkins by painting or coloring small paper bags orange, stuffing them with newspaper and tying bags closed with green yarn.

2. Challenge older students to roll an ear of dried corn through the obstacle course or to complete the course while walking on knees, hopping while holding on to one foot, etc.

3. Help younger students by allowing them to dictate responses for you to write on pumpkins.

• •

Discussion Questions

1. *What are some ways God cares for your family?*

2. *How can you show God that you are thankful for His love and care?* (Name the things you are thankful for when you pray. Write God a thank-you prayer. Sing praise songs to Him.)

3. *What is your favorite way to tell God thank-you?*

Art Center: Cornucopia Construction

Materials

Two large sheets of brown construction paper, tape, scissors, pencils, colored construction paper, staplers, newspaper, markers.

Prepare the Activity

Tape sheets of paper together and then roll and tape them to form cornucopia. Trim as shown (see sketch a). Make a sample stuffed vegetable shape, following directions below.

> *Giving thanks to God is something we can do every day of the year. Some countries have special holidays during which they remember to give thanks. Let's make something that was used by the earliest people who celebrated the Thanksgiving holiday.*

Lead the Activity

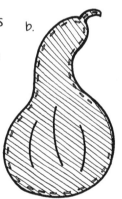

a.

Cut on dotted line.

tape

1. Show paper cornucopia. **What is this called?** (A cornucopia, or horn of plenty.) **Cornucopias are traditionally filled with lots of nuts and vegetables to show the good food God gives to eat. We're going to fill our cornucopia with some of the good things for which we're thankful to God.**

2. Students draw outlines of fruits, vegetables or nuts on colored paper (apple, pumpkin, zucchini, crookneck squash, walnut, pecan, corn, etc.). Students place second sheet of colored paper behind drawings and then cut around their drawing, making sure to cut through both layers of paper. Students staple around edges of cutout shapes, stapling layers together but leaving a gap (see sketch b).

b.

3. Students draw details of fruits, vegetables or nuts on one side of shapes and write or draw things for which they are thankful on the other side of the shapes. Students crumple up individual sheets of newspaper and stuff them in through the gap, filling their shapes before stapling them shut. Students place completed shapes in and around paper cornucopia.

Options

1. Students may make and decorate as many shapes as time allows. Students may also make their own paper cornucopias.

2. Encourage older students to help younger students with cutting, stapling and stuffing.

• •

Discussion Questions

1. *How does God care for you? For what would you like to thank God?*

2. *What other things does God give all people in the world?* (His love. Beautiful nature. Forgiveness of sins and eternal life when we believe in Jesus and ask for forgiveness.)

3. *What are some ways to give thanks to God?* (Sing Him a song of thanks. Tell Him what you are thankful for when you pray.)

Draw a picture of something you thank God for:

TAKE NOTE!

Exodus 15:2

The Challenge → Make a joyful noise to the Lord! For this puzzle, you have to be able to read music (sort of!). Use the music-note code to write out the verse that will be music to your ears!

Advent

Prophets Tell of Promise

Bible Verse

For to us a child is born, to us a son is given, and the government will be on his shoulders. And he will be called Wonderful Counselor, Mighty God, Everlasting Father, Prince of Peace. Isaiah 9:6

Bible Story Reference

Isaiah 9:1-7; Micah 1; 5:2-4

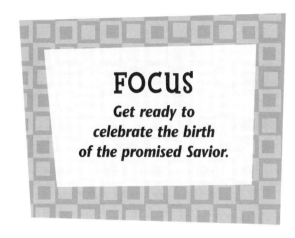

FOCUS

Get ready to celebrate the birth of the promised Savior.

Teacher's Devotional

In the modern world, we tend to be skeptical of a promise and may even steel ourselves for the sting of its never being fulfilled. We've learned to take a wait-and-see attitude toward promises, not wanting to trust them too deeply. However, Advent is the time when Christians all over the world celebrate promises being kept, expectations giving rise to reality.

"Advent" means coming or arrival. The Church celebration begins with the fourth Sunday before Christmas and continues through Christmas Eve. It is a time to celebrate Christ's coming, recalling His first advent as our Savior and preparing ourselves for His second coming as King of kings. Advent acknowledges that we live both in fulfillment and in expectation. Jesus has come to us in His first advent, fulfilling God's promises, but we still expectantly prepare ourselves for His return.

Although Advent may not be officially observed in some churches, it provides wonderful hands-on opportunities to pass on the truths and joys of seeing God's promises fulfilled! In many churches, colors of purple and royal blue are used to call to mind the arrival of royalty. The candles on an Advent wreath are lit each Sunday, each candle helping us focus on an aspect of waiting for the promised Savior.

For hundreds of years, promises of the coming Messiah were all that God's people had. Today we live in the fulfillment of those promises! Jesus has come, lighting the entire world with hope, illuminating our lives with His presence. Read John 1:1-9 for a description of Jesus' coming. There could be no more wondrous reason to celebrate!

Story Center

Materials
Bible.

Before the Story
Guide students to briefly practice signs for underlined words.

Tell the Story

As you tell the story, lead students in responding as shown when you say the underlined words.

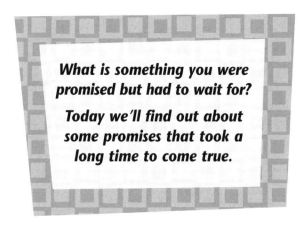

What is something you were promised but had to wait for?

Today we'll find out about some promises that took a long time to come true.

1. Many years after Solomon built the Temple in Jerusalem, there lived a man named Isaiah. Isaiah was a prophet, a person who told the people messages from God. God spoke to Isaiah about many things and Isaiah <u>wrote</u> them down. Isaiah <u>wrote</u> about things that would happen in the countries around Israel. He also <u>wrote</u> about terrible things that would happen to the people of Israel because they had not obeyed God.

2. Isaiah's book could have been a very sad book, but it wasn't. Here's why: In that book, God made wonderful <u>promises</u>! God <u>promised</u> that a baby would be born who would make everyone glad. This baby would be the Savior—the One who would save people from the punishment their sins deserved!

3. This Savior sent by God would be the greatest <u>King</u> of all time. His kingdom would never come to an end! This <u>King</u> would be known by many names. One name was the Wonderful Counselor, because He would teach His people how to follow God and He would give them wisdom.

4. Isaiah also called this Savior the Mighty <u>God</u>, the Everlasting Father and the Prince of Peace. All these names meant that the Savior would not be an ordinary man. He would be <u>God's</u> own Son. And He would be the One who would bring peace to those people who would let Him rule their lives.

1. Wrote: Touch thumb and right index finger; make wavy line across left palm.

2. Promises: Right index finger on lips; move to open hand on left fist.

3. King: Right thumb between index and middle fingers; move from shoulder to waist.

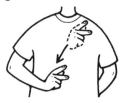

4. God: Point right index finger; lower and open hand at chest.

5. About the same time that Isaiah was telling God's messages, God sent another prophet to warn the people of Israel. Micah told the people that God wanted them to <u>stop</u> cheating each other and <u>stop</u> hurting the poor people. Micah also warned the people about terrible things that were going to happen very soon—things that really did happen, just as God said they would. But the most important thing Micah told about didn't happen until 700 years later.

5. Stop: Hit open left hand with edge of right open hand.

6. Micah told the people God's promise that a <u>ruler</u> would be born in Bethlehem, even though Bethlehem was a little town and didn't seem very important. Micah said that this <u>ruler</u> would be different from any other <u>ruler</u> they had ever known. When the people heard about this <u>ruler</u>, they knew that He would not be an ordinary man. He would be specially sent by God. It was another promise about the coming Savior!

6. Ruler: Move hands as though holding reins.

7. In many places in the Old Testament, God told His people things about the future and made <u>promises</u> about the coming Savior. Even at the very beginning of the Bible, when Adam and Eve had sinned, God had <u>promised</u> them that a Savior would come—a Savior who would make it possible for Adam and Eve and everyone in the world to be rescued from the punishment their sins deserved.

7. Promises: Right index finger on lips; move to open hand on left fist.

8. When the people heard God's promises to send a Savior, they were happy at the news. It wasn't long, however, before many people <u>forgot</u> to obey God. The sad things that God had said would happen, happened. But God did not <u>forget</u> His people. The GLAD things God promised happened, too! For 700 years later, in a little, unimportant town called Bethlehem, a great King WAS born. He is still the greatest King of all time! Do you know His name?

8. Forget: Move open hand on forehead to closed hand on the right.

• •

Discussion Questions

What do prophets do? (Tell God's messages to people.) **What are some of the things Isaiah told God's people?** (That God would send a Savior.) **What things did Micah tell the people?** (To obey God. That a ruler would be born in Bethlehem.)

   For hundreds of years after these prophets lived, God's people waited for God to keep His promise to send a Savior. And He did! While we get ready to celebrate Christmas, we can also get our minds and hearts ready to celebrate the birth of the King—Jesus!

Advent

Object Talk

Scripture Background
Isaiah 9:1-7

Materials
Bible with bookmark at Isaiah 9:6, Advent wreath and candles; optional—picture of Advent wreath, matches.

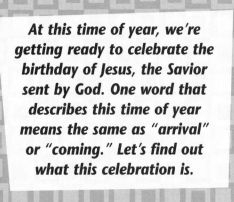

At this time of year, we're getting ready to celebrate the birthday of Jesus, the Savior sent by God. One word that describes this time of year means the same as "arrival" or "coming." Let's find out what this celebration is.

Lead the Activity

1. **What are some ways your family gets ready to celebrate Jesus' birth?** Volunteers answer. **A word that some people use when they talk about getting ready to celebrate Jesus' birth is the word "Advent." Advent not only describes the season of the year in which we celebrate Jesus' birth, but it also describes four Sundays before Christmas when we can especially look forward or get ready to celebrate Christmas.**

2. Show Advent wreath. (Optional: Show picture of Advent wreath.) **On the first Sunday of Advent only the first candle is lit.** (Optional: Light candles as you describe them.) **The first candle is called the Hope candle. It reminds us of Old Testament times when God's people hoped and waited for the Savior God had promised to send. On each of the following Sundays, another candle is lit. The second, or Peace candle, reminds us of the peace Jesus gives us. The third, or Joy candle, reminds us of the joy we feel at Jesus' birth. The fourth, or Love candle, reminds us of God's love for us and our love for God. Sometimes a fifth candle, called the Christ candle, is placed in the center of the Advent wreath. It is lit on Christmas Eve or Christmas Day to remind us of Jesus' birth.** (Optional: As each candle is explained, invite volunteers to suggest a motion for the name of each candle. Ask students to describe other objects used at Advent—calendars, daily Advent candle, etc.)

Conclude

The prophet Isaiah looked forward to the coming of God's promised Savior. Listen to what Isaiah wrote. Read Isaiah 9:6 aloud. **This verse reminds us that Jesus is the reason we celebrate!** Pray, thanking God for His love and for sending His Son, Jesus.

• •

Additional Information for Older Students

What colors of candles have you seen in Advent wreaths? Students tell. **Three purple candles are sometimes used in Advent wreaths to remind us of God's royalty. A pink or rose candle may be used for the Joy candle. The Christ candle is usually white and reminds us that Jesus is the light of the world.**

Advent not only celebrates Jesus' birth and the first time He came to earth, but it's also a time to look forward to His return! (Optional: Read Acts 1:9-11.)

Active Game Center: Ring Toss

Materials

Paper plates; scissors; measuring stick; stapler; butcher paper; marker; filled, small plastic water bottle; scratch paper; pencils.

Prepare the Game

Cut the center section out of two paper plates, leaving a ring at least 1 inch (2.5 cm) wide. Staple the plates together, one on top of the other, to create a sturdy ring (see sketch a). On a 3x3-foot (.9x.9-m) square of butcher paper, draw and number sections and place water bottle as shown in sketch b.

The season when people get ready to celebrate the birth of Jesus, the promised Savior, is called Advent. Let's play a game with things that will remind us of Advent and help us think about getting ready to celebrate Jesus' birthday.

Lead the Game

1. Students line up approximately 4 feet (1.2 m) from prepared paper. Give the paper-plate ring to the first student in line.

2. At your signal, the first student tosses the ring at the bottle. Student determines points based on where ring lands, retrieves ring and gives it to next student in line. (Note: A ring that circles the bottle scores 10 points.) Next student repeats action. Students keep track of points on scratch paper. Student with the highest score when you call stop answers one of the Discussion Questions below. Repeat play as time allows.

Options

1. Prepare a separate game for each group of eight students.

2. Use heavy-weight paper plates or poster board to make rings.

3. To challenge older students, group them in teams of two or three. Teams earn a letter in "Advent" with every 10 points scored. Continue until one team has earned all the letters in "Advent."

4. Use age and ability of students to determine distance from which ring is tossed.

. . . .

Discussion Questions

1. *What do you do to get ready for school? to go on a trip? to celebrate Christmas?*

2. *What do you and your family do to get ready to celebrate Christmas? Which of those celebrations especially remind you of Jesus' birth?*

3. *How can you get ready to celebrate Jesus' birth?* (Thank God that He sent Jesus. Sing songs to worship God. Prepare gifts for others to celebrate Jesus' birth.)

Art Center: Advent Wreaths

Materials

Materials for the wreath option of your choice; optional—a sample wreath.

Lead the Activity

Lead students in making wreaths.

Greenery Wreaths

Give each student a Styrofoam round or a green florist foam circle. Student pushes candles into round or foam. Students lay pine boughs or other greenery between candles, or stick greenery ends into base of wreath (see sketch a).

Paper-Plate Wreaths

Give each student a sturdy, white paper plate. Students use markers to decorate the plates as wreaths, drawing branches and other decorations such as holly berries. Each student attaches five small candles to his or her wreath using small mounds of green clay (see sketch b). (Optional: Place greens on plate instead of drawing greenery.)

Handprint Wreaths

Students trace and cut out handprints, gluing them together to form wreaths. Glue wreaths to individual sheets of paper. Students draw candles on wreaths (see sketch c).

> One of the ways to get ready to celebrate the birth of Jesus, the promised Savior, is to make wreaths with candles to light each Sunday before the celebration of His birth. These wreaths are called Advent wreaths because "Advent" means arrival or coming. Let's make our own wreaths to take home and use with our families.

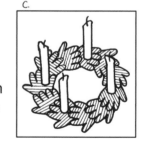

Options

1. Add additional decorations such as holly berries, miniature Christmas ornaments, strings of Christmas tree beads, Christmas ribbons or individually wrapped Christmas candies.

2. Students decorate classroom with evergreens, sometimes called "the hanging of the greens." Evergreens are the traditional symbol of the everlasting life we have in Christ, but any type of greenery can be used. Wrap greens around wire hangers that have been bent into a circle, or hang tied boughs of greens with a hook. Garlands of greens can also be strung around the room.

Discussion Questions

1. **Who was the promised Savior the Old Testament prophets told about?** (Jesus.)

2. **Because Jesus came to live on earth, what do we learn about God?** (God loves all people. God made a way for our sins to be forgiven.)

3. **Who has helped you learn about the coming of Jesus as our Savior?**

"For to us a child is born, to us a son is given." Isaiah 9:6

PROPHET-SHARING

Isaiah 9:1-7; Micah 5:2-5

The Challenge → God chose men called prophets to tell people about Jesus before He was even born! Can you trace this prophet's journey to Bethlehem to see Jesus?

Ready or not, here He comes!

The Super Challenge → Use the map to write down a special message from God for you. The first clue is done for you. Follow the clues to finish your message.

4-F   5-A   2-B   1-D   2-E   3-A   4-D   3-E   3-C   5-F

Cele _____ __ ___ ____ _____ _____ _____.

Christmas Story 1
An Angel Visits Mary

Bible Verse
My soul glorifies the Lord and my spirit rejoices in God my Savior. Luke 1:46,47

Bible Story Reference
Luke 1:26-56

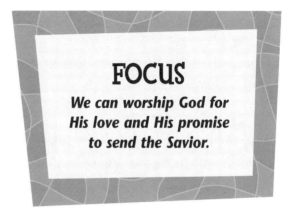

FOCUS

We can worship God for His love and His promise to send the Savior.

Teacher's Devotional

Have you ever been so astounded that you were unable to think or to speak? Mary certainly was! There before her stood the angel Gabriel! To her credit, Mary calmed down quickly and was able both to absorb Gabriel's announcement and to actually converse with the angel! After Gabriel made the astonishing claim that she would be the mother of the Son of the Most High whose kingdom will never end, she simply asked, "How will this be, since I am a virgin?" Once satisfied about the physical realities, encouraged by the news that her relative Elizabeth was also expecting a child and reminded that nothing is impossible with God, she replied with defining grace: "I am the Lord's servant. May it be to me as you have said." Many questions were yet unanswered; a myriad of painful implications would later come to mind. Yet she determined early on that she was the Lord's servant. Long before her Son prayed, "Your will be done" (see Luke 22:42), she lived a life in which every issue was clarified by her gracious, humble acceptance of God's will.

When Mary entered Elizabeth's door, John leapt for joy in Elizabeth's womb; and she was filled with the Holy Spirit, blessing Mary in the name of the Lord. Mary responded with a lyrical statement that has been the basis for songs ever since. This hymn of praise is often called "The Magnificat" (*magnificat*—"glorifies"—is the first word of the Latin translation). Like a psalm, it focuses on God, rejoicing in His deliverance of His people and of His mercy to Mary herself. Many versions of Mary's song have appeared over the centuries. Be alert to the versions you will hear at this season.

As the season of Advent celebration continues, take time to read (or listen to) Mary's song several times. How has the Mighty One done great things for you? List the gifts He has already given you, both every day and at this season. As you make time for quiet intimacy with Him in the midst of the holiday rush, you will find that your spirit, too, will rejoice in God, your Savior. Your outlook will be refreshed as you realize that if you are His, you are chosen. Celebrate that gift as you teach.

Story Center

Materials
Bible.

Before the Story
Guide students to briefly practice signs for underlined words.

Tell the Story
As you tell the story (or invite students to help tell the details of this familiar story), lead students in responding as shown when you say the underlined words.

What's something that makes you feel really happy?

Today we'll hear about a young woman who got a VERY big surprise that made her feel VERY glad!

1. In the dusty little town of Nazareth lived a young woman named Mary. She had promised to marry a man named Joseph. Maybe Mary was sweeping, brushing little clouds of dust, or weaving, sitting at the loom. But whatever she was doing, suddenly she STOPPED. The <u>angel</u> GABRIEL stood before her. Gabriel said, "Greetings! You are highly favored! The Lord is with you!" That meant that God loved Mary and wanted to honor her.

2. Mary must have DROPPED whatever she was doing! She was amazed and afraid and glad all at once! Then Gabriel said gently, "Do not be afraid! <u>God</u> is very pleased with you! You will have a son and will name Him Jesus. He will be great and will be called the Son of the Most High. He will rule forever!"

3. WELL! That was certainly a lot to take in! Perhaps Mary sat down, PLUNK, all at once. *A <u>baby</u>? The Son of the Most High…rule forever…? How can such a wonderful thing happen?* she must have wondered. She finally asked, "How will I have a <u>baby</u>?"

4. The angel answered, "God's Spirit will come to you. God's power will make it happen. That's the reason this baby will be called the Son of God." Mary <u>listened</u> carefully to the angel's words. The angel told Mary some other news: Mary's relative Elizabeth, who had NEVER had a child and was quite old, was going to have a baby, too—in only three more months! Mary <u>listened</u> as the angel said, "For NOTHING is impossible with God!" God can do anything!

1. Angel: Fingertips on shoulders; draw away and out, waving up and down.

2. God: Point right index finger; lower and open hand at chest.

3. Baby: Rock crossed arms.

4. Listened: Cup right ear; turn head to left.

5. WOW! Mary must have felt excited and scared! But she knew God had honored her and chosen her for the most important job a person had ever had. She looked up at the angel, took a deep breath and said, "I am the Lord's <u>servant</u>. May this happen just as you have said it will." Then the angel left.

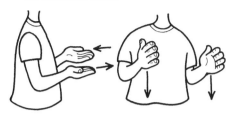

5. Servant: Face palms up, moving back and forth alternately; move hands down sides.

6. Soon after this, Mary traveled to visit her relative Elizabeth. As Mary walked into Elizabeth's house, Elizabeth said, "God has shown His love to you in a special way—you are <u>blessed</u>. And <u>blessed</u> is your baby, too! When I heard your voice, my baby jumped inside me for joy. You are <u>blessed</u> and honored for believing that God will do what He has promised!"

6. Blessed: Fists at mouth; open hands and move forward and down.

7. Mary answered Elizabeth's greeting with beautiful words that were like a <u>song</u>. She was so full of joy and amazement at the great things God had done for her, she just couldn't keep quiet! "My spirit rejoices in God, my Savior. The Mighty One has done great things for me," she said. Mary talked about what God had done for her and what wonderful things God was going to do to help His people. Mary talked about how God kept His promises and how He would make things right. It was a beautiful <u>song</u>.

7. Song: Move right hand back and forth in front of left palm.

8. Mary stayed with Elizabeth for about three months, probably until Elizabeth's <u>baby</u>, John, was born. Mary may not have wanted to go back to Nazareth. It could be very hard to face people who didn't understand why she was having a <u>baby</u>. But Mary knew what the angel had said. She knew that God can always be trusted. And she knew that NOTHING is impossible with Him!

8. Baby: Rock crossed arms.

• •

Discussion Questions

Who visited Mary? (The angel Gabriel.) **What did the angel tell Mary?** (God was pleased with her. She would have a son and name Him Jesus. Jesus would be great.) **What else did Mary learn?** (That nothing is impossible with God.) **What happened when Mary visited Elizabeth?** (Mary sang a beautiful song.)

Mary said those beautiful words as a way to worship and honor God. We can worship and honor God, too, for His love and for keeping His promise to send a Savior.

Object Talk

Scripture Background
Luke 1:46-56

Materials
Bible with bookmark at Luke 1:46-56, rhythm sticks or other rhythm instrument; optional—recording of "The Magnificat" and player.

> *God's love and His promise to send a Savior are good reasons to worship Him! Singing is one important way people worship God. Let's find out about one of the oldest songs ever sung about Jesus' birth.*

Lead the Activity

1. **What are some songs that people sing at Christmas?** ("Silent Night," "Jingle Bells," "Away in a Manger," etc.) Use rhythm sticks or other rhythm instrument to play the rhythms to several Christmas songs. Ask students to guess the names of the songs. (Optional: Lead students in singing one or more of the songs.)

2. **All of these songs are sung at Christmastime, but the very first Christmas song was sung by Mary after the angel told her she was going to be Jesus' mother. The words of Mary's song are now part of a song called "The Magnificat" (mahg-NEE-fee-kaht), which is a Latin word. "The Magnificat" is sung in many churches, not just at Christmastime, but all year long. It is said to have been set to music more often than any other hymn!** Read, or ask several students to take turns reading, Luke 1:46,47. (Optional: Also read verses 48-50 and/or play a portion of "The Magnificat.")

3. **What did Mary praise God for in this song?** (For being her Savior. For doing great things for her. For His mercy.) **How is this song the same or different from the other Christmas songs we named?** Volunteers respond.

Conclude

The word "magnificat" means "to magnify." When we magnify God, we are praising Him and telling others how wonderful He is. Pray, praising God for His wonderful gift of His Son, Jesus. Talk with interested students about becoming members of God's family (see "Leading a Child to Christ" on p. 253).

. . . .

Additional Information for Older Students

Mary's song of praise is similar to a song sung by Hannah in the Old Testament. Mary sang her song to praise God for the great things He had done for His people and for loving her and allowing her to be the mother of Jesus, the Savior of the world. In a similar way, Hannah was praising God for giving her a son, Samuel, who would be dedicated to God's work. Students read some or all of Hannah's song in 1 Samuel 2:1-10.

Active Game Center: Christmas-Tree Relay

Materials
Colored paper cups.

Lead the Game

1. Group students into teams of no more than six students each. Teams line up in single-file lines on one side of the playing area. Give each team six cups.

2. Demonstrate to the students how to stack cups to build a Christmas tree (see sketch). At your signal, the first student on each team runs to the opposite side of the playing area, sets down his or her cup, returns to his or her team and tags the next student in line. Team members repeat actions. Volunteer from the first team that finishes building Christmas tree answers one of the Discussion Questions below.

At Christmastime, we worship God because He loves us and promised to send Jesus, our Savior. Some people celebrate Christmas by decorating Christmas trees, singing special songs and giving gifts to one another. Let's play a game to build our own Christmas trees!

Options

1. Use Christmas cups for the relay.

2. For older students, provide 10 cups for each team. Print the letters of the sentence "Worship God" on paper cups, one letter on each cup. Team members complete relay in the correct order to build a tree that spells "Worship God" from the top down.

Discussion Questions

1. *What fun things do you and your family do to celebrate Christmas?*

2. *What can we thank God for at Christmastime?* (His love. Sending Jesus, the Savior.)

3. *How does giving and receiving gifts help us celebrate Jesus' birth?* (Jesus is God's gift to us.)

Art Center: Christmas Angels

Materials

Nine-inch (22.5-cm) white paper plates (one for every eight students), scissors, yellow construction paper, several caps from gallon milk jugs, pencils, several full masking tape rolls, glue; for each student—4-inch (10-cm) ice cream spoon (available at craft stores) and spring-type clothespin.

Prepare the Activity

Cut paper plates into eight wedges, trimming off the point of each wedge (see sketch a). Make a sample angel following the directions below.

We can worship God for His love and His promise to send Jesus, the Savior. Let's make angels to help us remember the angel that brought Mary the news that she was going to be the mother of the promised Savior!

Lead the Activity

1. Show students your angel sample. On yellow construction paper, each student first traces and cuts around a milk cap to form halo. (For a group of younger students, make halos ahead of time.) To make wings, two students work together to trace and cut around masking tape roll to make circle, fold circle in half and then cut on fold line. Each student keeps one half of circle.

2. Give each student a paper plate wedge. Student glues wings to the back of the wedge, lining up the flat edge of the wings with the flat top of the wedge. Student glues halo onto the large end of an ice cream spoon. Student glues wings and body onto the spoon on the opposite side from the halo so that the spoon end becomes angel's face (see sketch b). Then student glues a clothespin onto the back of the spoon (see sketch c). Angels may be used as ornaments for trees or packages.

Options

1. Bring a variety of papers (Christmas wrap, wallpaper, etc.) and Christmas paper plates for students to use in making halos, wings and angel bodies.

2. Attach a magnet strip to the back of the clothespin to form a refrigerator magnet.

3. Instead of masking tape rolls, substitute several small mixing bowls.

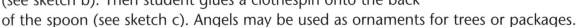

Discussion Questions

1. ***What are some reasons to worship and thank God at Christmastime?*** (He showed His love by sending Jesus as our Savior. He promised a Savior for many years.)

2. ***What are some ways to worship God at Christmastime?*** (Thank God in prayer and song for sending Jesus. Show God's love to others by giving gifts. Put up decorations that are reminders of Jesus' birth.)

3. ***What is one way you would like to worship God this week?***

"My soul glorifies the Lord and my spirit rejoices in God my Savior."
Luke 1:46,47

GOING AROUND IN CIRCLES!

Luke 1: 26-56

The Challenge

You might get dizzy doing this puzzle! Starting at the letter *F* in the balloon, go clockwise around the circle, skipping a letter each time. Write the letters you land on and you'll discover God's secret message to you, the same message the angel told Mary! Go around the circle twice until every letter is used.

__ __ __ __ __ __ __ __ __ __ __

__ __ __ __ __ __ __ __ __ __ __

__ __ __ __ __ __ __ __ __ __ .

See Luke 1:37.

The Super Challenge

Find 10 things in the picture that aren't in the original story of Mary and the angel.

____ ____ ____ ____ ____

____ ____ ____ ____ ____

Jesus Is Born

Bible Verse

This is how God showed his love among us: He sent his one and only Son into the world that we might live through him. 1 John 4:9

Bible Story Reference

Luke 2:1-20

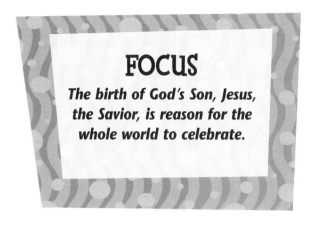

FOCUS

The birth of God's Son, Jesus, the Savior, is reason for the whole world to celebrate.

Teacher's Devotional

All over the world, babies are born every day. This isn't an earth-shattering fact. But when you are related to one of those babies, that child's birth brings wonder and excitement. There is no way to adequately describe that amazing moment when you gaze into a newborn's face for the first time.

In all of history, however, one birth offered not only the holy beauty of a newborn but also the reality that this particular baby had Himself created everything! Jesus, the express image of the Father, had come to live among us. When Jesus, God's Son, opened His eyes for the first time, all He saw was rightfully His because He had created it by the Word of His power! Thus, He could have come as a King in might and glory. But He chose to enter human history as a baby. By living out His perfect life and dying to make a perfect final sacrifice for sin, He fully obeyed the will of the Father and rose from the dead in a world where everything had been changed by His actions!

When Jesus was born, the shepherds immediately began to spread the good news of this amazing baby to the people of Bethlehem. A Savior has come to take away sin! The promised ruler has finally come! That same good news spread around the world. At this season, believers worldwide gather to celebrate Jesus' birth and more: to remember His life, sacrifice and resurrection, for they are all part of one grand celebration of God's grace!

Your traditional Christmas celebrations may include a *posada* (Mexico), the making of *lefse* (Norway), the leaving of gifts in shoes (Holland) or the singing of carols at midnight on Christmas Eve. Take time this week to research a few of the Christmas traditions you usually celebrate. Consider the ways in which each tradition enriches your understanding of who Jesus is. Consider also whether any of your traditions detract from your celebration of Christ's coming to our world. Then as you celebrate Christmas with the children you teach, help them see what you have seen of Jesus, the mighty creator come to live among us!

Story Center

Materials
Bible.

Before the Story
Guide students to briefly practice signs for underlined words.

Tell the Story

As you tell the story (or invite volunteers to help tell this familiar story), lead students in responding as shown when you say the underlined words.

What's the most exciting news you have ever heard?

Today we're going to find out about some VERY exciting news and who first heard the news!

1. For many hundreds of years, God had been promising to send a <u>Savior</u>, someone who would rescue people from their sin. Over the years, God's prophets had told more about the coming <u>Savior</u>. Then the day came when God sent an angel to talk to a young woman named Mary. The angel told her, "You will have a baby boy. Name Him Jesus." That baby would be God's own Son, the <u>Savior</u>!

2. Now it had been months since Mary had heard this exciting news. It was almost time for Mary's baby to be born. But the ruler of the country where Mary and Joseph lived had ordered all people to return to their family's home towns. The government was going to take a census, or <u>count</u> all the people. So Joseph and Mary traveled south from Nazareth to Bethlehem. Finally, they came into Bethlehem. But they were not alone! Many other travelers had come to be <u>counted</u>, too.

3. Mary and Joseph began looking for a place to stay. But everywhere Joseph asked, people said things like, "We don't have room. <u>Sorry</u>." There didn't seem to be room for them ANYWHERE. Joseph knew that Mary needed to get some rest. It was getting close to the time for her baby to be born! Mary needed a quiet, warm place. But where could they go?

4. Finally, one innkeeper had an idea. He said he had one place they could stay. "It's the stable where I keep my <u>animals</u>." Mary and Joseph were probably so tired they didn't care WHERE it was! <u>Animals</u> or not, they were just happy to have a place to stay that was warm and dry.

1. Savior: Cross fists and then pull apart; move hands down sides.

2. Count: With thumb and index finger touching, move right hand up left palm.

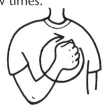

3. Sorry: Rotate right fist over chest a few times.

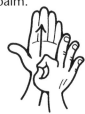

4. Animal: Keeping fingertips on chest, move hands back and forth.

5. And later that night, in that stable, something WON-DERFUL happened: God's Son, the Savior, was born! Joseph and Mary said, "We will call Him Jesus!" Mary wrapped her beautiful new baby in cloth to keep Him warm. Joseph added fresh hay to the manger, the place where the animals were fed. It made a perfect place for newborn baby Jesus to sleep!

5. Jesus: Touch palms with opposite middle fingers.

6. While Mary and Joseph were busy caring for baby Jesus in that quiet stable, some shepherds were sitting in a field outside of Bethlehem, watching their sheep. Suddenly there was a bright light all around them. An ANGEL appeared! The shepherds were stunned and afraid. But the angel said, "Don't be afraid. I bring some WONDER-FUL news!" The angel told them that God's Son had been born in Bethlehem that very night. They would find the baby lying in a manger. A MANGER?! That meant the baby was in a STABLE somewhere!

6. Sheep: Open and close right fingers, moving up left arm.

7. And then, MORE angels appeared! The sky filled with angels singing beautiful praises to God! Then, as suddenly as they had come, the angels disappeared. The light was gone. Everything was quiet again. Now the shepherds looked at each other and said, "Let's go to Bethlehem and see this thing that God told us about!" They ran all the way to Bethlehem and looked in every stable in town!

7. Angel: Fingertips on shoulders; draw away and out, waving up and down.

8. When the shepherds looked into the stable where Mary and Joseph were, they saw baby Jesus lying in a manger. There He was—the Savior God had promised to send! The shepherds knelt to see the baby. Then they left the stable. But as they walked down the road, they got very excited! The angel's news was TRUE! They began to tell EVERYONE they met, "Listen! Did you know? Have you heard? The Savior has been born today!" They spread the news far and wide about the baby—Jesus, God's own Son. And they thanked and praised God for the wonderful things that had happened that night!

8. Savior: Cross fists and then pull apart; move hands down sides.

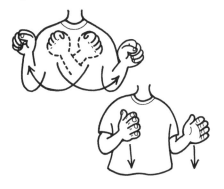

• •

Discussion Questions

What did God promise for many years? (To send a Savior.) **Where was the Savior born?** (Bethlehem.) **Who else heard about Jesus being born? How did they find out?** (Shepherds. An angel told them.) **How would they know the baby?** (This baby was sleeping in a manger in a stable.)

Now people all over the world celebrate Jesus' birth. The news the shepherds told has spread EVERYWHERE. Jesus is the Savior God promised to send. That's a BIG reason to celebrate!

Object Talk

Scripture Background
Luke 2:1-20

Materials
Bible with bookmark at 1 John 4:9, nativity scene; optional—Christmas object from your cultural heritage.

Lead the Activity

1. **What do you know about the place where Jesus was born?** Volunteers respond. Display nativity scene. **One of the objects we often see at Christmastime is a nativity scene like this one. People all over the world put up nativity scenes at Christmas to remind them of Jesus' birth.**

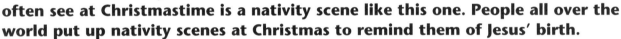

The birth of God's Son, Jesus, is reason for everyone to celebrate. Many of our Christmas traditions, or the ways we celebrate Jesus' birth, actually began in other countries. Let's find out how one Christmas tradition began.

2. **Nativity scenes were first made in Italy about 800 years ago. Since then, people in countries all over the world make nativity scenes. In France, the nativity scene is used in place of a Christmas tree. In South America, a whole room is often decorated as a nativity scene, including drawings of hills, shepherds, the wise men crossing the desert and even sailboats on the sea!** (Optional: Show object from your cultural heritage and explain its history and the customs surrounding it.)

Conclude

Nativity scenes are just one of the objects people all over the world use to celebrate the birth of God's Son, Jesus. Read 1 John 4:9 aloud. **What does this verse tell us is the reason God sent His Son to earth?** (God loves us.) Pray, thanking God for the gift of His Son, Jesus, and that we can celebrate Jesus' birth with people all over the world.

. . . .

Additional Information for Older Students

Most nativity scenes show the wise men worshiping Jesus at the stable. However, many people who study the Bible believe that the wise men actually arrived in Bethlehem when Jesus was between one and two years old. There are two reasons for this belief. First, it probably took the wise men a while to research the meaning of the star they saw, then to organize for their journey and then to travel a long distance. Second, when they arrived in Bethlehem, the Bible says they found Jesus in a house, not a stable. Read Matthew 2:11.

Active Game Center: Shepherd Relay

Materials

One shepherd costume (towels, bathrobes, fabric lengths, sandals, walking sticks, etc.) for each group of six to eight students, large paper bags.

Prepare the Game

Place the materials for each costume in a separate paper bag at one end of an open playing area.

The birth of God's Son, Jesus, the Savior, is reason for the whole world to celebrate! Let's play a game to dress up as some of the people who were among the first to celebrate Jesus' birth— the shepherds!

Lead the Game

1. Using the materials from one paper bag, demonstrate how to dress as a shepherd. When you are completely dressed up, hold the walking stick and call out, "Jesus the Savior is born today!" Return materials to bag.

2. Students form teams of no more than six to eight. Teams stand in single-file lines across the playing area from paper bags. At your signal, the first student on each team runs to his or her team's bag, dresses up in shepherd clothes, holds up the walking stick and calls out, "Jesus the Savior is born today!" Student puts clothes back in bag and returns to his or her team. The next student in line repeats the action. Students continue taking turns until all students have had a turn. A volunteer from the first team to finish answers one of the Discussion Questions below. Play again as time allows.

Options

1. Instead of shepherd costumes, bring angel costumes (white fabric to drape over body and silver garlands for halos). Angels say, "Glory to God and peace on earth!"

2. If your church has Bible-times costumes for a Christmas pageant, ask to borrow them for this game.

3. For younger students, limit dress-up items to three.

• •

Discussion Questions

1. *Why should the whole world celebrate Jesus' birth?* (He came as the Savior for all people. God showed His love for the whole world when He sent Jesus.)

2. *What are some ways you've seen or heard the Christmas story?*

3. *What are some ways you, your family or our church tell other people that Jesus has been born?*

Art Center: Christmas Ornaments

Materials

Materials for the ornament option of your choice.

Lead the Activity

Lead students in making ornaments.

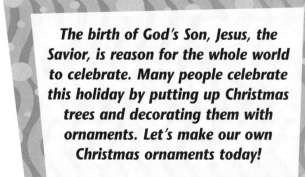

The birth of God's Son, Jesus, the Savior, is reason for the whole world to celebrate. Many people celebrate this holiday by putting up Christmas trees and decorating them with ornaments. Let's make our own Christmas ornaments today!

Fruit-Slice Ornaments

Give students ⅜-inch (.94-cm) thick slices of oranges, lemons or limes. Students gently blot slices with paper towels to absorb as much juice as possible. Students attach an ornament hanger to the top of each slice and tie a ribbon bow around the base of each hanger. Students take ornaments home and hang them in front of a sunny window until dry.

Christmas Card Ornaments

Students cut designs from old Christmas cards or wrapping paper and glue them onto colored felt pieces. Students trim around design, leaving a ½-inch (1.25-cm) felt border. Punch holes in the felt and insert ornament hangers.

Cinnamon Cookie-Cutter Ornaments

Before class, mix together 1 cup of applesauce, 1½ cups of cinnamon and ⅓ cup of nontoxic white glue. Form a ball and refrigerate it for at least 30 minutes or overnight. In class, roll out dough on a cutting board to a thickness of ¼ inch (.625 cm). Use additional cinnamon to prevent sticking. Students cut dough with Christmas cookie cutters and use a pencil to make a hole at the top of each shape. Students remove ornaments from cutting board with spatulas, placing ornaments on paper plates. Students take ornaments home and let them dry flat for a few days before inserting ribbon or hangers into holes. Recipe makes 30 medium-sized ornaments. (Optional: Make a garland by making two holes along the top of each ornament. String ornaments along a Christmas ribbon or length of twine.)

• •

Discussion Questions

1. *What objects or pictures come to your mind when you think of Christmas? How can (bells) help us celebrate Jesus' birth?*

2. *What are some ways we can help others celebrate Jesus' birth?* (Send Christmas cards picturing events from the story of Jesus' birth. Sing praise songs about Jesus.)

3. *What will you do with your ornament?*

"This is how God showed his love among us: He sent his one and only Son into the world that we might live through him." 1 John 4:9

SUPER STARS!

The Challenge

Luke 2:1-20

The birth of Jesus was heralded in the night sky by the star of Bethlehem. Unscramble the letters in each star cluster to read this celestial message.

_ _ _ _ _ _ _   _ _ _   _ _ _ _ _ _   _ _   _ _ _ _

The Super Challenge

Circle at least 15 things that are different between each scene.

New Year
Solomon's Prayer

Bible Verse

For the Lord gives wisdom, and from his mouth come knowledge and understanding.
Proverbs 2:6

Bible Story Reference

1 Kings 3

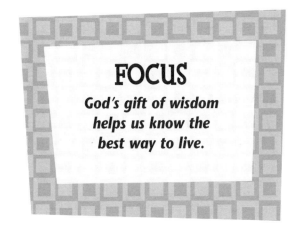

FOCUS

God's gift of wisdom helps us know the best way to live.

Teacher's Devotional

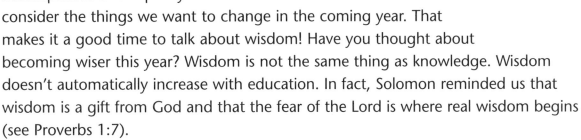

The celebration of a new year is a time to assess what we have accomplished in the past year and consider the things we want to change in the coming year. That makes it a good time to talk about wisdom! Have you thought about becoming wiser this year? Wisdom is not the same thing as knowledge. Wisdom doesn't automatically increase with education. In fact, Solomon reminded us that wisdom is a gift from God and that the fear of the Lord is where real wisdom begins (see Proverbs 1:7).

Wisdom is not only having knowledge but also the ability to use that knowledge to do God's will. It's godly knowledge coupled with gratitude and generosity that yields unselfish good. When God asked Solomon in a dream for anything he wanted, notice Solomon's response. First, he was grateful. He praised God for His mercy to David and the nation of Israel. Then, he was humble. He truly knew his need for wisdom and discernment—not so much for his own benefit, but for the benefit of the people God had given him, that he might rule them well and justly.

We often think that if we can be entertaining enough, we will reach children with God's Word. Children today, however, are surrounded by entertainers. Instead, consider this: When was the last time the students in your class had the opportunity to get to know a truly wise person? Could you be that person? After all, the same God who granted Solomon wisdom is completely able! Like Solomon, take time to thank God for the ways He has been gracious to you. Let gratitude fill your heart. Then tell God your need and ask Him in faith for wisdom. Trust Him to give it. How will you know if you are wise? James 3:17 tells us what the wisdom that comes from God looks like in action: pure motives, peace-loving words, considerate actions, submission, acts of mercy, a show of good spiritual fruit, fairness and sincerity. You can be wise! And your life lived in wisdom can more effectively teach wisdom to your kids than any words you say.

Story Center

Materials

Bible.

Before the Story

Guide students to briefly practice signs for underlined words.

Tell the Story

As you tell the story, lead students in responding as shown when you say the underlined words.

> *Who is a person you know who is very wise? What wise actions or words does that person do or say?*
>
> *Today we're going to meet the wisest man who ever lived. And we'll find out how he became so wise!*

1. David, the king of Israel, had lived to be a very old man. Before he died, he chose his son Solomon to be the next king. Solomon loved God and he wanted to obey Him. And God loved Solomon! One way Solomon showed his love for God was by <u>worshiping</u> Him. After one special time of <u>worshiping</u> God, Solomon was sleeping. God talked with him in a dream.

2. God said to Solomon, "Ask Me for whatever you want Me to give you." For ANYTHING? That meant Solomon could ask for all the money in the world or to be the most powerful king ever! But what do you think Solomon asked for?

    Solomon said to God, "You have been very kind to my father and to me. You have made me the king. But I'm so young! I don't know how to do this job. Please give me <u>wisdom</u>, so I'll know what is right and wrong. I don't know how to be king of all these people without Your help!"

3. God was glad to hear what Solomon had asked. God said, "I will <u>give</u> you wisdom. You will be the wisest person that ever lived. And since you have asked for wisdom instead of money or power, I will also <u>give</u> you riches and honor. If you obey Me, I'll <u>give</u> you a long life, too."

4. Solomon woke from his <u>dream</u>. He must have been excited! God was going to make him wise! But how would he know if he was really wise or not? Solomon's chance to find out came along soon.

1. Worship: Left hand over right fist; move hands to body and bow head.

2. Wisdom: Bend right index finger; move up and down on forehead.

3. Give: Hands down and fingertips touching, flip hands forward and open, palms up.

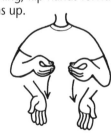

4. Dream: Right index finger at forehead; move up and out, repeatedly bending finger.

5. One day, two women came to Solomon in his throne room. The women were having a TERRIBLE fight. They wanted King Solomon to decide what should be done.

The first woman said, "Your majesty, this woman and I live together in the same house. We both had brand-new baby boys. This other woman's <u>baby</u> died. And while I was asleep, she took my little son and put him in her bed. Then she laid her dead <u>baby</u> beside me. When I woke up, I thought my <u>baby</u> was dead! But in the morning light, I could see it wasn't my <u>baby</u> at all."

5. Baby: Rock crossed arms.

6. The other woman broke in. "No! This baby is mine! Your baby is dead!" Solomon didn't argue with either woman. He said to his servant, "Bring me a <u>sword</u>." The two women didn't know why Solomon wanted a <u>sword</u>, but Solomon had a plan in mind in order to find out the real mother.

When the servant brought back a <u>sword</u>, Solomon said to the servant, "Cut this baby in half. Give half a baby to each mother!"

6. Sword: Slide right index and middle fingers off left index finger; pantomime drawing out sword and thrusting forward.

7. The woman who was NOT really the baby's mother said, "Fine. If I can't have him, YOU can't have him either. Cut him in two!" But the woman who was REALLY the baby's mother said, "Oh, no, Your Majesty! Give the baby to the other woman! <u>Don't hurt</u> him!"

Then Solomon said, "I have made my decision. Give the baby to the woman who said, '<u>Don't hurt</u> him!' She is his real mother. She would rather let someone else have him than let him be hurt."

7. Don't hurt: Uncross crossed hands; jab index fingers toward each other.

8. Everyone in the throne room looked at Solomon. Solomon had been very <u>WISE</u>! He figured out who the real mother was! Soon the story of Solomon's <u>wise</u> decision was heard all over Israel. Then the people knew that he was going to be a <u>wise</u> king! God had done what He promised. He had given Solomon GREAT <u>wisdom</u>!

8. Wise, wisdom: Bend right index finger; move up and down on forehead.

• •

Discussion Questions

How did Solomon show he loved God? (He worshiped God.) **What gift did Solomon ask God to give him?** (Wisdom.) **When a person is wise, he or she is able to make choices that show love for God and others. How was Solomon able to show God had given him wisdom?** (Solved a quarrel between two women. Found who the baby's real mother was.)

What are some times a kid your age needs God's wisdom? God's gift of wisdom is a gift we can ask for, too. God's wisdom shows us the best way to live. All we have to do is ask Him. That's a reason to celebrate!

New Year

Object Talk

Scripture Background
Proverbs 2:6

Materials
Bible with bookmark at Proverbs 2:6, variety of lists (grocery list, phone book, chore list, encyclopedia, dictionary, etc.).

Lead the Activity

1. Give each list you brought to a volunteer to describe. **What kind of list is this? How does this list help the person who wrote it or who is reading it? What kinds of lists do you or the people in your family make?** Volunteers respond.

2. **As part of their New Year's Day celebrations, some people make lists called New Year's resolutions. A resolution is something you plan or promise to do. When people write New Year's resolutions, they usually list wise ways of living.** (Optional: Ask students to tell items often listed as New Year's resolutions.)

3. **We can always think of good ways to live, such as eating healthy food or getting enough sleep, but because God loves us so much, He gives us the help we need to live the very best way. What are some ways we can find out the very best ways to live?** (Ask God for wisdom. Read God's Word. Listen to advice from people who love and obey God.)

Conclude

Read Proverbs 2:6 aloud. **What are some wise actions God will help us learn?** (How to show His love to others. How to be a good friend.) Pray, praising God for His gift of wisdom and asking for His help to live in wise ways.

> *If we ask God, He will give us wisdom to know the best way to live. When people celebrate the coming of a new year, they often think about better ways to live. Let's talk about how some people remind themselves of wise ways to live.*

• •

Additional Information for Older Students

King Solomon was known throughout the world for his wisdom. He wrote several books in the Bible, including Ecclesiastes. Ecclesiastes 3:1-13 is a list of different things that may happen to people. These verses are sometimes read at New Year's services. A volunteer reads Ecclesiastes 3:1-13 aloud.

Ask students to list wise ways to live that each begin with one of the letters in the words "Happy New Year." Print list on large sheet of paper. (Students may read Proverbs 10:8; 10:12; 12:18; 15:1 and 17:17 for ideas.)

Active Game Center: Hop and Talk!

Materials

10 Christmas cards, scissors, marker, masking tape, children's music CD and player.

Prepare the Game

Cut off the back of each card so that only the picture remains. On the back of one picture, write the word "wisdom." Use masking tape to outline a very large hop-scotch pattern on the floor. Place one card, picture side up, along outside edge of each section in the pattern.

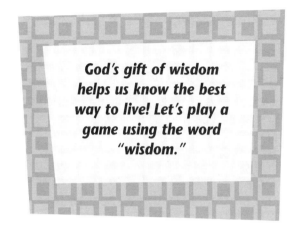

God's gift of wisdom helps us know the best way to live! Let's play a game using the word "wisdom."

Lead the Game

As you play music from CD, all students hop one after another through the pattern. After 10 to 20 seconds, stop the music. When music stops, students freeze. Each student in a section picks up card. Student holding the card with the word "wisdom" uses the word in a sentence to tell about God's wisdom. ("God's wisdom is best." "Ask God for wisdom." "God's wisdom helps you every day.") Repeat activity as time permits.

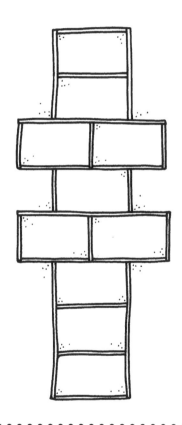

Options

1. Use Christmas wrapping paper squares instead of Christmas cards.

2. If you have more than 10 students, prepare more than one hopscotch pattern.

3. Vary the game by asking student holding the "wisdom" card to answer one of the Discussion questions below or to say the words of Proverbs 2:6.

• •

Discussion Questions

1. *What are some times kids your age need to be wise?* (When tempted to do something wrong. When making a choice about how to treat others.)

2. *The Bible tells us that God gives us wisdom. How can we get wisdom from God?* (Ask God to help us make wise decisions, and then trust Him to answer our prayers. Think about what God's Word says to do and how to obey it.)

3. *What does the Bible say are some wise ways to live?* (Love others. Be kind. Tell the truth. Be generous to others.) *Why is it wise to live those ways?*

Art Center: Confetti Words

Materials

Newspaper, paper, markers, glue, confetti in small paper bags.

Prepare the Activity

On one side of the classroom, cover floor with newspaper.

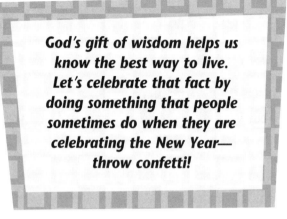

God's gift of wisdom helps us know the best way to live. Let's celebrate that fact by doing something that people sometimes do when they are celebrating the New Year—throw confetti!

Lead the Activity

1. Each student writes the word "wisdom" in large, colorful letters on a sheet of paper.

2. Students place papers on newspaper and squeeze dots or lines of glue onto paper around the letters. Students toss or sprinkle confetti onto glued sections of their paper. Additional glue may be added if needed. Students carefully shake papers onto newspaper to gather remaining confetti and toss confetti again. (Optional: Students shout "Happy New Year" while throwing confetti.)

Options

1. Purchase paper and metallic confetti, or use a hole punch to make confetti from colored paper or wrapping paper. (If making confetti, students punch holes over bowls or paper bags.)

2. Instead of writing the word "wisdom," older students draw symbols that remind them of wisdom (stars, light bulbs).

3. Make a group banner. Have an older student write the word "wisdom" in large block letters across a long length of butcher paper. Students fill letters with glue before tossing or sprinkling confetti onto the letters.

4. If you prefer not to use confetti, provide a variety of collage materials (cotton balls, ribbon, chenille wire, etc.) for students to glue onto papers.

Discussion Questions

1. ***What is wisdom?*** (The knowledge to make choices that show love for God and others.)

2. ***What can God's gift of wisdom help us do?*** (Know what to do when we have to make decisions. Know how to help others and how to be kind to them.)

3. ***What can we do to get wisdom from God?*** (Pray and ask Him for it. Talk to Him about the decisions you are making or the ways you are treating others. Read the Bible and ask God to help you act in the same wise ways some of the Bible people did.)

"For the Lord gives wisdom, and from his mouth come knowledge and understanding." Proverbs 2:6

GO FLY A KITE!

Proverbs 2:6

Follow Ann's kite string to the end, picking up the words you pass as you go. Write down each word in order. Then follow Sam's string and finally Hadiki's string, doing the same. You will find an awesome verse!

"_____

_____."

Valentine's Day

Parables of God's Love

Bible Verse

Love is patient, love is kind. 1 Corinthians 13:4

Bible Story Reference

Matthew 18:10-14; Luke 15:4-10

Teacher's Devotional

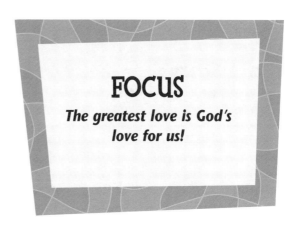

FOCUS
The greatest love is God's love for us!

We love our pets and our neighbors, our children, spouses and new shoes. And Scripture tells us to love God with all our hearts and souls, minds and strength (see Mark 12:30). Love can be used in many ways! As we celebrate Valentine's Day, however, we have a wonderful opportunity to clarify the word "love."

Although history is not absolutely precise on all points, we do know that a Christian named Valentine was imprisoned by Emperor Claudius the Goth around A.D. 270, during a sweep of arrests of those who were not worshiping Roman gods. (Valentine may have also been performing Christian marriages against the emperor's edict.) The story is told that through Valentine's prayers for and witnessing to his jailer, the jailer's whole family (46 people) came to know Christ! Needless to say, Valentine's praising God over this only further infuriated the emperor. On February 14, Valentine was martyred, probably clubbed to death and then beheaded. The feast to commemorate Valentine's love and martyrdom was decreed in the fifth century. A pagan love and fertility festival was already celebrated on the fifteenth; church leaders hoped that the feast of Valentine might help believers focus on true *agape* love.

Jesus said that no one has greater love than he who will "lay down his life for his friends" (John 15:13). Valentine followed Jesus' example, for he loved Jesus dearly. We can use our celebration of Valentine's Day to focus ourselves and our students on this kind of love, the greatest love the world has ever known. Take time to read carefully Jesus' parables of love in Matthew and Luke. God cares deeply about each individual; not only does He go to great lengths to bring any lost one to Himself, but He also rejoices exuberantly when that lost one is found! All of heaven rejoices!

Share with your students the ways God's love has made a difference in your life. Once we know His love in our lives, all other love pales by comparison. Take time during this session for kindness, genuine listening and keen observation. Make this a day when true love—God's love—is not only celebrated but also more fully understood!

Story Center

Materials
Bible.

Before the Story
Guide students to briefly practice signs for underlined words.

Tell the Story
As you tell the story, lead students in responding as shown when you say the underlined words.

Of all the things you have, what's your favorite? Have you ever lost it? What did you do?

Today we'll hear about two people who looked for what they had lost.

1. Jesus taught many things while He was living on earth. One time, some religious leaders were angry that Jesus spent time with people who did not follow God's laws. The religious leaders didn't understand that these people deserved God's <u>love</u>. But Jesus knew He was supposed to show God's great <u>love</u> to ALL people. So Jesus told two stories that helped show how much God <u>loves</u> everyone.

2. One story Jesus told was about a shepherd with 100 <u>sheep</u>. This shepherd took very good care of his <u>sheep</u>. Every day he took the <u>sheep</u> to places where they could find good things to eat and water to drink. Every night he gathered the <u>sheep</u> together and took them to a safe place where they could sleep. And he would count his <u>sheep</u> as they came to him, just to make sure that each <u>sheep</u> was there. The shepherd even had special names for each <u>sheep</u>!

3. One night, the shepherd was <u>counting</u> his sheep—*95, 96, 97, 98, 99.* What? He <u>counted</u> only 99 sheep! The shepherd started over and <u>counted</u> again. But there were STILL only 99. One sheep was MISSING! What could the shepherd do? That one sheep was IMPORTANT to the shepherd. So he left the 99 sheep in a safe place and went to find the lost sheep.

4. The shepherd probably looked down cliffs and in creek beds where the sheep might have fallen. He <u>searched</u> behind big rocks, up hills and along roads. He <u>searched</u> EVERYWHERE for his lost sheep. Every few minutes, he called for his sheep. He paused to listen, hoping he would hear his lost sheep bleating.

1. Love: Cross fists over heart.

2. Sheep: Open and close right fingers, moving up left arm.

3. Count: With thumb and index finger touching, move right hand up left palm.

4. Search: Curved right hand circles in front of face while moving to the side.

46

5. Finally, the shepherd heard the bleating of the frightened lost sheep. He was SO happy! He found his sheep, picked it up and carried it back to the safe place. Then he called to his friends and neighbors, "Come and see! Come and see! My lost sheep has been FOUND!" Everyone came to see and to CELEBRATE! The lost sheep had been FOUND!

5. Celebrate: Right index finger and thumb touching, make small circles.

6. Then Jesus told another story about a woman who had 10 silver coins. These were special coins she had received when she got married. The coins were worth a lot of money and were very important to the woman. One day the woman noticed that one of her coins was MISSING! *Oh no,* she probably thought. *What will I do?* The woman lit a lamp, so she could see in every dark corner. Then she took her broom and carefully swept the floor. She probably swept under the furniture, looked inside all the jars, shook her clothes and turned over her cups and dishes and pots.

6. Coin: With right index finger, make a small circle in left palm.

7. The woman searched and searched. She was so worried! She looked and looked, high and low, under and over. Then SUDDENLY, there it WAS! She had FOUND her coin. She was SO happy! She ran to tell her friends, "I found my coin! I found my coin! Come help me CELEBRATE!" All of her friends and neighbors came to see and to celebrate!

7. Celebrate: Right index finger and thumb touching, make small circles.

8. Then Jesus explained that God is like the shepherd and the woman. All people are like the sheep or the coin. People want to do things their own way instead of God's way, and that separates us from God. It's as though we're lost. So God sent Jesus to bring us into God's loving family. Jesus did that by dying on the cross to take the punishment for the wrong things we've done. When people receive God's forgiveness and become part of God's family, God is SO happy that He and the angels and everyone in heaven CELEBRATE!

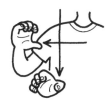

8. Cross: Move curved right hand down; then from left to right.

· ·

Discussion Questions

How many sheep were lost? (Only one.) **Why do you think the shepherd looked for just one sheep?** (He cared about the sheep.) **Why did the woman look for her lost coin?** (It was very important to her.) **What did the shepherd and the woman both do when they found what was lost?** (Invited others to celebrate with them.)

When someone becomes a member of God's family, what does God do? (Celebrates!) **God's love is the greatest love of all. That's the reason we celebrate!**

Valentine's Day

Object Talk

Scripture Background
John 15:13

Materials
Bible with bookmarks at John 15:13 and 1 Corinthians 13:4, 8½x11-inch (21.5x27.5-cm) sheet of paper, scissors, marker, variety of Valentine's Day gifts (heart-shaped candy box, valentine cards, flowers, etc.) in a large bag.

Prepare the Activity
Make pop-up card. Fold and cut paper (see sketch a). Keeping card closed, fold as shown in sketch b. Open the card, draw and cut heart and draw a cross (see sketch c). Fold top portion of heart down inside the card at an angle. Decorate the front of the card to resemble a valentine.

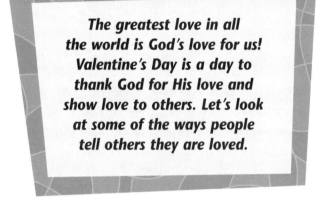

The greatest love in all the world is God's love for us! Valentine's Day is a day to thank God for His love and show love to others. Let's look at some of the ways people tell others they are loved.

Lead the Activity

1. **What kinds of things do people give each other on Valentine's Day?** As students suggest gifts, display examples from the Valentine's Day gifts you brought.

2. **On Valentine's Day we give cards and gifts to tell people that we love them. But the best, the greatest, gift of love ever given was not given on Valentine's Day.** Open pop-up card you prepared. **What gift does this card remind you of? When was it given?** Volunteers respond. **God's gift of His Son, Jesus, is the greatest gift of love ever given.** Read or ask an older student to read John 15:13 aloud.

Conclude
Listen to this verse which tells what we can do to show God's love to others. Read 1 Corinthians 13:4. **What are the ways to show love this verse tells us about?** (Be patient. Be kind.) **What are some ways you can show patience and kindness this week?** (Wait for someone else to share. Help someone who is hurt.) Pray, thanking God for His great love and His greatest gift, Jesus.

• •

Additional Information for Older Students
There are several stories about who Saint Valentine was. According to Church tradition, around A.D. 270 a man named Valentine was put in prison because he worshiped God. While in prison, he continued to show love for God by helping others. Because of his faith, Valentine was killed. After his death, Church leaders began a feast, or holiday, to help Christians remember God's love.

Active Game Center: Red-Hot Relay

Materials

Bible, disposable bowls, plastic spoons, small Valentine's Day candy (red hots, conversation hearts or red and pink M&Ms), sandwich-sized plastic bags.

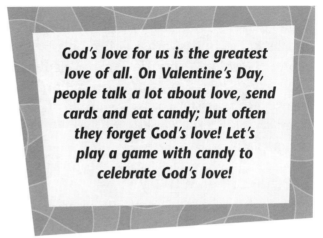

God's love for us is the greatest love of all. On Valentine's Day, people talk a lot about love, send cards and eat candy; but often they forget God's love! Let's play a game with candy to celebrate God's love!

Prepare the Game

Place two empty bowls on one side of open area in classroom. On the other side of the room, place two bowls filled with equal amounts of candy.

Lead the Game

1. Group students into two teams. Teams line up by empty bowls. Give the first student on each team a spoon.

2. At your signal, the first student on each team walks quickly to his or her team's bowl of candy, fills spoon with candy and returns with the candy, dumping candy into team's empty bowl. If student drops any candy, student picks it up and returns to the candy bowl to begin again with new candy. (Students throw away dropped candy.) Next student in line repeats the action. Play continues until both teams have transferred all candies from one bowl to the other. Volunteer from the first team to complete the relay answers one of the Discussion Questions below. Repeat relay as time permits.

3. Students take home candy in plastic bags.

Options

1. Limit number of students on each team to six. If you have more than 12 students, form additional teams and provide additional materials.

2. Use large spoons for younger students.

- -

Discussion Questions

1. ***What are some ways God's love is different than the love people have for one another?*** (God always loves us no matter what. We don't have to do anything to earn God's love for us. God's love is shown by His forgiveness of our sins.)

2. Have an older student read 1 Corinthians 13:4-7 aloud. ***How do these verses describe love?*** Volunteers name characteristics. ***These are the ways God loves us!***

3. ***What are some ways we can show God's love to others?***

Valentine's Day

Art Center: Frosted Art

Materials

Bible, plastic tablecloth, one or more colors of frosting in bowls, other edible decorative materials (colored sprinkles, small Valentine's Day candy like red hots or conversation hearts, etc.), plastic knives, two unfrosted heart-shaped sugar cookies for each student, paper plates.

Prepare the Activity

Cover table with tablecloth. Place bowls of frosting, other edible decorative materials and plastic knives evenly around table.

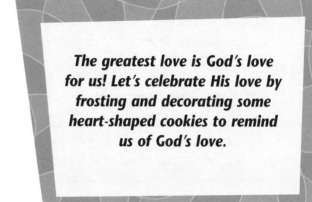

The greatest love is God's love for us! Let's celebrate His love by frosting and decorating some heart-shaped cookies to remind us of God's love.

Lead the Activity

1. Give each student two cookies and a paper plate. Students frost and decorate cookies with materials provided. Ask the Discussion Questions below as students work on cookies.

2. Each student eats one cookie and takes the other cookie home on a paper plate to give away as a way of sharing God's love.

Option

Bring small Valentine's Day plates, clear or colored cellophane, scissors and curling ribbon. Student places cookie to give away on plate, wraps cellophane around plate and secures cellophane with ribbon.

Discussion Questions

1. **Why is God's love the greatest love of all?** (He always loves us, no matter what. He is always patient and kind toward us. We may forget to love people all the time, but God always loves us.)

2. **How does God show His love for us?** (Sent Jesus to teach people about God and to die on the cross for our sins. Cared for people since the world began. Hears and answers our prayers. Gives us families and friends to love us.)

3. **What words would you use to describe God's love to someone else?** (Huge. The greatest. Faithful. Patient. Kind.) Ask an older student to read 1 Corinthians 13:4-7 aloud.

"Love is patient, love is kind." 1 Corinthians 13:4

LOST AND FOUND

Luke 15:3-7

The Challenge

The shepherd has lost a sheep, and like the Good Shepherd, he will search high and low for it. In the blanks, write the letters you find on the sheep. Read the hints for help. It's a word that tells what God feels for us.

___ ___ ___ ___ ___ ___ ___ ___ ___ ___

(Hints: The first letter is a curve. The sixth and seventh letters are the same consonant. The fourth letter has a straight line and a curve in it. The last letter is a consonant made of three straight lines.)

The Super Challenge

The shepherd is looking for one specific sheep. It looks just like the one in his picture. Can you find it? When you do, circle it.

Maundy Thursday

The Last Supper

Bible Verse

This is how we know what love is: Jesus Christ laid down his life for us. 1 John 3:16

Bible Story Reference

Matthew 26:17-30; Mark 14:12-26; Luke 22:7-20; John 13:1-17

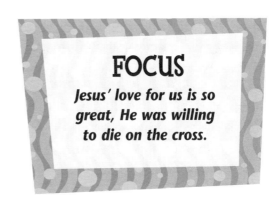

FOCUS

Jesus' love for us is so great, He was willing to die on the cross.

Teacher's Devotional

The Israelites celebrated the Passover with complete involvement! Whether in the countryside, in the villages or in Jerusalem, the entire nation was on the same schedule, cooked the same foods and enjoyed the same celebration. In this lesson, we remember and examine a Passover-related event. (Note: You may want to teach this Last Supper lesson directly after the Passover lessons to help children understand the new meaning Jesus gave to the Passover celebration and so that the Palm Sunday and Easter lessons may be taught on the Sundays on which those holidays are celebrated.)

The memorializing of this particular Passover meal, the final one Jesus shared with His disciples, is done on Maundy Thursday. The word "maundy" derives from the Latin word *mandatus,* "command," and refers to the words Jesus spoke at this unique *seder*: "A new command I give you: Love one another. As I have loved you, so you must love one another" (John 13:34). While the rest of the nation looked back at the great things God had done for them, Jesus' eleven friends sat at a *seder* where they slowly absorbed a new significance to Passover. The familiar celebration was being entirely changed and deepened right before their eyes! At the *seder* Jesus conducted, new meaning was given to the unleavened bread: that symbol of sinless purity was broken apart—and given to each of them! The wine of the old covenant became the symbol of a new covenant, made with God through Jesus, the Messiah. He passed the cup and said, "Drink from it, all of you" (Matthew 26:27).

New purity was available. New promise was about to supersede the old covenant, the one broken over and over by the fallible humans who couldn't maintain their end of the agreement. The Passover Lamb, the High Priest, the Redeemer and Anointed One stood before them and declared that all of what had gone on before, as significant as it was, was only a shadow of what He was about to do. Is there any more astounding reason to celebrate?!

Maundy Thursday • Matthew 26:17-30; Mark 14:12-26; Luke 22:7-20; John 13:1-17

Story Center

Materials
Bible.

Before the Story
Guide students to briefly practice signs for underlined words.

Tell the Story
As you tell the story, lead students in responding as shown when you say the underlined words.

> *What does your family eat when you have a special meal? What other things does your family do when you have a celebration?*
>
> *Today we'll hear about what Jesus and His friends did at a special meal they ate together.*

1. The roads to Jerusalem were full of people. Everyone was coming into the city to <u>celebrate</u> Passover, when all the Israelites remembered how God freed their ancestors from slavery in Egypt. Passover was one of the three times every year when people came from all over the country to <u>celebrate</u>, feast, sing and pray at the Temple.

2. Jesus and His friends were coming to celebrate Passover, too. Jesus told Peter and John to get everything ready for the special Passover meal, called the *seder,* they would <u>eat</u> together. This was to be the last time the disciples would <u>eat</u> with Jesus before He died on the cross. (That's why many people call this Passover meal the Last Supper.)

3. Toward evening, Jesus and the rest of the disciples gathered around the low table. But no servant was there to <u>wash</u> their dusty, dirty feet. Much to everyone's surprise, Jesus got up from the table, poured water into a bowl and began to <u>wash</u> their feet. At first, Peter didn't want Jesus to <u>wash</u> his feet. But Jesus explained that letting Him <u>wash</u> Peter's feet meant that Peter wanted to follow Jesus. <u>Washing</u> the dirty feet of His friends was an example of Jesus' love and caring.

4. Soon after, Jesus and the disciples began to eat and sing together and to listen once again to the story of how God had freed the Israelites. While He ate with His disciples, Jesus told them that He would die soon. He said that one of them would <u>betray</u> Him to the men who would kill Him. Jesus knew that Judas would be the one to <u>betray</u> Him by leading soldiers to arrest Him later that night.

1. Celebrate: Right index finger and thumb touching, make small circles.

2. Eat: Fingertips touching, move right hand to mouth a few times.

3. Wash: Rub knuckles together in circles.

4. Betray: With thumbs, index and little fingers extended, slide right hand back and forth over left.

5. The disciples were horrified and <u>sad</u>. One of them would BETRAY Jesus? Eleven of them thought, *I wouldn't do such a thing—would I?!* But Judas got up and left. Jesus told His disciples that even this <u>sad</u> thing was part of God's plan. It was going to happen in just the way the prophets in Old Testament times had said it would so that salvation from sin could be offered to all people.

5. Sad: Palms in, drop hands down face.

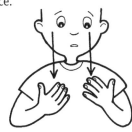

6. As Jesus and the disciples finished the special <u>meal</u> and its story, Jesus tried to help the disciples understand why He would die on the cross. As He spoke, Jesus broke off the unleavened bread used for the *seder* and shared the wine from one of the Passover cups with His disciples. From now on, Jesus wanted His followers to celebrate the Passover <u>meal</u> in a new way. It was now more than a reminder of God freeing the Israelites from Egypt. It would always remind Jesus' followers of His death.

6. Meal: Fingertips touching, move right hand to mouth a few times.

7. Jesus also explained how much He loved His disciples. He promised to send the Holy Spirit to help them after He died and rose again. The disciples <u>listened</u> carefully. They <u>listened</u> so that they would remember the words Jesus spoke that night.

7. Listen: Cup right ear; turn head to left.

8. When they finished the meal, they <u>sang</u> together. At the end of the *seder* it was traditional to <u>sing</u> a song that began, "Blessed is the One who comes in the name of the Lord . . ." They had <u>sung</u> it at the end of Passover meals for years. But now as they <u>sang</u>, they must have begun to understand that those words meant even more. That song was about Jesus! Quietly, they went out to pray in a garden on the Mount of Olives. It was the beginning of the end of Jesus' time on earth with His disciples.

8. Sing: Move right hand back and forth in front of left palm.

● ●

Discussion Questions

What meal did Jesus and His disciples eat? (The Passover meal.) **What did Jesus tell His friends?** (That He was going to die.) **What did Jesus want His friends to remember when they ate the unleavened bread and shared the cup?** (Jesus' death.)

Jesus' love for us is so great, He was willing to die on the cross to take the punishment for our sins. That's great love. And it's a BIG reason to celebrate! Talk with students about becoming Christians (see "Leading a Child to Christ" on p. 253).

Object Talk

Scripture Background

Matthew 26:17-30; Mark 14:12-26;
Luke 22:7-20

Materials

Bible with bookmarks at John 13:34,35
and 1 John 3:16; objects used by your
church for communion (plates, cups,
chalice, bread or wafers, juice, etc.).

> *Because He loves us so much, Jesus was willing to die on the cross so that our sins could be forgiven. The night before He was killed, Jesus ate a special supper with His disciples. Let's look at the way our church family remembers that special supper and Jesus' death on the cross.*

Lead the Activity

1. Show objects one at a time. **What is this object? What are some ways to use it?** (Optional: Students taste food items.)

2. **We use these objects when we celebrate the Lord's Supper. One of the names for this celebration is "communion," which means to share something with others. When we celebrate communion together, we share in celebrating and remembering the last supper Jesus ate with His disciples before He died on the cross to take the punishment for our sins.** Explain and demonstrate use of objects. (Optional: Invite your pastor or other church leader to talk with students about how your church celebrates the Lord's Supper.)

3. **One special day each year, many Christians celebrate Jesus' last supper with His disciples; this day is called Maundy Thursday. The word "maundy" comes from the Latin word *mandatus* which means "command."** Read or ask an older student to read John 13:34,35 aloud. **What is the new commandment Jesus gave His followers during the Last Supper?**

Conclude

Read 1 John 3:16 aloud. **What does this verse tell us that love really is?** (Jesus cares so much for us that He died for us.) Pray, thanking Jesus for dying on the cross for our sins. Talk with interested students about becoming members of God's family (see "Leading a Child to Christ" on p. 253).

. . . .

Additional Information for Older Students

The day on which Jesus died is sometimes called Good Friday. No one knows for sure where the name Good Friday came from. Some people think that the word "good" came from the phrase "God's Friday." Other people, however, believe the name came about because even though Jesus' death was very sad, so much good happened as a result of His death. What are some of the good things that happened as a result of Jesus' death and resurrection? (Our sins can be forgiven. We can experience God's love.)

Maundy Thursday

Active Game Center: Amazing Feet

Materials

Two large sheets of butcher paper, crayons.

Prepare the Game

Place sheets of butcher paper and crayons on the floor in an open area of the room.

Lead the Game

1. All students take off shoes and place them in a large pile on one side of the playing area. Group students into two equal teams. Assign each team a paper on the floor.

> *Jesus showed His great love for us by being willing to die on the cross for us! He showed His love to His disciples and served them by washing their feet during the last meal He ate with them. Let's play a game where we serve each other, too.*

2. Students on each team line up in pairs. At your signal, the first pair in each line runs to his or her team's paper. Students trace each others' feet on the paper and return to their team. Continue until all students have had their feet traced.

3. When tracing is completed, pairs take turns running to the shoe pile. Students must find partner's shoes (with help from partner as needed) and put shoes on partner's feet. Game continues until all students have had their feet traced and are wearing their shoes.

Options

1. If you have more than 14 to 16 students, form more than two teams and limit each team to eight students.

2. If a team has an uneven number of students, play the relay with them.

Discussion Questions

1. *What are some ways Jesus loved and served people when He was here on earth?* (Healed them. Fed them. Taught them the best way to live. Washed the disciples' feet.)

2. *How does Jesus show love for us today?* (Answers our prayers. Promises to always be with us.)

3. *What are some ways we can show Jesus' love to people today?* (Be patient with brothers or sisters. Help others at school. Play games fairly.)

Art Center: The Jesus Story

Materials

Four different colors of 9x12-inch (22.5x30-cm) construction paper (four sheets of each color for each student), ruler, paper cutter, markers, several staplers, large sheet of paper.

Jesus' love for us is so great, He was willing to die on the cross so that our sins could be forgiven. Let's make books to celebrate Jesus' life and all His love for us.

Prepare the Activity

Cut all paper in half lengthwise, and then cut each color of paper a different length: 6 inches (15 cm), 7 inches (17.5 cm), 8 inches (20 cm) and 9 inches (22.5 cm). Make a sample book following directions below.

Lead the Activity

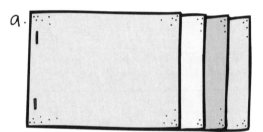

a.

1. Show students the book you made. **How does this event remind you of Jesus' love? What else did Jesus do to show His love for people here on earth?** List events you illustrated and others suggested by students on a large sheet of paper. (Optional: List events in chronological order as much as possible.)

2. Each student takes a sheet of each color of paper. Students arrange papers and staple as shown in sketch a.

b.

3. Students title and decorate the top page of the book as a cover. Then students choose three events from Jesus' life which show His love for us, and illustrate or write descriptions of the events on the pages of their books. Students write (or dictate) descriptions of events on the edge of the pages (see sketch b).

Options

1. Students create decorative covers for books using wrapping paper, specialty paper and/or decorating materials such as stamps, metallic pens, etc.

2. Students dress up in Bible-times costumes and pose scenes which picture events from Jesus' life. Take instant photos and display photos in a time line. During the next two lessons students add to the time line to show the events of the last week of Jesus' life.

• •

Discussion Questions

1. *What were some of the important events in Jesus' life?* (Birth in a stable. Baptism by John the Baptist. Calling disciples to follow Him. Feeding a crowd of 5,000. Healing a blind man. Dying on the cross and coming back to life.)

2. *What are some things we know about Jesus' love for us?* (He loves us so much, He was willing to die on the cross to take the punishment for our sins. He loves us so much, He will always help us.)

Draw a picture of a way to show God's love to others.

UP CLOSE AND PERSONAL!

Matthew 26:17-30

The Challenge Number Jesus' disciples alphabetically, and then write the word below each disciple in the matching blank. Read the words in order to discover some good news about Jesus. (Hint: Save the two disciples with the same name for last.)

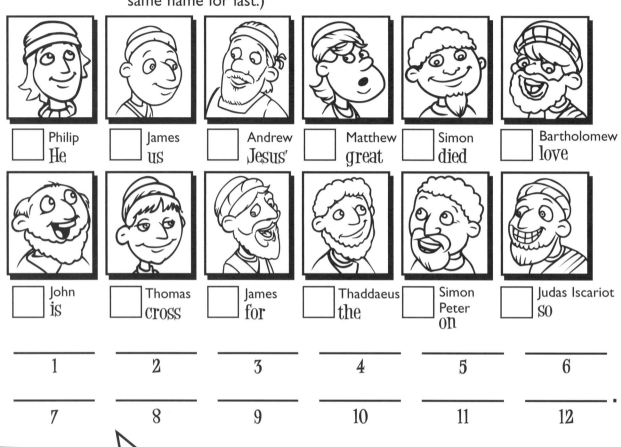

☐ Philip	☐ James	☐ Andrew	☐ Matthew	☐ Simon	☐ Bartholomew
He	us	Jesus'	great	died	love

☐ John	☐ Thomas	☐ James	☐ Thaddaeus	☐ Simon Peter	☐ Judas Iscariot
is	cross	for	the	on	so

___ 1   ___ 2   ___ 3   ___ 4   ___ 5   ___ 6

___ 7   ___ 8   ___ 9   ___ 10   ___ 11   ___ 12 .

The Super Challenge — Can you identify the 12 disciples in their close-ups below? Write each one's name below the box.

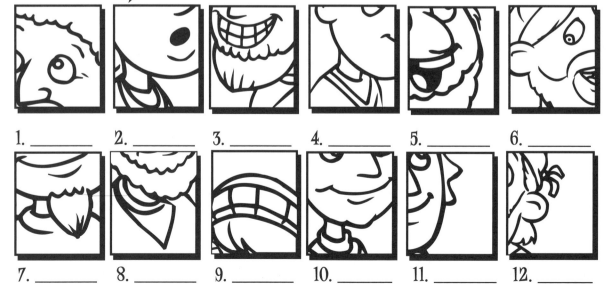

1. _____ 2. _____ 3. _____ 4. _____ 5. _____ 6. _____

7. _____ 8. _____ 9. _____ 10. _____ 11. _____ 12. _____

Palm Sunday

Jesus Enters Jerusalem

Bible Verse

Praise the Lord. How good it is to sing praises to our God, how pleasant and fitting to praise him! Psalm 147:1

Bible Story Reference

Matthew 21:1-17; Mark 11:1-11; Luke 19:28-40; John 12:12-19

Teacher's Devotional

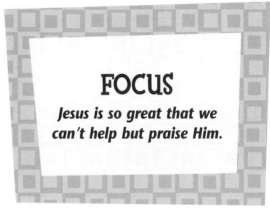

FOCUS

Jesus is so great that we can't help but praise Him.

Most of us enjoy being part of a cheering crowd. We cheer at parades and applaud at performances; even when we watch televised sports, we find ourselves shouting in the living room along with those in the stands! We love to cheer for a winner!

In ancient Israel, cheers and shouts were associated not just with sport but also with praising God. Certain psalms were sung at particular feasts and everyone involved in a celebration would shout praises to God together. The words of the crowd in today's familiar story are first found in Psalm 118—an example of a psalm used at a festival. The words "Blessed is he who comes in the name of the Lord" (Psalm 118:26) roared around Jesus as He rode into Jerusalem. Perhaps few of the people who shouted the words understood their far-reaching significance, but the words were shouted nevertheless—as ritual psalm, as hero's welcome and as God's sweet yet ironic confirmation that here, indeed, was His beloved Messiah. Jesus understood both the human fickleness and the heavenly confirmation of this praise, yet He never held it against the crowd that they cried "Hosanna!" that day and "Crucify!" not long after. He had no illusions about human beings; their praise or blame never swayed Him. At that last Passover meal with His disciples, He clearly declared that praised or cursed, adored or crucified, His purpose remained firm: to give His life as a ransom for many.

Why do we find ourselves shouting along with the Palm Sunday crowd? Do we praise Jesus because it's exciting? Do we praise Him because it's a familiar ritual? Take time to read through the entire Passion Week narrative in at least one Gospel. Consider the awesome price Jesus paid, not in some general effort to save the world, but in a specific act to save *you*. Take time to praise Him as the One who endured the cross, despising the shame, to gain your soul! Then you'll be truly prepared to help your students celebrate Jesus' greatness by praising Him!

Palm Sunday • Matthew 21:1-17; Mark 11:1-11; Luke 19:28-40; John 12:12-19

Story Center

Materials
Bible.

Before the Story
Guide students to briefly practice signs for underlined words.

Tell the Story
As you tell the story, lead students in responding as shown when you say the underlined words.

> *What kinds of parades have you seen? What did you do as you watched the parade?*
>
> *Today we'll find out what some people did when a parade happened right in front of them!*

1. As Jesus and His disciples <u>walked</u> toward Jerusalem, they were part of a great big crowd! The roads were full of excited, happy people on their way to Jerusalem to celebrate Passover, the holiday when the Israelites remembered how God freed their ancestors from slavery in Egypt. People were <u>walking</u> from all over the country to attend the special services at the Temple and to eat the meal God had commanded.

1. Walk: Alternately move hands back and forth.

2. As Jesus and His friends were walking, Jesus said to two of them, "Go on ahead into the next town. There you will find a young <u>donkey</u>. Untie it and bring it to Me. If anyone asks where you are taking the <u>donkey</u>, tell him that the Lord needs it and He will send the <u>donkey</u> back when He's finished."

2. Donkey: Flat right hand at ear; bend fingers at knuckles.

3. Jesus' friends went to the town. There stood the donkey tied up just as Jesus had said it would be. They untied the donkey and began to <u>lead</u> it away. When the owners asked what they were doing, the disciples said the Lord needed it. And sure enough, there was no trouble. They <u>led</u> the donkey to Jesus and spread their coats over the young donkey's back to make a place for Jesus to sit.

3. Lead: Right hand pulls left forward.

4. Jesus climbed onto the donkey and began to <u>ride</u> down the road. His friends walked along beside Him. The news passed quickly through the crowd: "Jesus is coming!" One person and then another shouted, "Jesus is coming!" Soon the crowd was looking around, buzzing with excitement. Then Jesus <u>rode</u> through the crowd and the people all shouted praises to Jesus.

4. Ride: Right index and middle fingers on either side of left palm; hands move forward in short arcs.

5. Some people began spreading their coats on the <u>road</u> like a colorful carpet! Other people cut branches from trees and laid them on the <u>road</u>. People were welcoming Jesus the way they would welcome a KING! They wanted Jesus to know they thought He was important! The <u>road</u> must have looked like a beautiful tapestry!

6. Some people ran on ahead of Jesus, shouting and singing. As they told others, "Jesus is coming! JESUS is coming!" the crowd of people around Jesus got even BIGGER! Soon there was a crowd in front of Jesus and a crowd behind Him. It was looking more and more like a <u>parade</u>! Everyone from children to old people joined the <u>parade</u>, shouting and singing: "Hosanna! Hosanna! God bless the One who comes in the name of the Lord!" (Hosanna means, "Save us!")

7. The people inside the city heard the singing and <u>shouting</u>. They ran out to see what was going on! "Who's coming? What's causing so much excitement?" they asked.

"It's Jesus! Jesus is coming!" people <u>shouted</u> as they came through the gate. More and more people came! The people wanted Jesus to be their new King. Everyone was singing and waving branches in the air as Jesus rode the donkey through the big gate into Jerusalem.

8. Jesus rode up the hill to the Temple, where He got off the donkey. As Jesus went into the Temple, the children danced around Him, singing and shouting <u>praise</u> to Him. The children's songs made some of the religious leaders angry. These men did not believe Jesus really was the Savior. And they were jealous! "Do you hear what these children are saying about You?" they angrily asked Jesus.

"Yes!" Jesus said. "God's Word says that God planned for even children to <u>praise</u> Me!" Jesus had come as the King, and the children knew it, even if the leaders did not!

5. Road: Facing palms move forward with wiggling motion.

6. Parade: Swing bent hands sideways while moving forward, right hand behind left.

7. Shout: Wiggle curved right hand up and away from mouth.

8. Praise: Clap hands a few times.

• •

Discussion Questions

Why were people coming to Jerusalem? (To celebrate Passover.) **What did the people say when they welcomed Jesus? Why?** ("God bless the One who comes in the name of the Lord." They praised Jesus. They wanted Jesus to be their King.) **What did the religious leaders think about Jesus?** (Didn't believe in Him. Were jealous.) **What did the children do?** (Praised Jesus.)

People of all ages are glad to praise Jesus today, too! Jesus is so great and He loves us so much, we can't help but praise Him and celebrate!

Palm Sunday
Object Talk

Scripture Background
Matthew 21:1-17; Mark 11:1-11;
Luke 19:28-40; John 12:12-19

Materials
Bible with bookmark at Psalm 147:1;
optional—objects used to welcome and
praise others (medal, red carpet, confetti,
pennants, pom poms, etc.).

> *We can't help but praise
> and honor Jesus because
> He is so great! Let's look
> at some of the ways great
> people are honored.*

Lead the Activity

1. One at a time, pantomime, or ask volunteers
to pantomime, ways to praise or honor people. (Lay out a red carpet, drop
flower petals down an aisle, cheer for a sports team, salute, bow, curtsy, throw confetti, etc.)
As each action is pantomimed, students guess the action. **Who might be honored that
way?** (Optional: Show objects used to honor others and ask students to describe how
objects could be used to praise others.)

2. **Why do we do special things to praise people?** (To show they are important to us.
To show that we admire or love them.) **On the first Palm Sunday, people praised and
honored Jesus when He arrived in Jerusalem. They clapped and cheered, waved
palm branches in the air and laid palm branches and their coats on the road
for Jesus to ride on. Every year we remember and
celebrate Palm Sunday because it was the beginning
of the time when Jesus died for our sins and then
rose again to give us new life.**

Conclude

**During the week that followed Jesus' kingly parade into
Jerusalem, Jesus died on the cross to make a way for all
of us to become members of God's family. He deserves
all the honor we can give Him!** Read Psalm 147:1 aloud.
**What are some of the things God has done in your life
for which you would like to praise and honor Him?**
Praise God in prayer, mentioning students' responses.

• •

Additional Information for Older Students

**We may not think of a donkey as a royal animal, but in Bible times, the donkey
was considered a sign of humility, peace and royalty! Read 1 Kings 1:38-40 to
learn about a kingly parade similar to the one we celebrate on Palm Sunday.**

   **In Zechariah 9:9, you can read the Old Testament prophet Zechariah's pre-
diction of a King coming to save God's people—riding on a donkey! Now we
know the King he wrote about was Jesus!** Volunteer reads verse aloud.

Palm Sunday

Active Game Center: Palm Branch Pass

Materials

A chair for each student, small branch from a tree or bush for every six to eight students, garden clippers.

Prepare the Game

Set the chairs in lines of four to eight, creating at least two lines of chairs as shown in the sketch. Trim off any sharp twigs from branches.

Lead the Game

1. Group students into teams of four to eight. Assign each team a line of chairs. Students sit on chairs.

We can't help but praise Jesus because of who He is and what He came to do! When Jesus entered Jerusalem the week before He died, people praised Him by waving palm branches in the air. Let's play a game with palm branches to remember a way Jesus was praised!

2. Give a branch to the student sitting in the first chair on each team. At your signal, the student passes the branch down the row. When the branch reaches the last student in the row, he or she carries the branch and runs to the first chair in the row. While student is running, all the other team members move down one chair, leaving the first chair empty for the running student to sit on. After he or she is seated, student passes branch to the next student and branch is passed down the row again. Process is continued until all students have returned to their original chairs.

3. A volunteer from the first team to finish the relay answers one of the questions below. Mix up teams and play game again if time allows.

Options

1. If possible, use palm branches (available at flower shops).

2. If you cannot get a branch from a tree or bush, cut a palm branch out of green paper.

3. If there are not an even number of players, play the relay along with the students.

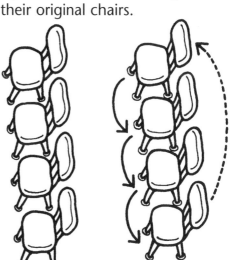

• •

Discussion Questions

1. ***What are some of the reasons we want to praise Jesus?*** (He is God's Son. He was willing to die on the cross to pay the punishment for all people's sins. He rose from the dead. He loves us all. He taught us the best way to live.)

2. ***What are some ways we can praise Jesus?*** (Sing songs to Him. When we pray, tell Him why we love Him or what we are thankful for. Tell others how wonderful He is.)

3. ***What is your favorite way to praise Jesus?*** Volunteers respond.

Palm Sunday

Art Center: Palm Praises

Materials

Green construction paper, pencils, scissors, markers, straws or thin 8-inch (20-cm) wooden dowels, tape.

Lead the Activity

1. Give each student a sheet of construction paper. Students fill papers by tracing their hands on papers. Students cut out hand shapes.

2. On each hand shape, students write prayers of praise to Jesus. Ask the Discussion Questions below to help students think of reasons to praise Jesus. Students may also write the words of Psalm 147:1.

3. Each student tapes together in a vertical row the hand shapes he or she prepared to make a "palm branch." Students tape straws or wooden dowel to branches (see sketch). Invite students to wave palm branches in the air and to read their prayers aloud. Students take home their palm praises to share with family members, or tape branches to wall or over doorways.

We are glad to praise Jesus because of who He is and what He came to do. The people in Jerusalem were glad to praise Jesus, too, when they saw Him entering Jerusalem. They waved palm branches to praise Him! Let's make our own palm praises.

Back

Options

1. Students tape each hand shape onto a separate straw or dowel and place them into the ground or grass outside the church or their home.

2. Encourage older students to read Psalm 100 and 148 to find phrases to use for their prayers of praise.

3. Bring sugar cookies for students to decorate with green frosting or sprinkles. Students may also use tubes of green icing to draw palm branch shapes on cookies.

Discussion Questions

1. **Who is Jesus?** (God's Son. The Savior of the world.)

2. **What has Jesus done?** (Paid for our sins by dying for us. Shown His great love. Made it possible for us to be forgiven and be members of God's family.)

3. **What could you say to praise Jesus for who He is and what He has done?** Volunteers tell ideas.

"Praise the Lord. How good it is to sing praises to our God, how pleasant and fitting to praise him!" Psalm 147:1

HOSANNA!

The Challenge → **Mark 11:1-11**

Can you solve the rebus? It's going to echo the shouts of joy that followers of Jesus made when He entered Jerusalem on a donkey.

(tape)-e + (ant)-t (nail)-il
_____

(yo-yo)-al + ES (sled)-L
_____

(fist)-ft (muscle)-el W + (horse)-of
_____

(comet)-t + S (fish)-f (spool)-rad
_____

N(camel)-cl (on/off switch)-f 3-re
_____

L + (sword)-sw.
_____

The Super Challenge On the back of this paper, make your own rebus for the phrase "We want to praise Jesus."

Easter Story 1

Jesus' Death and Resurrection

Bible Verse

God has given us eternal life, and this life is in his Son. 1 John 5:11

Bible Story Reference

Matthew 26:36—28:15; Mark 14:32—16:8; Luke 22:47—24:12; John 18—20:18

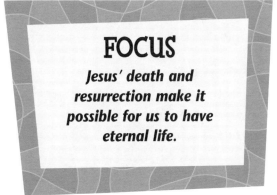

FOCUS

Jesus' death and resurrection make it possible for us to have eternal life.

Teacher's Devotional

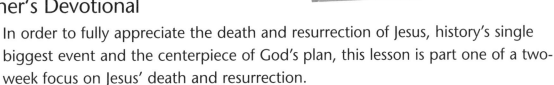

In order to fully appreciate the death and resurrection of Jesus, history's single biggest event and the centerpiece of God's plan, this lesson is part one of a two-week focus on Jesus' death and resurrection.

Passion Week, also called Holy Week, begins with Palm Sunday and ends with Easter. Many churches are open for services daily or at least on Thursday and Friday. This is the week during which Lent culminates, the week during which Christians around the world consider the depth of God's love revealed in Christ's actions, actions which would be considered irrational in anyone but Him! Anyone else in the same situation would naturally try to save his life, to reason with the jealous leaders, to bargain with the Roman ruler for his freedom. But no one else in all of history was charged with the profound task of giving His own life as a ransom for the sins of the world. No one else was qualified; no one else had lived a perfect life. And no one else could die His perfect death. As Jesus prayed in the garden of Gethsemane, He agreed to drink this cup of suffering. All that followed was the fulfillment of that commitment, the outflow of that choice to be obedient—even to death by the most horrible torture known in the Roman world.

Jesus endured the horrors of crucifixion and counted the shame as something insignificant because He valued your soul so deeply. Jesus loved you with such an intensity that all else was unimportant. Jesus proved Himself not only the only One qualified to redeem us but also the only One able to overcome death itself, the final fear! Because He lives, we can share in that life, both now and forever! Take time to consider Jesus' actions and then to thank and praise Him. Communicate your excitement with your students as you celebrate together. He is alive and offers us life at its fullest!

Easter Story 1 • Matthew 26:36—28:15; Mark 14:32—16:8; Luke 22:47—24:12; John 18—20:18

Story Center

Materials
Bible.

Before the Story
Guide students to briefly practice signs for underlined words.

Tell the Story
As you tell the story, lead students in responding as shown when you say the underlined words.

> **When has something you thought was going to be really BAD turned out to be something really GOOD?**
>
> **Today we'll hear about a really BAD thing that God turned into a really GOOD thing!**

1. Jerusalem was crowded! It was the biggest celebration of the year. God's people were eating the special Passover dinner with their families and singing and praying to God. While <u>Jesus</u> and His friends were eating their Passover meal, <u>Jesus</u> broke some bread into pieces and said, "This bread is My body. I give it for you." <u>Jesus</u> picked up a cup and said, "This is my blood, shed for you."

2. Jesus wanted His friends to understand God's <u>plan</u> for Him. Jesus knew that He had to be killed. By His death, Jesus would take the punishment for all the sins, or wrong things, people had done. And Jesus loved us so much, He was willing to go through with the <u>plan</u>. He was willing to die so that we can be forgiven.

3. Even though many people had praised Jesus, some of the <u>leaders</u> hated Him. They said to each other, "We must STOP Jesus. Too many people love Him. If we don't get rid of Him soon, WE won't be the <u>leaders</u> anymore!" They decided to take Jesus away when no one was around and KILL Him. Judas, one of Jesus' disciples, went secretly to these <u>leaders</u>. He offered to take them to Jesus, and the <u>leaders</u> paid Judas money to do this.

4. Jesus knew what Judas had done secretly. And He knew that God would turn this horrible thing into something VERY GOOD. You see, even though Jesus had shown love and taught about God and healed people, His main reason for coming to earth was to <u>take</u> the punishment for sin. So when Judas led people to Jesus to <u>take</u> Him away, Jesus let them <u>take</u> Him.

1. Jesus: Touch palms with opposite middle fingers.

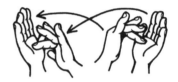

2. Plan: Move hands left to right, bouncing slightly.

3. Leader: Right hand pulls left forward; move hands down sides.

4. Take: Sweep open right hand to form a fist.

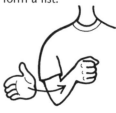

5. Jesus let these people tell lies about Him and hurt Him and make fun of Him. And He let them kill Him on a cross. Most of Jesus' friends had run away when Jesus was arrested. But now they stood sadly watching as Jesus died. *Can't Jesus make this STOP?* they must have wondered. At noon, when the sun should have been brightest, it got <u>dark</u>. Jesus' friends must have felt <u>dark</u> inside, too, for Jesus' friends didn't yet understand what Jesus had told them. They didn't know yet the good that God had planned!

5. Dark: Cross palms downward in front of face.

6. After Jesus was dead, two of His <u>sad</u> friends put His body into a tomb in a little garden. (A tomb was a little room dug into the side of a hill.) A HUGE rock was put in front of the tomb's doorway. And Jesus' friends went home feeling VERY <u>sad</u>. It looked like EVERYTHING had gone wrong. Now Jesus was dead. But something more was going to happen!

6. Sad: Palms in, drop hands down face.

7. On Sunday, the third day after Jesus died, some women who had been Jesus' friends got up at dawn and went to the tomb. When they got there, they could see that the big rock had been rolled away from the tomb's doorway! Mary, one of the women, was so surprised, she <u>ran</u> back to get Peter and John, two more of Jesus' friends. Peter and John <u>ran</u> to the garden and looked inside the tomb. They could see that it was EMPTY! But Peter and John didn't understand. They sadly left.

7. Run: Hook right index finger to left thumb; move forward and repeatedly bend fingers.

8. Mary had followed Peter and John back to the garden. She stayed there, crying. But then she saw and heard someone. *Is this the gardener?* she wondered. But then He said her name. Mary knew that voice. It was JESUS! He was ALIVE! She was so <u>happy</u>! Jesus told her to go tell the others that He was alive. She ran back, full of <u>joy</u>! Jesus was ALIVE! And God's plan was good!

8. Happy, joy: Move hands in forward circles, palms touching chest.

• •

Discussion Questions

Why did Jesus let people arrest Him, hurt Him and kill Him? (It was part of God's plan. He loves us. He was willing to die to take the punishment for our sins.) **How did people know Jesus was alive again?** (Stone was moved. Tomb was empty. Mary saw Jesus.)

Jesus died to take the penalty for our sins. And He is alive. That means anyone who believes in Jesus and asks for forgiveness can have eternal life. What a reason to celebrate! Talk with students about becoming members of God's family (see "Leading a Child to Christ" on p. 253).

Object Talk

Scripture Background

Matthew 26:36—28:15; Mark 14:32—16:8;
Luke 22:47—24:12; John 18—20:18

Materials

Bible with bookmark at 1 John 5:11, children's
music CD or music video and player.

> *Because Jesus died for our sins and rose again, we can have eternal life! Let's look at one way we remember Jesus' great gift every year at Easter.*

Lead the Activity

1. Wave hand at students. **What does it
mean when I wave my hand at you?** (Waving is a way to say hello or greet someone.)
Demonstrate, or ask students to demonstrate, other ways to greet people. (Say hello. Give a
high five. Shake hands.)

2. **During Easter, many Christians greet each other in a special way. One person
says "Christ is risen," and the other says "He is risen indeed."** For several minutes,
play children's music CD as students walk around room and greet each other in the manner
described above. (Note: If there are other Easter traditions followed in your church family,
explain these traditions to students.)

Conclude

**Jesus' resurrection makes it possible for us to
become members of God's family!** Read 1 John 5:11
aloud. **Eternal life means we can live with God in
heaven, experiencing His love forever. According
to this verse, where can we get eternal life?** (From
God's Son, Jesus.) Pray, thanking Jesus for dying on the
cross and rising from the dead so that we can have eternal
life. Talk with interested students about becoming members
of God's family (see "Leading a Child to Christ" on p. 253).

Christ is risen!

He is risen indeed!

Discussion Questions

1. *Why was Jesus the only One who could take the punishment for our sins?* (Jesus is
the only person who never sinned. He is the One God promised to send.)

2. *When we choose to become members of God's family, what does He give us?*
(Forgiveness for our sins. Eternal life.)

3. *What are some ways we remember Jesus' death and celebrate His resurrection?*
(Thank Jesus for His love. Sing special songs. Celebrate Easter with our church families at
special worship services.)

4. *How does your family celebrate Jesus' resurrection at Eastertime?*

Active Game Center: "He's Alive!" Relay

Materials

Large sheets of brown or gray paper, scissors, black markers; optional—Post-it Notes, pencils.

Prepare the Game

Cut paper into rock shapes, creating one "rock" for every four to six students. Place paper rocks on one side of the playing area. Place a black marker next to each paper rock.

> *Jesus' death and resurrection make it possible for us to have eternal life! What a wonderful gift to celebrate! Let's celebrate by playing a game in which we say the good news about Jesus' resurrection.*

Lead the Game

1. **When Mary Magdalene went to Jesus' tomb on Easter morning, what did she find?** (The stone had been rolled back and the tomb was empty.) **Mary, Peter and John discovered that the tomb was empty because Jesus had risen from the dead and was alive! What did they all do next?** (Told everyone that Jesus had risen!)

2. **What are some things we can say to share the good news about Jesus' resurrection?** ("Jesus is alive!" "He is risen!" "Christ conquered death!" "Hallelujah!" "Jesus rose!") List students' responses on a large sheet of paper. (Optional: Each student writes one phrase on a Post-it Note.)

He is risen! hallelujah Jesus is alive!

3. Group students into teams of four to six, creating at least two teams. Teams line up across the playing area from the paper rocks. At your signal, the first student from each team runs to his or her team's paper rock, writes one good news phrase on the rock, calls out the phrase and returns to his or her line, tagging the next student, who repeats the action. (Optional: Student sticks Post-it Note phrase on rock.) Students refer to list of responses during relay if necessary. Relay continues until all students have had a turn. Repeat relay as time permits.

Option

1. Suggest that each student think of and remember one phrase to write on the team's rock before the relay begins.

2. Bring a large rock for each team. Students stick Post-it Notes on the rocks.

• •

Discussion Questions

1. *What does Jesus' death and resurrection mean for us?* (Our sins can be forgiven when we believe in His death and resurrection. Jesus has the power to forgive our sins.)

2. *What do you want to do when you hear the good news about eternal life through Jesus' death and resurrection?* (Tell others. Thank God. Celebrate.)

3. *With whom can you share this good news?*

Art Center: Creative Crosses

Materials

Scissors, ¼-inch (.625-cm) ribbon, measuring stick, craft sticks, several emery boards, fine-tipped markers.

Prepare the Activity

Cut a 3-foot (.9-m) length of ribbon for each student.

> *Jesus' death and resurrection make it possible for all people to live forever with Him! Let's celebrate that great news by making cross necklaces.*

Lead the Activity

1. Give each student two craft sticks.
Students cut or break in half one craft stick and then use the rougher side of an emery board to round the broken edge.

2. On one side of their craft sticks students use fine-tipped markers to draw designs and write messages about Jesus' resurrection.

3. Students place craft sticks together to form crosses. Beginning at the middle of the ribbons, students wrap ribbons around the two sticks several times in an X-shaped pattern. Students knot the ribbons at the back of their crosses, leaving enough ribbon to knot the ends together and slip over their heads.

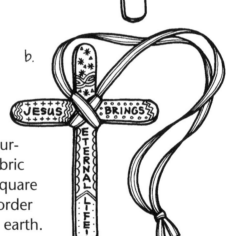

Options

1. Provide a variety of materials (horseshoe nails and lengths of thin leather, short twigs and twine, etc.) from which students can make cross necklaces.

2. During this lesson and the next, celebrate the life, death and resurrection of Christ by leading students to make a Resurrection Story quilt. Each student first uses pencil and then fabric marker to illustrate an event of Passion week on a separate square of fabric. Sew completed squares together in chronological order so that students can review the events of Jesus' last week on earth.

3. If time in class is limited, break craft sticks before class.

Discussion Questions

1. *What does the cross remind you of?* (Jesus' death and resurrection.)

2. *What can happen for anyone because of Jesus' death on the cross and His resurrection from the dead?* (We can live forever with Jesus when we believe in Jesus' death and resurrection.)

3. *What might you say if people ask you about the cross you made today?* (Tell them the good news that Jesus is alive and gives us forgiveness.)

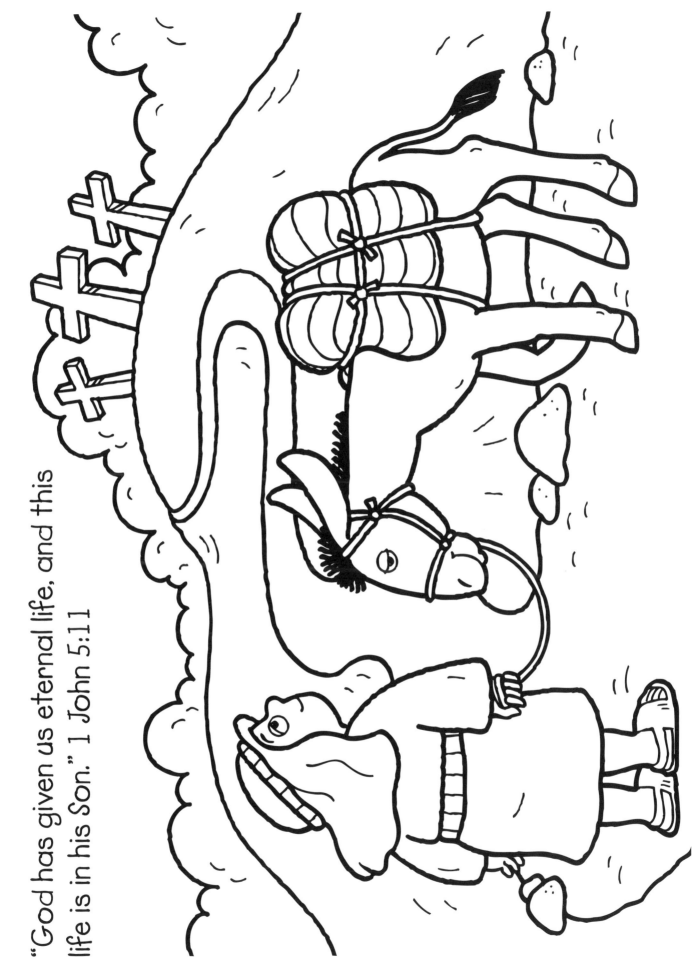

"God has given us eternal life, and this life is in his Son." 1 John 5:11

LIFE SUPPORT SYSTEM

1 John 5:11

Solve this rebus telling about God's incredible gift to us.

 " −L    −T   G + 5 − F + N

_____   _____   _____

 −B   ⬛ − M + 🖊 − I

_____   _____

L + 🔪 − KN   🖐 − H   𝟯rd − RD + S

_____ , _____   _____

L + 🔪 − KN   🐟 − FH

_____   _____

 − CH   🐛 − VE + S    − PGE "

_____   _____   _____ .

76   © 2005 Gospel Light. Permission to photocopy granted. *The Big Book of Holiday and Bible Celebrations*

Easter Story 2

Jesus Appears to Thomas

Bible Verse

For God so loved the world that he gave his one and only Son, that whoever believes in him shall not perish but have eternal life.
John 3:16

Bible Story Reference

John 20:19-31

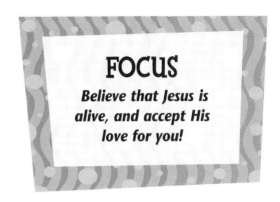

FOCUS
Believe that Jesus is alive, and accept His love for you!

Teacher's Devotional

In this lesson celebrating the miracle of Jesus' resurrection, we take time to consider the actions of Thomas. We don't know why Thomas was not present when the risen Jesus appeared to and talked with the other disciples. But when the others told Thomas that Jesus was alive, Thomas refused to take their word for it! Even the word of 10 of his dearest friends was not authority enough when it came to such a life-shaking issue. Thomas would not say that he believed what he did not understand!

At first look, Thomas's stubborn honesty seems negative. Where was his faith? He certainly would have seemed more spiritual if he had listened to his friends' testimony and believed right away. However, in another sense, Thomas's attitude is a very positive one, for all too often we say we believe or understand something when we really don't. This is partly due to peer pressure (after all, the others all seem to understand) and partly due to fear that others will think we aren't spiritual (best to agree quickly, look spiritual and not ask questions). But as time goes on, our actions sometimes prove that we really didn't believe or understand at all! Thomas was humble enough not to grab the chance to look spiritual. His honesty said, "This is not something I can believe. I'm not there yet. I need proof."

There are answers to all our doubts—but we shouldn't accept something on the word of others simply because we fear that we won't look spiritual. We need to humbly take our doubts to the Lord and ask Him to reveal His truth to us. Then we need to search God's Word until our own hearts are satisfied. While Jesus commented that those who do not see and yet believe are blessed (see John 20:29), He did not withhold His love and blessing from the doubter! When we are honest with our doubts and faithful in seeking truth, the end result will be, as it was for Thomas, a commitment to Jesus that is thought-out and genuine—yielding the fruit of a living, growing relationship with the same Jesus who invited Thomas to put his finger into His nail prints. Let's celebrate the journey to belief!

Story Center

Materials
Bible.

Before the Story
Guide students to briefly practice signs for underlined words.

Tell the Story
As you tell the story, lead students in responding as shown when you say the underlined words.

> *Have you ever heard about something and wondered whether it was true or not?*
>
> *Today we're going to hear about someone who didn't believe what his friends told him.*

1. There was a time when most of Jesus' disciples and friends were very <u>scared</u>. The Romans had killed Jesus, and His friends were <u>afraid</u> they might be killed, too. They didn't know what to do. So Jesus' friends were hiding in an upstairs room of someone's house. They locked all the doors, so no one could get in.

2. Ever since morning on this third day after Jesus died, Jesus' friends had been hearing exciting but confusing reports about Jesus. First, they had heard that His tomb was empty. Then some people actually claimed to have seen Jesus. They said He was <u>alive</u> again! But most of the people who were hiding weren't at all sure they could believe that Jesus was <u>ALIVE</u>.

3. SUDDENLY, there was Jesus standing in the room with them! He didn't come through the door. He was just THERE!

   "Peace be with you," He said. Jesus' friends thought they were seeing a ghost! They couldn't believe their eyes!

   "I am not a ghost," said Jesus. "Come and <u>touch</u> Me. I'll show you that I am alive." His friends <u>touched</u> Him.

4. Then just to be sure His friends knew it was really Him and not a ghost, Jesus asked them to bring Him some <u>food</u>. One of His friends gave Jesus some fish. Jesus <u>ate</u> it right there in front of them. Jesus' friends were amazed. Since only living people could <u>eat</u>, they knew that Jesus was really ALIVE!

1. Scared, afraid: Fingertips touching, open hands and cover chest.

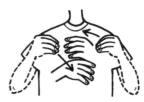

2. Alive: Thumbs and index fingers extended, move hands up body.

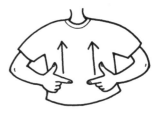

3. Touch: Touch left hand with right middle finger.

4. Food, eat: Fingertips touching, move right hand to mouth a few times.

5. Jesus' friends looked at each other. It really WAS Jesus! The room began to buzz with excited questions. Jesus explained to them again how it had been God's plan for Him to die and come back to life so that people could be forgiven for their sins and become part of God's family. Then Jesus was gone, just as quickly as He had appeared.

5. Jesus: Touch palms with opposite middle fingers.

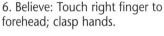

6. One of Jesus' friends named Thomas was not there when Jesus visited. The other disciples could hardly wait to see Thomas and tell him, "WE HAVE SEEN JESUS!"

Thomas didn't believe them. It sounded too good to be true! "Until I put my fingers in the nail prints in Jesus' hands and touch the place where the sword pierced His side," Thomas said, "I will not believe!"

6. Believe: Touch right finger to forehead; clasp hands.

7. Nothing anyone said could change Thomas's mind. But Jesus loved Thomas and wanted him to know He was alive. A full week later, Jesus' friends were meeting in the same house. This time, Thomas was with them. Just like before, the doors were all locked. And SUDDENLY, just like before, there was Jesus, RIGHT there with them in the room!

7. With: Touch fists together.

8. Jesus turned to Thomas first.

"Thomas!" said Jesus. "Come and touch Me. I want you to believe that I am really alive." All of Thomas's doubts suddenly were gone. Thomas knelt down and said, "MY LORD AND MY GOD!"

Now Thomas truly believed that Jesus was alive!

Jesus said to Thomas, "You believe now that you have seen me." Then Jesus said something about all of us who weren't there that night. Jesus said, "Imagine the happiness of those who believe without being able to see Me." When we believe that Jesus truly is alive, we share in the same happiness Jesus' friends enjoyed that night they saw Jesus.

8. Alive: Thumbs and index fingers extended, move hands up body.

• •

Discussion Questions

What did Jesus' friends tell Thomas? (That Jesus was alive. That they had seen Him.) **Why didn't Thomas believe his friends?** (He said he wanted to touch Jesus.) **What did Thomas say when Jesus invited him to touch Him?** ("My Lord and my God!")

Jesus will help us believe He is alive and accept His love for us. He showed that love by dying for us and rising again. And that's a GREAT reason to celebrate!

Easter Story 2

Object Talk

Scripture Background

John 20:19-31

Materials

Bible with bookmarks at John 3:16 and John 20:29; objects for students to describe (unusual stuffed animal, kitchen utensil, tool, etc.), placed in a bag.

We accept Jesus' love for us and believe that He is alive, even though we didn't see Him for ourselves! Let's try an experiment to discover why it sometimes might be hard to believe what other people tell us about something we didn't see for ourselves.

Lead the Activity

1. Several volunteers leave the room (or close eyes). Show one of the objects and give students several moments to look at it. **When the volunteers return, describe the object to them, but don't use the words ("stuffed" or "animal").** Volunteers return and try to guess what the object is based on student descriptions. Repeat for each object you brought, reminding students not to use obvious words that would give away the object's identity.

2. **What made it difficult to figure out what the object was?** Volunteers respond. **Sometimes it's hard to believe something is true if you haven't seen it yourself. When Jesus rose from the dead, Thomas, one of His disciples, didn't believe Jesus was really alive because he hadn't seen Jesus with his own eyes.**

Even though we didn't see what Jesus did or hear what He said when He lived on earth and even though we didn't see Him after He rose from the dead, we believe all these things happened. That's why we celebrate Easter! We can read God's Word that tells us exactly what the disciples saw and that they believed Jesus was alive! What did Jesus say about people who believe in Him without seeing Him? Read John 20:29.

Conclude

Because we know Jesus is alive, we can also have eternal life—life that lasts forever with God in heaven. Read John 3:16 aloud. Pray, thanking God that Jesus is alive and that He loves us.

• •

Discussion Questions

1. *What are some of the things you believe about Jesus?* (He loves me. He forgives the wrong things I do. He makes it possible for me to be part of God's family.)

2. *Who has helped you learn to believe in Jesus?* (Sunday School teacher. Parent.)

3. *In what ways do kids your age show they believe that Jesus is alive?* (Pray to Him. Obey His commands. Read the Bible to learn more about Him.)

Active Game Center: Believe It or Not!

Materials

Children's music CD and player, index cards, marker.

Prepare the Game

Print each letter of the word "believe" on a separate index card and mix them together with enough other blank index cards to provide one card for each student.

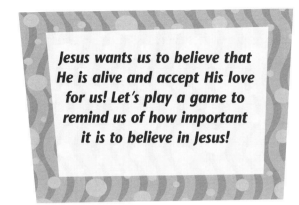

Jesus wants us to believe that He is alive and accept His love for us! Let's play a game to remind us of how important it is to believe in Jesus!

Lead the Game

1. Students sit or stand in a circle. Give each student an index card facedown.

2. As you play children's music CD, students pass cards facedown around the circle. Stop the music after a short while. When music stops, students look at their cards. Students with blank cards do five jumping jacks. Students with letters on their cards move quickly to stand in the correct order to spell "believe." Student holding the letter *B* answers one of the Discussion Questions below. Collect index cards, mix cards together and redistribute to play again. Continue game as time allows, varying which students are to answer questions and changing the actions of students holding blank cards (high-five a friend, turn around twice, etc.).

Options

1. For older students, prepare cards for other words or phrases from John 3:16. Call out which word or phrase to spell when you stop the music. You may also prepare enough cards so that each student has a card with a letter from one of the words in the verse. Students group themselves into words. Give help as needed (identify first letters of words, etc.).

2. Bring a stopwatch and time how quickly it takes each set of students to form the word(s).

3. For younger students, number the cards with the letters of "believe" on them. Students refer to numbers on cards if they need help lining up in the correct order.

Discussion Questions

1. ***What does John 3:16 say about believing in Jesus?*** Have a student say or read the verse aloud and then invite volunteers to answer the question.

2. ***How did Jesus show He loves us?*** (Died for our sins. Came to earth as a baby.)

3. ***What can you do to show you believe that Jesus rose from the dead and to show that you want to accept His love?*** (Thank Him for His love. Ask Him to forgive my sins and believe that He will. Learn more about Jesus' love for me and how He wants me to live by reading the Bible.)

Art Center: Ceiling Signs

Materials

Poster board in several colors; scissors or paper cutter; one or more of these art supplies: neon markers, metallic pens, glitter pens, glow-in-the-dark pens or paint; masking tape or tacks.

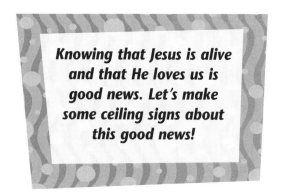

Knowing that Jesus is alive and that He loves us is good news. Let's make some ceiling signs about this good news!

Prepare the Activity

Cut poster board into a variety of shapes (rectangles, squares, triangles, squiggles, etc.), making at least one shape for each student.

Lead the Activity

1. Each student chooses one or more poster-board shapes.

2. Using the supplies you have provided, students write on their shapes messages about Jesus' love and that He is alive. To help students think of messages ask, **What is something about Jesus everyone ought to know? What are some reasons Jesus is so great? What are some words you would use to describe Jesus' love? How does Jesus show His love for us today? Why are you glad Jesus is alive?** Students may also draw designs of their own choosing on the shapes.

3. Display completed signs on the ceiling of your classroom, or students may take home the signs to display on the ceilings of their bedrooms.

Options

1. If students will be taking their signs home, provide glow-in-the-dark stars for students to attach to their signs.

2. Older students may prefer to cut their own poster-board shapes.

• •

Discussion Questions

1. *What are some important things to believe about Jesus?* (He is God's Son. He lived on earth. He died for the sins of all people. He rose from the dead. He loves us.)

2. *How can we learn more about Jesus' love for us and His resurrection from the dead?* (Read the Gospels in the Bible. Ask people who love Jesus to tell you about Him.)

3. *Where can you put your sign(s) to remind you of the good news about Jesus?*

"For God so loved the world that he gave his one and only Son, that whoever believes in him shall not perish but have eternal life." John 3:16

DIZZY SPELLS!

The Challenge ➜

John 3:16

These kids are getting dizzy trying to solve this puzzle! Start at the center of the spiral and fill in the missing vowels. After you do, memorize the verse. (Hint: Read the verse in your Bible for help.)

Ruth Listens to Naomi

Bible Verse

Trust in the Lord with all your heart and lean not on your own understanding; in all your ways acknowledge him, and he will make your paths straight. Proverbs 3:5,6

Bible Story Reference

Ruth

FOCUS
God gives us people to guide and care for us.

Teacher's Devotional

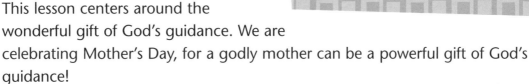

This lesson centers around the wonderful gift of God's guidance. We are celebrating Mother's Day, for a godly mother can be a powerful gift of God's guidance!

The connection of the story of Ruth to Mother's Day is found in Naomi, a mother used by God to guide her daughter-in-law Ruth into a prominent place in the messianic line of David. Ruth was a pagan girl who had learned the ways of Israel's God from her husband's family. Ruth's full embracing of the God of Israel and her devotion to her mother-in-law made her a role model of unselfish care. As a result, she was also the recipient of God's blessing and honored as an ancestor of the Messiah. Ruth and Naomi's story illustrates how God provides people in our lives to guide us in coming to know and love Him. (In addition, the story of Ruth has come to be associated with the Feast of Firstfruits because it took place during the barley harvest, which took place during May or June.)

Mother's Day in the United States was first suggested by Julia Ward Howe (who wrote the words to the "Battle Hymn of the Republic") in 1872; the official national observance dates from 1914. Other countries around the world (such as France and Yugoslavia) have also established spring days to honor mothers; and England observes Mothering Sunday, a custom dating back to the Middle Ages when worshipers returned to their "mother" churches for special services.

Today as you help your students honor their mothers and other significant people in their lives, help your students see that loving adults whom they trust, whether mothers, grandmothers or even teachers, can be a source of wise counsel and godly experience—people through whom God guides us.

Story Center

Materials
Bible.

Before the Story
Guide students to briefly practice signs for underlined words.

Tell the Story
As you tell the story, lead students in responding as shown when you say the underlined words.

When was a time you really needed someone's help? What happened?

Today we'll find out what happened when someone needed help just to have food to eat!

1. For years in Israel, there had been famine—no rain and no food. Many Israelites had moved from Israel to nearby Moab in search of food. Ruth was a young woman who grew up in Moab. She met and married one of these Israelite men. Ruth and her <u>husband</u> lived with her <u>husband's</u> family. After a time, her <u>husband's</u> father died and then her <u>husband</u> and his brother died. Now Ruth, her <u>husband's</u> mother, Naomi, and Ruth's sister-in-law were widows! They had no <u>husbands</u>.

2. In those days, a woman who had no husband usually had no way to make a living. All three women must have wondered, *Who will help us now that our husbands are gone?*

   Naomi told her daughters-in-law, "Go back to your own families. Perhaps you will marry again. I will <u>leave</u> for Israel." Ruth and her sister-in-law did not want to <u>leave</u> Naomi. But finally, Ruth's sister-in-law <u>left</u> for home.

3. Ruth, however, said, "I'm going <u>with</u> you! I will be like your daughter. Your people will be my people, and your God will be my God. I have promised God that I will not leave you!" Naomi could see that Ruth WASN'T going to change her mind! So Ruth set off <u>with</u> Naomi for Bethlehem, Naomi's hometown. During this hard time in her life, Ruth must have been glad that God had provided her <u>with</u> a caring mother-in-law like Naomi.

4. When they got to Bethlehem, the farmers were just beginning to harvest, or cut down, the ripe barley <u>plants</u>. Barley is a grain, like wheat. In Bible times, people harvested the barley and tied the <u>plants</u> into bundles.

1. Husband: Close fingers of right hand while moving out from forehead; clasp hands.

2. Leave: Flat hands move up and into fists.

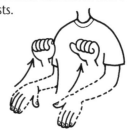

3. With: Touch fists together.

4. Plant: Open right hand as it comes up through left.

5. Ruth must have been VERY glad there was a harvest going on! God had made laws about harvesting food. God said that grain that fell to the ground and grain that grew in the corners of the fields were to be left for <u>poor</u> people to gather (called gleaning). Well, Ruth and Naomi were <u>poor</u> people now, so Ruth could glean enough barley so that she and Naomi could eat for a while.

5. Poor: Right hand cups left elbow; move hand down and close fingers.

6. Ruth went to a barley field where she saw people harvesting grain. She followed the harvesters, picking barley off the ground and cutting barley stalks in the corners of the field. Ruth didn't mind the hard work. Naomi had been <u>kind</u> to her and helped her. Ruth wanted to make sure that she was <u>kind</u>, too, and that she had enough food for Naomi.

6. Kind: Left hand at chest level; right hand circles left.

7. The field where Ruth gleaned belonged to a relative of Naomi. His name was Boaz. When Boaz saw Ruth <u>working</u> in his field, he asked his helper about her. "She's the woman from Moab who came with Naomi," the helper said. "She asked if she could glean in our field, and she's <u>worked</u> very hard since she got here!" Boaz had already heard about Ruth and how she had taken care of Naomi. Boaz went to Ruth and invited her to stay and glean in his fields.

7. Work: Hands in fists, tap left wrist with right.

8. So Ruth gleaned in Boaz's fields all during the harvest. And once Naomi heard that it was her relative Boaz who owned the field where Ruth was gleaning, she made a <u>wise</u> plan. Her plan would mean that she and Ruth would be able to get back some of her family's land. Naomi guided Ruth in following Naomi's plan exactly. And as a result of Naomi's guidance, Boaz bought back the land Naomi's family had owned. Now Naomi and Ruth had a home! And Boaz also MARRIED Ruth! When Ruth and Boaz had a baby, Naomi's friends came to celebrate with her. Because of her <u>wise</u> plan, Naomi and Ruth had a home and family again!

8. Wise: Bend right index finger; move up and down on forehead.

● ●

Discussion Questions

Why did the Israelites go to Moab? (There was no food in Israel.) **When Naomi decided to go back to Israel, what did Ruth decide?** (To go with Naomi and care for her.) **When Naomi found out that Boaz was her relative, what did she do?** (Made a plan to get Boaz to help her.) **How did Naomi help and guide Ruth?** (She brought her back to Bethlehem. She told her what to do to get some land and a home.)

Even in hard times, God gives us people to love and care for us. It's one way God guides us. And it's a great reason to celebrate!

Mother's Day
Object Talk

Scripture Background
Proverbs 3:5,6

Materials
Bible with bookmark at Proverbs 3:5,6; several gifts traditionally given on Mother's Day (candy, flowers, cards, etc.).

Lead the Activity

1. One at a time, display the gifts you brought. **Who might you give this gift to? Why would you give this gift?** Repeat for each of the gifts you brought.

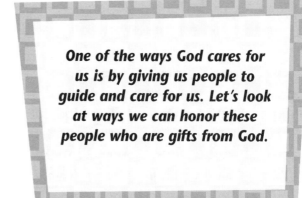

One of the ways God cares for us is by giving us people to guide and care for us. Let's look at ways we can honor these people who are gifts from God.

2. **On Mother's Day, we give gifts like these to mothers and other people who care for us. We do this to honor them and let them know we appreciate all that they do for us. There are lots of types of mothers—grandmothers, stepmothers, foster mothers and people who act like mothers! They are all given to us by God to guide and care for us. Who are some other people God has given to care for you?** (Fathers. Aunts. Older brothers or sisters. Teachers.) Invite volunteers to tell ways people care for them.

3. **This year on Mother's Day, you can honor your mother or anyone else who guides you and cares for you. What are some special or unusual ways to honor this person?** (Say "I love you." Give a back massage. Water flowers. Clean your room and bathroom. Cook dinner.)

Conclude

Read Proverbs 3:5,6 aloud. **According to these verses, whose directions should we follow?** (God's directions.) **How can we know what God wants us to do?** (By reading God's Word. By listening to parents and other people who guide and care for us.) Pray, thanking God that He gives us people to guide and care for us.

• •

Discussion Questions

1. *Who are the people you want to honor today?*

2. *How have these people helped you?*

3. *What special gifts will you give them?*

Mother's Day

Active Game Center: Ball Bounce

Materials

Ball, container (wastebasket, large bowl, cardboard box).

Lead the Game

1. Students line up approximately 3 feet (.9 m) from container.

2. Students take turns bouncing a ball at least once while attempting to get ball into container. If the ball goes into the container, student tells the name of someone who guides and cares for him or her. If ball does not go into the container after three tries, next student takes a turn. Continue play as time allows.

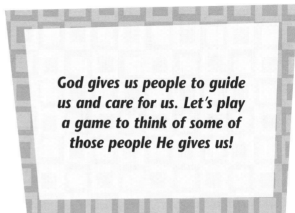

God gives us people to guide us and care for us. Let's play a game to think of some of those people He gives us!

Options

1. Instead of naming people who care for them, older students give clues ("This person taught me to ride a bike." "This person helps me do math problems.") about the people for others to guess.

2. Consider the age and ability of your students and adjust distance students stand from container accordingly.

3. If you have more than six students in your group, provide additional balls and containers in order to limit the time students spend waiting in line.

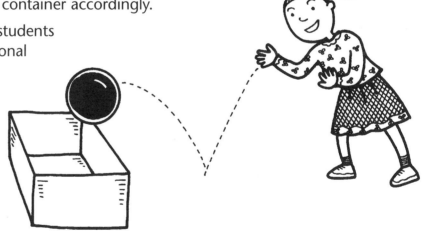

Discussion Questions

1. *How does (your mother) guide and care for you?* Volunteers respond. Repeat with other people named by students.

2. *What are some ways we need to be cared for? What are some good reasons to have people to guide us?* (To help us know what to do in our lives. To teach us good ways to live.)

3. *Who are some people who teach you about God? What can you do to thank God for giving you people to guide you in knowing Him?*

Art Center: Gifts Galore!

Materials

Materials needed for gift of your choice.

Prepare the Activity

Make a sample of the gift of your choice.

Lead the Activity

Lead students to complete one of the following gifts. As students are making gifts, ask students to tell to whom they plan to give gifts.

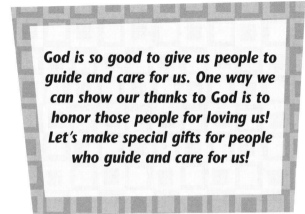

God is so good to give us people to guide and care for us. One way we can show our thanks to God is to honor those people for loving us! Let's make special gifts for people who guide and care for us!

Corsage Pins

Give each student a small bunch of fabric flowers. Students trim and arrange flowers, making stems at least 2 inches (5 cm) long. Students tightly wrap colored vinyl tape or green chenille wires around the flower stems and a large safety pin (see sketch a). (Optional: Older students use green florist's tape, stretching it to make it adhere as they wrap it.) Add ribbons to trim.

Magnets

Provide Fun Foam in one or more colors. Give each student a piece of Fun Foam approximately 4 inches (10 cm) square. Students use pencils to draw shapes of their own choosing (stars, suns, flowers, hearts, triangles, circles, birds, etc.) on Fun Foam pieces (see sketch b). Students cut out shapes and then draw designs on shapes with markers. Students attach adhesive-backed magnets to the back of their shapes.

Discussion Questions

1. ***Who are some of the people God has given to guide and care for you?*** Volunteers respond.

2. ***In what ways do these people guide and care for you? How do they help you?*** (Provide food, clothing and a home. Teach me about God. Help me learn to get along with other people. Help me with homework.)

3. ***What might happen if God didn't give us anyone to guide and care for us?***

Trust in the Lord with all your heart...and he will make your paths straight." Proverbs 3:5,6

COMPUTER VIRUS!

The Challenge

Proverbs 3:5,6

The computer has some sort of a glitch. When the verse was input, the words ran together in places and became difficult to read.
Can you separate the words and write out the verse correctly?

"Trus tint he Lordwithal lyour

_____

hea rtand leanno ton youro wn

_____

understa nding; inallyour

_____

waysack nowle dgehi mand

_____

hewi llma keyou r

_____

pat hsstr aight."

_____

Jairus and His Daughter

Bible Verse

Dear friends, since God so loved us, we also ought to love one another. 1 John 4:11

Bible Story Reference

Mark 5:21-43; Luke 8:40-56

Teacher's Devotional

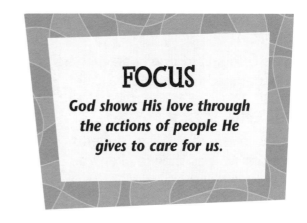

FOCUS

God shows His love through the actions of people He gives to care for us.

There is much talk today about fathering; many children grow up without positive fathering influences. But fathering—not the biological act but the committed act of lovingly rearing a child—is tremendously powerful, for a person's view of God is often shaped by interactions with his or her father.

Father's Day, the holiday discussed in this session, was first celebrated in the early 1900s, largely through the efforts of a woman, Sonora Louise Smart Dodd, who felt she had an outstanding father. A Civil War veteran, William Jackson Smart had reared six children alone after the death of his wife. His now-grown daughter wanted to honor his selfless love and devotion to his family. It later became a national holiday in the United States.

Jairus was such a father. His devotion to his child drove him, a synagogue ruler, to humble himself before an itinerant rabbi reported to be a healer. He begged Jesus to come to his home. He despaired when he heard his little girl had died. But Jesus looked him in the eye and said, "Don't be afraid. Just believe!" Even in the midst of this horrifying situation, Jesus had control of the circumstances and was able to return the dead to life!

Whether reared by a wonderful father, a distant father, an abusive father or no father at all, each of us who are children of the living God now have a perfect Father! He is always available and always thinking of us. Even when He seems to be handing us a hard assignment, we can be confident that He will do wonderful things in us through that difficulty. This Father TRULY knows best!

Whatever the circumstances of the students in your class, encourage each of them to realize that in God's family, there are no fatherless children. God's love for them is greater than they can imagine. It's a Father-child relationship that will never end! Take time this week to pray for those children who have difficulty with Father's Day. God longs to father each of us. What a reason to celebrate!

Story Center

Materials
Bible.

Before the Story
Guide students to briefly practice signs for underlined words.

Tell the Story
As you tell the story, lead students in responding as shown when you say the underlined words.

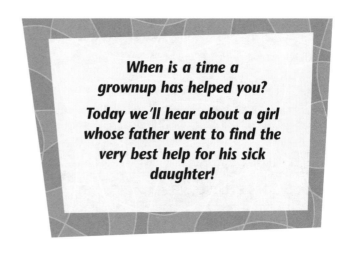

When is a time a grownup has helped you?

Today we'll hear about a girl whose father went to find the very best help for his sick daughter!

1. One day a large crowd of people <u>watched</u> as a boat came to the shore of the Sea of Galilee. As the boat came near, Jesus and some of His disciples got out. The crowd was excited. THIS was the person they were <u>watching</u> for! They pushed in eagerly around Jesus. They all wanted to see Him.

2. In this crowd was a very important man. His name was Jairus and he was a <u>leader</u> in the synagogue (the place where people met to worship God). This important <u>leader</u> pushed and pressed and SQUEEZED through the crowd, trying to get to Jesus. When he reached Jesus, he bowed down on the ground at Jesus' feet. Then he looked up at Jesus and said, "Jesus, my little girl is DYING. Please come quickly to my house. I know if you touch her, she will be healed and live."

3. Jesus immediately turned to go with Jairus to his house. But as they went, people tried to get as close to Jesus as they could. In this crowd was ANOTHER person who needed Jesus, a woman who had been <u>sick</u> for 12 YEARS. She knew that if she could just get close enough to Jesus to touch His robe, she would not be <u>sick</u>. So when she got quite close, she reached out and touched His robe. And she was WELL!

4. Jesus stopped. "Who <u>touched</u> My clothes?" He asked.

One of His disciples answered, "There are LOTS of people here. MANY people have <u>touched</u> You!"

But Jesus kept looking to see who had <u>touched</u> Him. The woman who had <u>touched</u> Jesus finally, fearfully spoke up.

1. Watch: Move right two fingers away from eyes.

2. Leader: Right hand pulls left forward; move hands down sides.

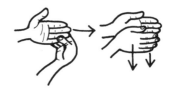

3. Sick: Right middle finger on head; left middle finger on stomach.

4. Touch: Touch left hand with right middle finger.

5. The woman told Jesus how she had touched Him because she believed she would be <u>healed</u>. Jesus kindly said, "Your faith has <u>healed</u> you. Be happy, you are <u>well</u>!"

Meanwhile, Jairus was waiting. While Jesus was still talking to the woman, some men came and told Jairus, "Don't bother Jesus anymore. Your daughter is dead."

DEAD? Poor Jairus! He had tried so hard to hurry. Now it was too late.

5. Healed, well: Curved hands on chest move forward to fists.

6. Jesus just kept walking toward Jairus's house. He looked at Jairus and said, "Don't be afraid. Just <u>believe</u>!"

When they got to the house, neighbors and friends had gathered there with the family and were crying loudly.

Jesus called out, "Why all this crying? The girl isn't dead; she's just asleep." Jesus meant that the girl would live again. But the people laughed at Him. They knew she was dead! They didn't <u>believe</u> Jesus could help this girl.

6. Believe: Touch right finger to forehead; clasp hands.

7. Jesus <u>told</u> the neighbors and friends to leave the room. Jesus, a few of His disciples and the girl's parents stood quietly by the bed where the dead girl was lying.

Jesus took her hand. He gently <u>said</u> to her, "Little girl, get up now."

The girl opened her eyes. She sat up. Then she got out of bed and walked around the room. She was ALIVE! Her parents were full of joy! Their little girl was not dead!

7. Tell, say: With right index finger, make circular movement from mouth.

8. Jesus told Jairus and his wife to get their girl some food. Imagine what all those people who had laughed at Jesus thought when the girl came laughing and running out of the house! Jesus <u>loved</u> the girl and her family. He had time to care about the woman on the way and still had plenty of time to bring this girl back to life. His <u>love</u> and power are greater than ANY bad thing that can ever happen to us—even greater than death itself!

8. Love: Cross fists over heart.

• •

Discussion Questions

How did Jairus show love for his daughter? (Went to get Jesus.) **Why didn't Jesus get there before the girl died?** (Crowd slowed Him down. A woman was healed.)

Jairus was a loving dad. He cared for his daughter and found the BEST help for her ever! One way God shows His love to us is by giving us people who love us, too. And Jesus loves us more than ANYONE! That's a big reason to celebrate!

Object Talk

Scripture Background
1 John 4:11

Materials
Bible with bookmark at 1 John 4:11, variety of neckties; optional—one or more medals.

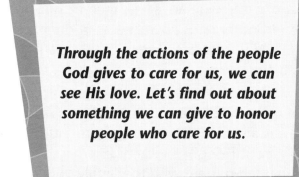

Through the actions of the people God gives to care for us, we can see His love. Let's find out about something we can give to honor people who care for us.

Lead the Activity

1. (Optional: Show one or more medals.) **What kinds of things do people receive medals for?** (Winning a game or contest. Courageous action in rescuing someone.) **Some medals are called badges of honor.** Display neckties you brought. **A necktie is also a badge of honor. In 1660, King Louis XIV of France saw brightly colored silk handkerchiefs around the necks of some war heroes from a country called Croatia. He decided to make silk neckwear a sign of royalty. Over time, men everywhere started wearing ties.**

2. **Who do you know who wears neckties? When are some times you might give a necktie as a gift? Many people give their fathers and other important men in their lives neckties on Father's Day. The next time you give someone a necktie, remember that you are giving a badge of honor for all the ways that this person cares for you!** (Optional: Distribute neckties to students and allow them to experiment with tying them around their own necks.)

3. **Who is someone who cares about you? What might you give that person to honor him or her?** Volunteers respond.

Conclude

God loves us so much that He gives us fathers and other people to take care of us. Read 1 John 4:11. **What are some ways you can show love to others? By showing love to others, we are showing our love for God! Loving and caring for others is one of the best ways we can show God's love.** Pray, thanking God for all the people He gives to care for us and asking for His help in showing love to others.

• •

Additional Information for Older Students

When we say the word "father," we are usually talking about our parents. In the Bible, instead of referring only to parents, the word "father" is used as a title of respect for rulers, elders and priests. Students find and read Scriptures about men who were called father as a way of showing respect for them: Joseph—Genesis 45:8; Elijah—2 Kings 2:11,12; Elisha—2 Kings 13:14.

Father's Day

Active Game Center: Care-Full Question

Materials

Large sheet of paper, marker, masking tape, blindfold.

Lead the Game

1. Students name specific people who care for them. List students' responses on a large sheet of paper. Display paper for students to refer to during the game.

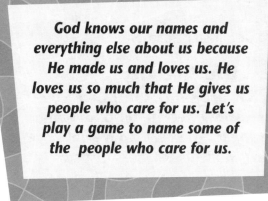

God knows our names and everything else about us because He made us and loves us. He loves us so much that He gives us people who care for us. Let's play a game to name some of the people who care for us.

2. Students stand in a circle. Volunteer puts on a blindfold or closes his or her eyes. Students standing in the circle begin walking clockwise. When volunteer stamps his or her feet twice, students stop moving. Volunteer points in any direction and says, "Good morning, Mr. Brown. Who cares for you?" (Note: Volunteer may substitute any last name for "Brown.")

3. Student to whom volunteer pointed responds by saying "(My parents) care for me," referring to list made earlier if needed. If volunteer can identify the speaker, they change places. If not, play another round of the game. If volunteer does not identify speaker after two rounds, allow another student to have a turn.

Option

Before the game, review students' names by grouping students in pairs and asking each student to introduce his or her partner to the whole group. Or play game in groups of no more than eight so that students will easily be able to remember each others' names.

Discussion Questions

1. *How have some of the people we talked about in this game cared for you?*

2. *As you grow older, how do you think parents and teachers will continue to care for you?* (Help me learn to do new things like driving a car. Help me choose which college to attend.)

3. *What can you do this week to thank someone who cares for you?*

Art Center: Ties of Love

Materials

Large sheet of paper, marker, discarded neckties, fabric paint or markers; optional—instant camera.

Lead the Activity

1. **What are some things we could say to show people who love and care for us that we appreciate them?** Students tell ideas. List students' ideas on large sheet of paper.

2. Distribute neckties to students. Students use fabric paint or markers to write messages they choose from large sheet of paper and decorate ties. (Optional: Take pictures of students wearing ties. Students give pictures and ties to people they wish to honor.)

Options

1. Ask several parents and others in your church to donate old ties, or buy ties at thrift stores or garage sales.

2. Instead of using fabric neckties, cut tie shapes from construction paper. Students use markers to decorate ties.

3. Make bolo ties. Students braid three long strands of yarn together. Before knotting ends, thread a large coat button or clasp through both ends of yarn. Then knot both ends of yarn.

Father's Day is a great time to say thank-you to people who show God's love by caring for us. Neckties originally were worn by people who were royalty and worthy of honor and respect. Let's make neckties to give to people we honor and respect for loving and caring for us.

• •

Discussion Questions

1. *How does knowing that God gives us people who care for us make you feel? Why do you think God wants us to have people who care for us?*

2. *What are some ways that fathers care for their children? Who are some people who care for you in this way?*

3. *How can you thank people who care for you? Why do you think these people want to care for you?*

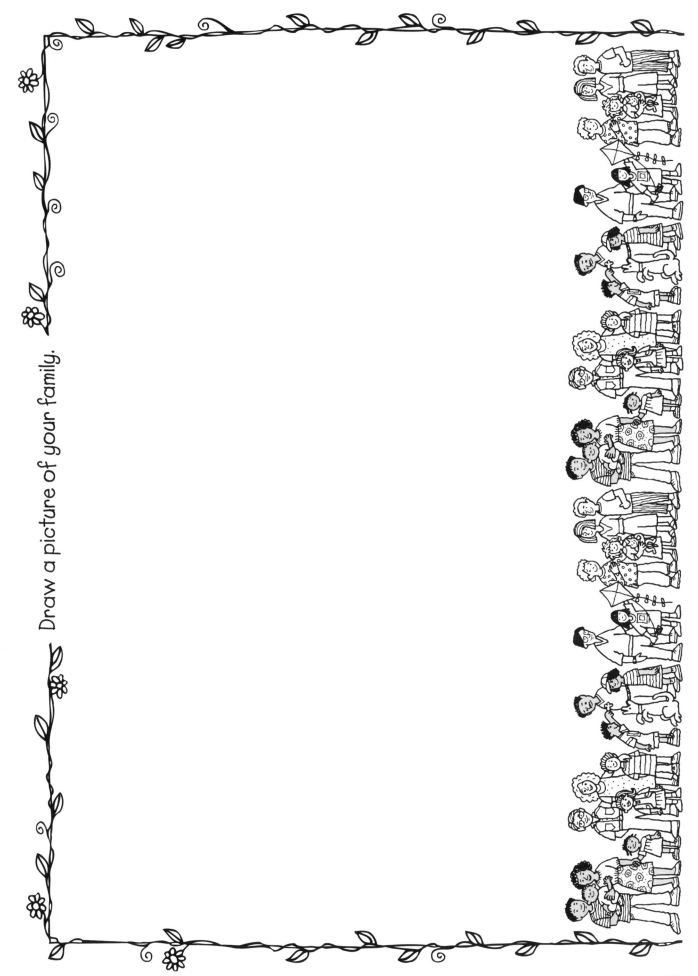

Draw a picture of your family.

A-MAZE-ING LOVE

1 John 4:11

The Challenge

"Dear friends, since God so loved us, we also ought to love one another."

Find your way through the maze by finding the words of 1 John 4:11 in order and then try to memorize the verse!

Crossing the Jordan River

Bible Verse

I will remember the deeds of the Lord.
Psalm 77:11

Bible Story Reference

Joshua 3—4

Teacher's Devotional

FOCUS
God's people remember His love and care.

One special day in the Old Testament, God gathered His people together to celebrate the keeping of His promise to give the people a land of their own. He was also reminding them of His love and care for them as He brought them out of Egypt and through the wilderness. This moment, like the Passover, was to be remembered by Israel for generations to come.

The people were first commanded to prepare themselves and watch in obedience because "the Lord will do amazing things among you" (Joshua 3:5). As the priests, following God's directions given through Joshua, stepped into the flooded Jordan River, the waters were cut off and piled up a distance upstream. The ground dried up and all of Israel crossed on dry ground into the Promised Land. God's promise was kept.

Then it was time for celebration! This was an important day for the nation of Israel and God wanted the people to create a reminder, a memorial, of what God had done for them in this place. One member from each tribe of Israel carried a large stone from the middle of the Jordan and Joshua set them up to create a memorial.

When future generations saw the stones and asked, "What do these stones mean?" the story of God's love, care and power could be shared. "He did this so that all the peoples of the earth might know that the hand of the Lord is powerful and so that you might always fear the Lord your God" (Joshua 4:24).

Most countries have at least one holiday that draws their people together as a nation. It is a time to express patriotism and remember their nation's history and development. In the United States, Independence Day is celebrated on the Fourth of July and Canada celebrates Canada Day on July 1.

A national holiday is a great occasion to remember God's love and care in the past. It is also an opportunity to focus on obedience to God in the future.

Story Center

Materials
Bible.

Before the Story
Guide students to briefly practice signs for underlined words.

Tell the Story
As you tell the story, lead students in responding as shown when you say the underlined words.

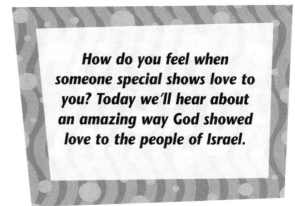

How do you feel when someone special shows love to you? Today we'll hear about an amazing way God showed love to the people of Israel.

1. God's people were excited! God had helped them escape from Egypt and had <u>promised</u> them a land of their own. And now, after many years, they were getting close to their new land. They were camped by the Jordan River and on the other side was the land God had <u>promised</u> them. The river was flooded at this time of the year, and the water was moving very quickly. Any animal or person who fell into the river would certainly drown!

1. Promises: Right index finger on lips; move to open hand on left fist.

2. After three days of waiting, Joshua, the new leader of these people, sent helpers to tell the people to get <u>ready</u> for a really big move. They said, "Tomorrow is the day you will see God do some amazing things!" As they rolled up their tents and packed their things, they must have wondered, *How will God help us get across the river? Will THAT be the amazing thing God does?*

2. Ready: Facing hands bounce left to right.

3. <u>God</u> had told Joshua exactly what to do. So Joshua told the people, "Follow the Ark of the Lord!" (The Ark of the Lord was a beautiful box covered with gold. It had God's laws inside it.) The priests carried the Ark on poles to the edge of the river. As soon as the priests' feet touched the river, <u>God</u> made something amazing happen!

3. God: Point right index finger; lower and open hand at chest.

4. The water stopped flowing down the <u>river</u> and piled up like a wall. Now the riverbed was dry! The people must have been amazed as they watched the priests carry the ark into the middle of the <u>river</u> on dry ground.

4. River: Extend three fingers; touch mouth a few times; flow fingers horizontally.

5. The priests stayed in the middle of the dry riverbed as the <u>people</u> of Israel crossed over to the other side. They hurried past the priests, and even though the <u>people</u> moved quickly, it must have taken hours for the hundreds of thousands of Israelites to cross the river!

5. People: With index and middle fingers extended, hands touch upper and then lower chest.

6. It was probably late in the day when all the Israelites, their belongings and animals stood safely on the other side of the river. The priests still stood with the Ark in the middle of the river. What was Joshua waiting for? Just then, Joshua sent 12 men into the riverbed to do a special job. Each one chose a large <u>stone</u>, lifted it onto his shoulder and carried it to the shore.

6. Stone: Strike left fist with right; turn curved hands inward.

7. Finally Joshua gave the word, "Tell the priests carrying the Ark to come up out of the Jordan." The very second the priests stepped out of the riverbed, CRASH! The <u>water</u> came rushing back to fill up the riverbed! By looking at the rushing mighty river, no one would ever have guessed that just a second ago it had been dry! But God's people knew!

7. Water: Extend three fingers of right hand; touch mouth a few times.

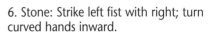

8. The people found a place to set up camp, and Joshua gathered together the 12 <u>stones</u> that were taken from the Jordan River. God had told Joshua to build a reminder of the wonderful way He had held back the river for them. The <u>stones</u> were laid just as Joshua directed and a monument was made. Whenever the people saw the stones, they must have praised God by telling the story of His love, care and power.

8. Stone: Strike left fist with right; turn curved hands inward.

• •

Discussion Questions

What had God promised to give the people of Israel? (A land of their own.) **How did God show His love and care to the Israelites?** (God kept His promise to the people. He provided a way for them to cross the Jordan River.) **What helped the people remember what God had done for them?** (They set up a memorial made from 12 stones taken from the river.) **How do you think the people felt about what God had done?**

God helps people today. He provides places for us to live, food for us to eat and families for us to belong to. The good things we have in our country are also ways God provides for us. When we remember God's love and care, we can thank God.

Object Talk

Scripture Background

Joshua 3—4

Materials

Bible with bookmark at Joshua 3, large sheet of paper, tape, marker, light brown paper rock shape for each student, magazine pictures of items that can remind students of God's love and care (at least one picture for each student), scissors.

> *Many countries celebrate important events in their histories. One of the most important celebrations in our country is* (name of holiday). *We can use this holiday to remember what God did for His people in the Bible and how He loves and cares for us today.*

Prepare the Activity

Attach the large sheet of paper to an open wall space. Print "Remember God's Love and Care" across the top of the paper. Trim pictures to fit rock shapes.

Lead the Activity

1. Ask a volunteer to select a picture and identify the item for the group. **How can a (house) remind you of God's love and care?** Student answers then keeps the picture. Repeat with other students.

2. When each student has a picture, say, **A memorial is a reminder of something important that has happened. The Israelites built a memorial from stones to remember how God helped them cross the Jordan River. We are going to build a memorial to help us remember God's love and care.** Read aloud the words written on the large sheet of paper. Guide each student to tape his or her picture to a rock shape. Then students take turns to tape their rocks to the large sheet of paper you have prepared, starting at the bottom of the paper and stacking the rocks up to make a pile.

3. **Our country has built many memorials to tell about important parts of our history.** (Tell or invite students to tell about two or three well-known memorials.) **When we see memorials in our nation, they can also remind us of God's love and care for us.**

Conclude

Read Psalm 77:11 aloud. **What are some of the good things God has helped our country have? What can you do to thank God for His love and care?** (Pray. Tell others what God has done for you. Show love and care to others.)

• •

Additional Information for Older Students

Most countries have a special day to celebrate becoming a nation. In Canada, Canada Day is celebrated on July 1, and in the United States Independence Day is celebrated on July 4. Mexico celebrates Mexican Independence Day on September 16. Celebrations are held throughout these countries and often include displaying the national flag, fireworks, parades and special performances.

Active Game Center: Parade Relay

Materials

Two buckets ⅓ full of sand, small national flag on a stick for each student, rope or tape, small noise-maker (whistle, kazoo, etc.).

Prepare the Game

Poke the sticks of half of the flags into the sand of one bucket. Repeat, placing remaining flags in the second bucket. Place the buckets about 6 feet (1.8 m) apart at one end of an open area in the room or outdoors. Use rope or tape to mark a line parallel to the buckets and about 10 feet (3 m) away.

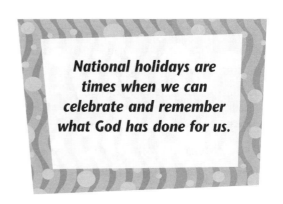

National holidays are times when we can celebrate and remember what God has done for us.

Lead the Game

1. Group students into two teams. Teams line up behind the line, each team facing a bucket.

2. On your signal from the noisemaker, the first member of each team races to his or her bucket and removes a flag. He or she must then wave the flag and march, not run, back to the next team member in line and tag him or her. The next student repeats the process, and so on, until all members of a team have crossed the line with a flag. Repeat the game as time allows. At the end of the game, students may keep the flags.

Options

1. Give specific instructions for how students should march or carry their flags during the game (hold flags above head, high step march, sing a familiar patriotic song while marching, etc.).

2. Form new teams after each round. Teams can be arranged by colors children are wearing, birthdays or the first letters of their names.

Discussion Questions

1. What are some reasons you are glad to live in our country?

2. What are some ways God shows His love and care for your family?

3. What things remind you of what God has done for you? (Songs of praise to God. Pictures of family. Bible verse. Your house, clothes, pet, toys, food.)

4. What can you do when you remember how God has helped you? (Say a prayer of thanks. Sing a song of praise. Tell others what God has done. Share what God has given with others.)

Art Center: Patriotic T-Shirt

Materials

Corrugated cardboard, craft glue, scissors, newspapers, plain white T-shirt for each child plus an extra for a sample, fabric paint in patriotic colors, wide shallow containers (such as pie pans), small sponge brushes, permanent marker.

Prepare the Activity

Cut the cardboard into patriotic shapes (stars, stripes, etc.) approximately 4 to 6 inches (10 to 15 cm) across. Peel away the top layer of paper from one side of the cardboard to expose the corrugated ribs. To make shapes easier to handle, cut 1-inch (2.5-cm) squares from cardboard and glue to the center of unribbed side of each shape. Let dry. Place a pad of newspaper inside each shirt to prevent paint from bleeding through fabric to the back of shirt. Cover the work area with newspaper. Lay shirts out over newspaper. Pour small amounts of paint into shallow containers—a different color in each container. Prepare enough containers and shapes for groups of 4 to 6 students to share.

> *Remembering what God has done for us is something we can do every day. Many countries have special days to remember important events. Let's decorate special shirts to help us celebrate God's love and care for our country, as well as His kindness to us.*

Lead the Activity

1. Show the shapes and colors of paint you have prepared. **How do these shapes and colors remind you of our country?** (They are on our flag and other symbols of our country.) **Holidays that our country celebrates remind us of important events that have happened. We can also remember ways God has helped our country and our families on these special days. We are going to paint T-shirts that remind us of our country and can help us remember God's love and care for us.**

2. Demonstrate how to paint the shirt by brushing paint onto the ribbed side of a cardboard shape. Firmly press the painted surface against the shirt, and then carefully lift up the shape.

3. Help children as they stamp their shirts, refilling paint as needed. Let paint dry completely before moving shirts. Use permanent marker to write child's initials on the tag of the shirt.

• •

Discussion Questions

1. *What are some ways you like to celebrate a national holiday?* (Fireworks, parades, special music, picnics, barbeques.)

2. *What are ways we can ask God to help our country?* (Help our leaders do what is right. Protect us from enemies.)

3. Read Psalm 77:11. *How does God show His love and care for you? What can you do to remember what God has done for you?* (Write Psalm 77:11 down and hang in your home. Thank God each day for what He has done. Tell others what God has done for you.)

Draw a picture of something God has done to show His love and care.

SHARD SEARCH

The Challenge ➤ Cross off all the pieces of pottery with Y, T, K, S, A or L written on them.

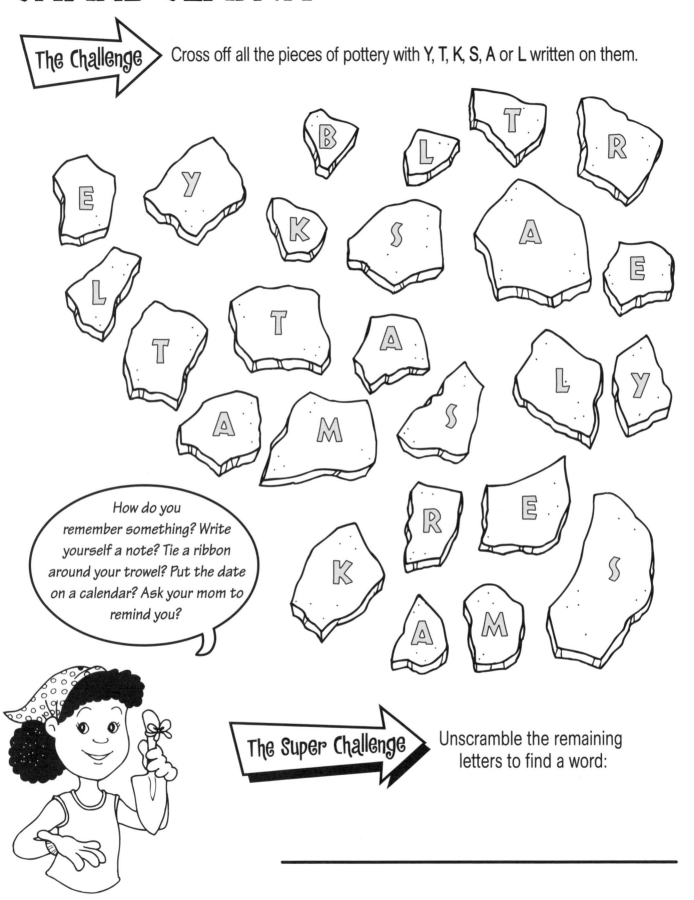

How do you remember something? Write yourself a note? Tie a ribbon around your trowel? Put the date on a calendar? Ask your mom to remind you?

The Super Challenge ➤ Unscramble the remaining letters to find a word:

_____

Birthdays

God Creates People

Bible Verse

Know that the Lord is God. It is he who made us, and we are his. Psalm 100:3

Bible Story Reference

Genesis 1:26-31; 2:4-7,15-23

Teacher's Devotional

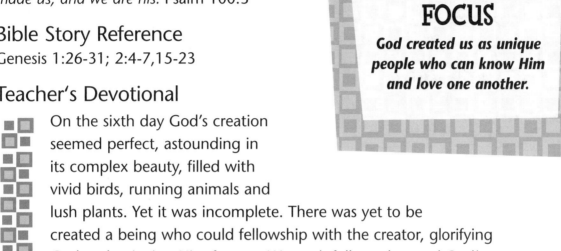

FOCUS
God created us as unique people who can know Him and love one another.

On the sixth day God's creation seemed perfect, astounding in its complex beauty, filled with vivid birds, running animals and lush plants. Yet it was incomplete. There was yet to be created a being who could fellowship with the creator, glorifying God and enjoying Him forever. We can't fully understand God's own reasons for creating humans, but there is a sense in Scripture that God's glory would not be complete until beings were created who could communicate with Him (see Isaiah 43:7). Thus God brought forth a human who loved to walk and talk with Him. When that man understood how much he needed a human counterpart, God provided woman. These two lived in full and open fellowship with their creator until their sin.

Today we celebrate birthdays, the annual events when friends and family focus on the uniqueness of each person God created. We do not yet fully understand what God's glory may mean. Nor can we tell where our lives are headed. But one thing we know: Our creator loves each of us as individuals. He deeply desires to know us and be known by us, to have a one-on-one relationship with each of us!

In a world where many don't understand why they are here or what to do with the lives they have been given, the deep need to know and be known are often not satisfied. God created us for fellowship with Him and made sure that nothing short of that can make us truly happy! As you talk about birthdays and celebrate each student's uniqueness, remember that God made each one, whether shy or bold, silly or serious, for His own glory. He longs to bring each of them into that relationship of knowing and being known. What a deeply satisfying reason to celebrate!

Story Center

Materials
Bible.

Before the Story
Guide students to briefly practice signs for underlined words.

Tell the Story
As you tell the story, lead students in responding as shown when you say the underlined words.

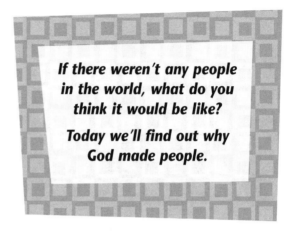

If there weren't any people in the world, what do you think it would be like?

Today we'll find out why God made people.

1. God's creation of the world was off to an amazing start! By the sixth day of God's work of creating the world, it was a <u>beautiful</u> place. It was no longer dark and empty. Now the world was filled with growing plants. Animals of all kinds ran and jumped; colorful, flying birds flew through the air and fish swam through the waters. It was all brand-new and <u>beautiful</u>. The sun shone in the daytime and the moon and stars at night. But there was still more to do.

2. On the sixth day, God said, "Let us make <u>humans</u> in our likeness. They can rule and take care of the whole world."

   Then the Bible says that God took dirt from the ground. He used the dirt to form a <u>human</u> body. God breathed His breath into the body. That body became a living person who could love and worship God!

3. God named that person Adam. God had planted a beautiful <u>garden</u> that He called Eden. God put Adam in this <u>garden</u> and gave Adam important and interesting work to do. Adam took care of the <u>garden</u>, watching over it carefully.

4. God brought every animal to Adam and let Adam give each animal its <u>name</u>. That must have been fun! But as Adam said the <u>names</u>, he saw that there were none that could talk with him, none that could be a companion for him. Adam began to realize he was the only one of his kind.

1. Beautiful: Right hand opens and then closes as it moves around face.

2. Human: With index and middle fingers extended, hands touch upper and then lower chest.

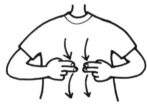

3. Garden: Starting together in center, hands make outward circle; right hand touches beneath each nostril.

4. Name: Index and middle fingers extended, right fingers tap top of left fingers a few times.

5. Out of all the animals God had created, there was no animal that could be a partner or friend just right for Adam. There was no one around who could talk <u>together</u> with Adam or be with him the way he saw all the other animals running <u>together</u>. Of course, God had known all along that it wasn't good for Adam to be alone. Now Adam knew it, too!

5. Together: Place fists together; move in circle to the left.

6. God had a plan. He made Adam fall <u>asleep</u>. Then He opened up Adam's side. God gently took a rib out of Adam's side. He closed up the place again while Adam <u>slept</u> on. From that rib, He formed ANOTHER person. Now there was another person who could love and worship God.

6. Sleep: Draw hand down to chin, closing fingertips.

7. But this person wasn't JUST like Adam. This person was female, and she was a perfect <u>match</u> for Adam! Adam woke up and saw her. He said, "THIS person was made from my bones and flesh. She came from me. I'll call her woman."

Later, Adam named the woman who was a <u>match</u> for him. He called her Eve, which sounds like the Hebrew word for "life."

7. Match: Interlock bent, spread fingers.

8. God loved these people He had made. He blessed them and told them, "Be fruitful and have children. I <u>give</u> you permission to be in charge of this world and the animals and fish and birds. I <u>give</u> you every seed-bearing plant on the earth and the fruit of every tree for food."

The people God made loved God, too. They walked with God in the evening and talked with Him. Even later, after Adam and Eve had sinned, God continued to love them and made it possible for their sins to be forgiven. God wanted Adam and Eve to know Him. He wants us to know Him, too!

8. Give: Hands down and fingertips touching, flip hands forward and open, palms up.

• •

Discussion Questions

From what did God make the first person? (The dirt of the earth.) **What work did God give Adam to do?** (To watch over and work in the garden. To name the animals.) **Who else did God make? How?** (Woman. From Adam's side.)

God loved the people He had made. God made each and every one of us, too. And He loves us just like He loved Adam and Eve. He made us to love Him and know Him and to love each other. And that's a GREAT reason to celebrate!

Birthdays

Object Talk

Scripture Background
Genesis 1:26-31; 2:4-7,15-23

Materials
Bible with bookmark at Psalm 100:3, one or more objects used to celebrate birthdays (choose from those listed below).

> *God created all the people in the world so that we would know Him and love one another. One way we show love to others is by celebrating their birthdays. Let's look at some ways birthdays are celebrated around the world!*

Lead the Activity

1. **What do you like to do to celebrate your birthday?** Volunteers tell. **Birthdays are good times to show love to people and to celebrate the unique ways in which God made them.**

2. Display and discuss objects you brought that are associated with some of the following birthday traditions: *China*—friends and relatives join in a lunch of noodles to wish the birthday child a long life; *Denmark*—a flag is flown outside a window to show someone in the house is having a birthday; *Japan*—the birthday child wears all new clothes; *Mexico*—the birthday child uses a bat to break open a piñata which is stuffed with candy and small toys to be shared; *Philippines*—blinking lights decorate the home of the birthday child; *Russia*—the birthday child receives a birthday pie with a greeting carved in the crust; *United States*—the birthday child receives a birthday cake with one candle for each year of the child's age. (Optional: Students reenact one or more of the traditions.)

Conclude

Read Psalm 100:3 aloud. **According to this verse, to whom do we belong? Why?** (God. Because He made us.) **God created us and wants us to know and love Him. God also wants us to show His love to others. No matter what the tradition, birthdays are a time to celebrate and show love to people we care about.** Pray, thanking God for creating us and asking His help in loving each other.

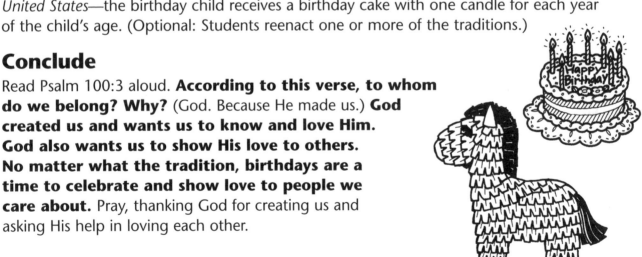

Additional Information for Older Students

The most important birthday ever was the day Jesus Christ was born. How did the shepherds celebrate the birth of the baby Jesus? Volunteers answer or students may read Luke 2:16-20. **Who else came to celebrate the birth of Jesus?** (The wise men.) **How did they worship Jesus?** Students tell about the gifts given by wise men or read Matthew 2:9-11.

Birthdays

Active Game Center: The Name Game

Materials

None.

Lead the Game

1. Group students into teams of six to eight students each. Teams line up in single-file lines leaving at least 4 feet (1.2 m) between each team.

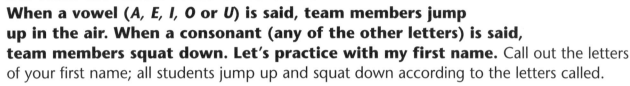

God created us to know Him and love each other. One way to care for others is to learn their names. Let's play a fun game with everyone's name.

2. **In our game today, each person will take a turn to call out to his or her team the letters of his or her name. When a vowel (*A, E, I, O* or *U*) is said, team members jump up in the air. When a consonant (any of the other letters) is said, team members squat down. Let's practice with my first name.** Call out the letters of your first name; all students jump up and squat down according to the letters called.

3. At your signal, the first student on each team begins calling out the letters of his or her first name while the other students on the team jump up or squat down according to the letter called. When the first student is done, the second team member calls out the letters of his or her name with teammates responding as above. Each team continues the process as quickly as possible, sitting down as soon as all members of the team have spelled out their names. Ask a volunteer from the first team to finish to answer one of the Discussion Questions below. Students form new teams and play again as time allows.

Options

1. Print "Vowel = Jump" and "Consonant = Squat" on a chalkboard or a large sheet of paper for students to refer to during the game.

2. With older students, you may wish to play a different game: Half the group writes their names on separate strips of paper, inserts papers into balloons and blows them up. Tie balloons. Place balloons in center of playing area. At your signal, each student in the other half of the group gets a balloon, pops it and finds the person whose name is on the paper. Repeat game, reversing roles.

• •

Discussion Questions

1. ***What are some ways we can get to know God?*** (Read the Bible. Listen to older people who love God talk about Him. Ask your parents, pastor or teacher questions about God.)

2. ***What are some of the things you already know about God?*** Volunteers respond.

3. ***Why should we show love to other people?*** (To show God's love. Jesus tells us that loving God and loving others are the most important things to do.) ***What are some ways to show love to other people?***

Birthdays

Art Center: Birthday Bash

Materials

Large sheet of white butcher paper, markers; optional—glue sticks, colored tissue paper, chenille wire.

Prepare the Activity

Cover a large tabletop with butcher paper. Draw 12 candles on the paper. Label one candle for each month of the year.

Lead the Activity

1. Students draw designs on paper as if decorating a birthday cake.

2. Each student writes his or her name near the birthday candle labeled with the month of his or her birth. (Optional: Students glue tissue paper and chenille wires to create more designs around the cake.)

3. Students gather around finished cake in order of their birth dates and sing "Happy Birthday" to each other.

Options

1. Bring a large sheet cake and tubes of colored frosting. Students write their names with frosting on the cake. Students decorate room with crepe paper. Lead students to join in a birthday party, playing one or two party games and eating the cake. Give each child a bag of party favors to take home.

2. Cover sides of table and invite students to draw decorations representing layers of cake.

> God created us to know Him and love one another. One of the ways we can show love to each other is by celebrating birthdays. Let's decorate a big pretend cake for everyone's birthday!

. . . .

Discussion Questions

1. *Why did God create people?* (To know and love Him. To show His love to each other.)

2. *How did God show His love in the ways we are created?* (Made our bodies in amazing ways. Gave us minds to think.)

3. *What are some ways to show love to other people?* (Be kind to them. Help them with tasks they are doing. Care for them when they are upset. Be patient with people who sometimes annoy you.)

"Know that the Lord is God. It is he who made us, and we are his." Psalm 100:3

MADE IN THE SHADE!

Genesis 1:26-31

The Challenge ➡

God created Adam and Eve and gave them the Garden of Eden to live in. Unscramble the words on each insect, and then write the word from each one below the matching insect at the bottom of the page. You'll find out why God created Adam and Eve and you!

Jesus Forgives Zacchaeus

Bible Verse

Everyone who believes in him receives forgiveness of sins through his name.
Acts 10:43

Bible Story Reference

Luke 19:1-10

Teacher's Devotional

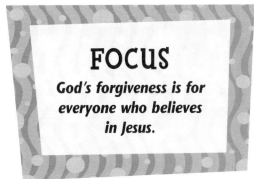

FOCUS
God's forgiveness is for everyone who believes in Jesus.

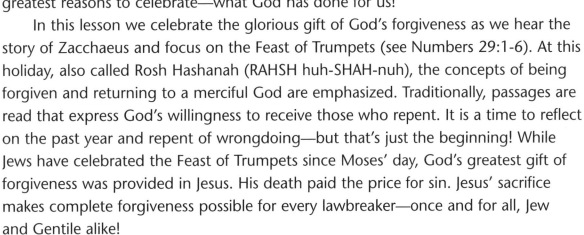

While sports victories or the change of calendar years may be cause enough for some celebrations, God's followers are offered the world's greatest reasons to celebrate—what God has done for us!

In this lesson we celebrate the glorious gift of God's forgiveness as we hear the story of Zacchaeus and focus on the Feast of Trumpets (see Numbers 29:1-6). At this holiday, also called Rosh Hashanah (RAHSH huh-SHAH-nuh), the concepts of being forgiven and returning to a merciful God are emphasized. Traditionally, passages are read that express God's willingness to receive those who repent. It is a time to reflect on the past year and repent of wrongdoing—but that's just the beginning! While Jews have celebrated the Feast of Trumpets since Moses' day, God's greatest gift of forgiveness was provided in Jesus. His death paid the price for sin. Jesus' sacrifice makes complete forgiveness possible for every lawbreaker—once and for all, Jew and Gentile alike!

Free access to this forgiveness is God's great gift and a great reason to celebrate! Ask God to give you a heart of joy and praise. His kindness and forgiveness always await. Live out God's loving acceptance as you teach children God's forgiveness by your words and actions!

Story Center

Materials
Bible.

Before the Story
Guide students to briefly practice signs for underlined words.

Tell the Story
As you tell the story, lead students in responding as shown when you say the underlined words.

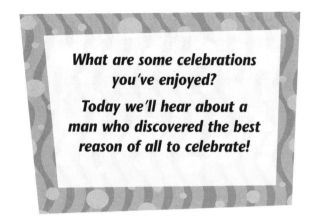

What are some celebrations you've enjoyed?

Today we'll hear about a man who discovered the best reason of all to celebrate!

1. When Jesus lived on earth, the people in Israel had to pay <u>taxes</u> to the Romans. The Israelites weren't happy about paying these <u>taxes</u>. First of all, they didn't LIKE the Romans. And second of all, paying <u>taxes</u> to Rome took money that they needed for buying food and clothes. And WORST of all, every time they paid <u>taxes</u> it just REMINDED them of how UNHAPPY they were that the Romans were in charge!

1. Tax: Move crooked right finger down left palm.

2. But one man WAS happy about people paying taxes to Rome. This man was the tax collector. His name was Zacchaeus; and not only was he a tax collector, but he was also <u>RICH</u>. He had a big house and nice clothes. But he had NO friends.

2. Rich: Put right hand in left palm; then lift up, curve open and face down.

3. Zacchaeus was rich because he took more <u>money</u> from people than they were supposed to pay in taxes to Rome. Then Zacchaeus kept the extra <u>money</u> for himself! Everyone in town could see that he had extra <u>money</u> because of his rich-looking house and clothes. NO one liked him!

3. Money: Touching, right fingertips strike left palm a few times.

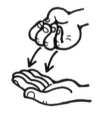

4. But one day <u>Jesus</u> came to the town where Zacchaeus lived. People crowded along the road, waiting to see <u>Jesus</u>. Zacchaeus wanted to see <u>Jesus</u>, too. But Zacchaeus was so short that he couldn't see past all the people. And nobody would let him through the crowd! He couldn't see <u>Jesus</u> at all!

4. Jesus: Touch palms with opposite middle fingers.

5. Zacchaeus REALLY wanted to <u>see</u> Jesus. He had probably heard many wonderful things about Jesus. So he ran past the crowd. He could <u>see</u> a big tree up ahead! Quickly Zacchaeus climbed up the tree. NOW he could <u>see</u>! He could <u>see</u> Jesus—coming closer and closer!

5. See: Move two right fingers away from eyes.

6. When Jesus was right under the tree where Zacchaeus was sitting, Zacchaeus got a big <u>surprise</u>. Jesus looked up right at him! Then he got another <u>surprise</u>! Jesus called, "Zacchaeus, come down! I want to go to your house." The crowd was <u>surprised</u>, too. They were <u>surprised</u> that Jesus would want to be with that greedy, cheating tax collector! *Why would Jesus want to be friends with a man like that?* But Jesus did! And Jesus' love CHANGED Zacchaeus!

6. Surprise: Index fingers and thumbs touch at temples; flick up.

7. Zacchaeus said, "I want to <u>give</u> half of everything I have to poor people. And if I have cheated anyone, I will <u>give</u> back FOUR TIMES as much money as I took!" Zacchaeus wanted EVERYONE to know that Jesus was now his friend. Zacchaeus was different now. He wanted to <u>give</u>, not take!

7. Give: Hands down and fingertips touching, flip hands forward and open, palms up.

8. Jesus knew that Zacchaeus was sorry for cheating and stealing and doing other wrong things. Jesus <u>forgave</u> Zacchaeus. He was glad to <u>forgive</u> Zacchaeus and be his friend. And Zacchaeus was VERY glad Jesus had <u>forgiven</u> HIM! Now EVERYTHING would be so much better for Zacchaeus!!

8. Forgive: Stroke edge of left palm with right fingertips.

Discussion Questions

How did Jesus show He cared about Zacchaeus? (By talking to him. By forgiving him.) **How did Zacchaeus show he was sorry for his cheating?** (Promised to give back more than he took.) **Jesus forgave Zacchaeus and because of Jesus' loving forgiveness, Zacchaeus had a reason to celebrate.**

If you admit that you've disobeyed God and if you believe that Jesus died for you, God will forgive all your sins. That's a great reason to celebrate! Invite children to talk with you about becoming members of God's family (see "Leading a Child to Christ" on p. 253).

Object Talk

Scripture Background
Leviticus 23:23-25; Numbers 29:1-6

Materials
Bible with bookmark at Acts 10:43, apples, knife, bowls, lemon juice, honey, napkins.

Prepare the Activity
Slice apples and place slices in bowls. Drizzle apple slices with lemon juice to prevent browning. Pour approximately ⅓ cup honey into bowls. (Prepare one bowl of slices and one bowl of honey for every six to eight students.)

> *No matter how old or young we are or how many good or bad things we've done, we can receive God's forgiveness when we believe in Jesus. Since Bible times, God's people (called Hebrews, or Jews) have celebrated a holiday that reminds them of their need for forgiveness. This holiday is called the Feast of Trumpets.*

Lead the Activity

1. **The Feast of Trumpets got its name because it began with the sounds of a trumpet, called a** *shofar* **(SHOH-fahr) in Bible times.** (Optional: Older students read Leviticus 23:23,24.) **This holiday was the beginning of a time of year when God wanted His people to turn away from their sins—the wrong things they had done. This was a time to realize that they needed God's forgiveness for their wrong actions.**

2. **Rosh Hashanah (RAHSH huh-SHAH-nuh) is another name for this celebration; it means "new year." The Hebrew calendar started a new year in the fall. Rosh Hashanah reminds people to start the new year by celebrating God's loving forgiveness. To celebrate the new year, special foods are eaten. What are some special foods you eat at parties or celebrations?** (Birthday cake. Thanksgiving turkey.) **Apples dipped in honey are eaten at Rosh Hashanah to show that a sweet or good new year is hoped for.** Students dip apple slices into honey before eating.

Conclude
Apples and honey remind us that God gives us many good things. God's greatest gift is that when people believe in Jesus and admit their sin, God forgives them. Read Acts 10:43 aloud. Thank God for His forgiveness.

• •

Additional Information for Older Students
In the Old Testament book of Micah we can read about God's forgiveness of sin. Ask a volunteer to read Micah 7:18,19. **How do these verses describe God's forgiveness of sin? As a reminder that God takes away all sin, on Rosh Hashanah Jewish people throw bread crumbs into the ocean or a river and watch the crumbs disappear.**

Active Game Center: Forgiveness Frenzy

Materials

Children's music CD and player, index cards, markers, stopwatch or watch with second hand.

Prepare the Game

Print the word "forgive" on index cards, one letter on each card. Make at least one set of cards for every three to six students. Mix up all cards and place them facedown in a large circle on the floor.

> *Let's play a game to celebrate the fact that God's forgiveness is for everyone!*

Lead the Game

1. Students form teams of three to six students. Assign a name or number to each team. Members from all teams stand in mixed-up order around the circle of cards.

2. As you play children's music CD, students walk around the circle. Stop the music after 15 or 20 seconds. When the music stops, each student picks up the card closest to him or her and finds other team members. Team members compare cards collected, keeping cards with letters needed to spell "forgive" and placing duplicate cards facedown back in the circle. Add blank cards to the circle as needed so that there is always a card for each student.

3. When one or more teams have collected a complete set of cards to spell "forgive," ask one or more of the Discussion Questions below. Repeat game as time allows.

Options

1. Students prepare cards in class.

2. If you have fewer than six students in your class, students form pairs or play individually.

3. For older students, add a few cards with letters not used in "forgive" (*s, m, b,* etc.).

• •

Discussion Questions

1. ***What are some things people might think they have to do to be forgiven?*** (Go to church. Read their Bibles.) ***Those are all good things to do, but who does Acts 10:43 say can have their sins forgiven?*** (Anyone who asks God for forgiveness of sin and who believes in Jesus.)

2. ***What does it mean to believe in Jesus?*** (To believe that Jesus is God's Son and that He died to take the punishment for our sins.)

3. ***How can we be sure our sins are forgiven?*** (God always keeps His promises.)

Art Center: Personalized Place Mats

Materials

Materials for one or more of the place mats described below.

Lead the Activity

Lead the students to make place mats as directed below, writing on the place mats messages about God's forgiveness. Ask the Discussion Questions below to help students think of messages.

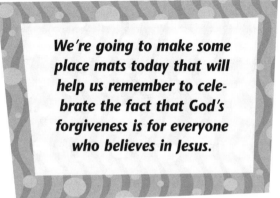

We're going to make some place mats today that will help us remember to celebrate the fact that God's forgiveness is for everyone who believes in Jesus.

Paper Place Mats

Give one 12x18-inch (30x45-cm) sheet of colored paper to each student (or use paper place mats purchased from a restaurant supply store). Students decorate place mats with markers, pictures of party decorations (such as horns, streamers, hats) and decorative-edged scissors (see sketch a). Assist students in covering both sides of their place mats with clear adhesive-backed paper. Then students cut designs around the place mat edges: scallops, curved corners, points, etc.

Vinyl Place Mats

Purchase inexpensive, solid-colored vinyl place mats. Students decorate place mats using permanent markers (see sketch b).

Options

1. Cut one 12x18-inch (30x45-cm) piece of unbleached muslin for each student. Students use pencils to sketch designs that remind them of God's forgiveness (cross, heart, Bible) onto fabric and then cover sketch lines with fabric markers or crayons. Fray the edges by pulling out three or four threads from each side of the place mat.

2. Provide a snack for students, or use snack prepared in Celebration Object Talk. Students use place mats while eating.

3. Younger students may dictate their messages for you to write. Older students may want to write Acts 10:43 on their place mats.

• •

Discussion Questions

1. ***Why is God's forgiveness such good news?*** (We all need forgiveness for our sins. God's forgiveness is for everyone! God's forgiveness makes it possible for us to live with Him forever.)

2. ***What happens when God forgives our sins?*** (We become members of God's family.)

3. ***How would you describe God's forgiveness?*** (Great. Awesome. Eternal.)

"Everyone who believes in him receives forgiveness of sins through his name." Acts 10:43

IN STEP WITH JESUS

Acts 10:43

"Everyone who believes in him receives forgiveness of sins through his name."

The Challenge →

Start at the stone the boy is standing on and trace each letter of the verse until you reach Jesus at the end of the maze.

Jesus Forgives Peter

Bible Verse

Therefore, if anyone is in Christ, he is a new creation; the old has gone, the new has come! 2 Corinthians 5:17

Bible Story Reference

Matthew 26:31-35,69-75; John 21:1-24

FOCUS

God's forgiveness helps us make a new start.

Teacher's Devotional

The Feast of Trumpets marks the beginning of a month-long festival that presents a wonderful picture of God's forgiveness, His mercy and His provision. This holiday helps us remember and celebrate the new start we receive with God's forgiveness.

While in Bible times the Feast of Trumpets did not include a celebration of the new year, over the years it became known as Rosh Hashanah (RAHSH huh-SHAH-nuh), which means "new year." The date for Rosh Hashanah varies from year to year because the Jewish calendar is a lunar calendar of 360 days a year, while the western world operates on a solar, 365-day calendar. (And remember, Jewish holidays always begin at sundown the night before the day marked on our calendars!)

The biblical name for this holiday, Feast of Trumpets, came about because of the special use of the *shofar* (SHOH-fahr), or ram's horn trumpet. The *shofar* was traditionally used to call the people together, to warn of danger, to declare war and to herald the start of a new month at the first glimpse of a new moon. At the Feast of Trumpets, the Bible prescribed *shofar* blasts to call the people together for rest and worship (see Leviticus 23:24,25). Today, the ram's horn also reminds us of the ram in the thicket who took Isaac's place as a sacrifice on Mount Moriah (see Genesis 22). Just as the ram was substituted for Isaac, Jesus is our substitute, taking the penalty for sin once and for all and offering forgiveness to all who believe.

This holiday signals us to gather for worship and celebration, too. We can experience a new start, just as Peter did after his sad betrayal of Jesus. Because Jesus became the sacrifice for our sins, because He made forgiveness possible and because God's mercy and provision are around us every moment, blow the trumpets, clap and shout! Join your students in joyously celebrating all that God has done for us!

Story Center

Materials
Bible.

Before the Story
Guide students to briefly practice signs for underlined words.

Tell the Story
As you tell the story, lead students in responding as shown when you say the underlined words.

What is something you've done that you wished you could do over again?

Today we'll meet a man who wished he could go back and change something he did. And we'll hear what Jesus did about it!

1. When Jesus lived on earth, He had many friends. But from them, He chose 12 men, called <u>disciples</u>, to follow Him and learn from Him. Jesus said to these men, "Come and follow Me!" One <u>disciple</u> was named Peter. Peter loved Jesus very much. Peter was one of the first people to tell Jesus, "You are the Son of God!"

1. Disciple: Move left fist ahead of right; move open hands down sides.

2. After Jesus had been with His friends for three years, He told them that He would be arrested and sent to die. Jesus also told His disciples that they were going to run away and say they did not know Him. Well, Peter spoke right up. He said, "I will <u>NEVER</u> say I don't know You!" And each of Jesus' other disciples said the same thing: "I will <u>NEVER</u> say I don't know you!"

2. Never: Move right hand in half circle; then drop to right.

3. Things happened just as Jesus said they would. Soldiers came and arrested Him. All His friends DID run away. But Peter followed at a distance. While Jesus was being questioned inside the high priest's house, Peter stood outside. While he warmed himself by a little fire, a servant girl said to him, "You were with Jesus!" Peter replied, "I <u>don't know</u> what you're talking about!"

3. Don't know: Fingers of right hand on forehead; move hand away, flipping palm out.

4. Then another girl said to someone else, "He's one of Jesus' friends." Peter answered, "I am <u>NOT</u>!" In a little while someone else said, "I'm sure you're one of Jesus' friends. You're from Galilee!" Peter cursed and said, "I <u>don't KNOW</u> this man you're talking about!"

4. Not: Move fist sharply away from chin. Don't know: Repeat #3.

5. Just then, a <u>rooster</u> crowed; and Peter remembered Jesus' words: "Before the rooster crows, you will deny three times that you know Me." Peter began to cry. He had told Jesus he would NEVER say he didn't know Him. Now he had done just that—THREE TIMES!

5. Rooster: Place right thumb against forehead with two fingers extended.

6. A few hours later, Jesus was crucified. He died on a <u>cross</u> to pay the price for sin. All of Jesus' friends were VERY sad. And where was Peter? He was hiding out, sorry and so afraid. He had done something so AWFUL! But three days later, Jesus came back to life! He wasn't dead anymore! And one of the first things Jesus said was, "Tell my disciples—and Peter—to meet Me in Galilee!"

6. Cross: Move curved right hand down; then from left to right.

7. WELL! When Peter heard that, he felt better. And when he himself saw Jesus alive again, Peter must have been over-joyed! But in the days after Jesus' resurrection, he still wasn't sure what to do. So one day he told the other disciples, "I'm going <u>fishing</u>." They said, "We're going, too." They went to Galilee and <u>fished</u> all night. They caught NOTHING. But at dawn, someone on shore said, "Throw out your net on the other side!" They did, and they caught LOTS of fish!

7. Fishing: Left fist over right; move hands as though holding fishing pole.

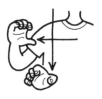

8. "It is the LORD!" John shouted. When Peter heard these words, he jumped in the water and swam to shore to be with Jesus. Jesus wanted Peter to know he was <u>forgiven</u>. Jesus said to Peter, "Feed My sheep. Feed My lambs." Jesus meant that He wanted Peter to tell others about God's love. Jesus hadn't given up on him! Jesus had given Peter impor-tant work to do. But best of all, Peter knew that Jesus had <u>FORGIVEN</u> him and that he could make a brand new start with Jesus!

8. Forgive: Stroke edge of left palm with right fingertips.

• •

Discussion Questions

Why did Peter need to be forgiven? (Broke his promise to Jesus and said three times he didn't know Jesus.) **How did Jesus show Peter he was forgiven?** (Helped him catch fish. Asked him to tell others about God. Didn't give up on Peter.)

God doesn't give up on us, either. He loves us and wants to forgive us. And every time we ask God to forgive us, He will help us make a new start! That's a GREAT reason to celebrate!

Object Talk

Scripture Background

Leviticus 23:23-25; Numbers 29:1-6

Materials

Bible with marker at 2 Corinthians 5:17; optional—*shofar,* trumpet or horn, or prerecorded trumpet sounds (see pattern below) and player, rhythm instruments.

> *When we believe in Jesus, God's forgiveness helps us make a brand-new start. God forgives the wrong things we have done. In the Old Testament the sound of a trumpet reminded the people of their need for forgiveness. Let's find out what happened.*

Lead the Activity

1. (Optional: Play blasts of *shofar,* trumpet or horn.) **When do you hear trumpets blow?** (Parades. Concerts. Church.) **In Bible times, God's people played trumpets as signals. On the holiday called Feast of Trumpets, the sound of a trumpet called a *shofar* signaled the people to remember their need for God's forgiveness. *Shofars* were made from the horns of rams.**

2. **At the Feast of Trumpets, also called Rosh Hashanah (RAHSH huh-SHAH-nuh), the *shofar* is played in a special way.** Clap hands in this pattern: one clap followed by a long pause, three claps, nine fast and short claps, one clap. Invite students to clap hands in this same pattern, repeating the pattern several times. (Optional: Blow pattern on *shofar* or any single note of trumpet or horn or play prerecorded trumpet sounds. Students play pattern with rhythm instruments.)

Conclude

In Bible times at the Feast of Trumpets, God's people would think about the wrong things they had done. When we think about our sins, we can ask God to forgive us, and He will! Jesus' death on the cross makes it possible for our sins to be forgiven. Read 2 Corinthians 5:17 aloud. Lead students in prayer, thanking God for forgiving our sins.

Additional Information for Older Students

The sound of the trumpets not only signaled a time to get ready for the forgiveness of their sins but also signaled a new year was beginning. (In Bible times, the people didn't have calendars to keep track of what day of the week or year it was.) The words "Rosh Hashanah" actually mean "new year." When do we celebrate the beginning of the new year? (New Year's Eve in the month of December.) **Find out the season of the year in which the Hebrew people in Bible times celebrated their new year.** Students read Leviticus 23:23-25 to find information: the Hebrew people's seventh month, which is the fall of our year—the months of September or October.

Active Game Center: Fresh-Start Tag

Materials
Masking tape or chalk, party horn.

Prepare the Game
Make two masking-tape lines about 30 feet (9 m) apart. Make each line at least 10 feet (3 m) long. (Use chalk if you are playing on asphalt.)

> **When God forgives the wrong things we have done, we can make a new start. We're going to play a game in which we can practice making new starts, too!**

Lead the Game
1. Choose one volunteer to be "It." "It" stands between the two lines. All other students stand behind one line.

2. **In the Old Testament, when God wanted to get the Israelites' attention, the priests blew the *shofar*—a ram's horn—like a trumpet. In our game today, the horn is your signal to run back and forth between the two masking-tape lines without getting tagged.** Blow the horn. Students run past the opposite line, trying not to be tagged by "It." Students who are tagged stay in the middle and help "It" tag other students. Students who have not been tagged continue running back and forth between the two masking-tape lines. When most students have been tagged (or after several minutes of play), blow the horn again and call out "forgiven." All the students who were tagged get to make a new start and be runners again. Choose a new volunteer to be "It." Repeat game as time allows.

Options
1. Allow a student who cannot participate in the game to blow the horn. Bring several party horns if you want to give more than one student an opportunity to blow the horn.

2. If space is limited, students jump or hop between the two lines.

3. Play game outdoors if possible.

• •

Discussion Questions
1. *What happened when I called "forgiven"?* (The game started over. Everyone got a new chance to be a runner.) *How is that like what happens when God forgives us?*

2. *When are some other times we get to make a new start?* (Beginning of a school year. Begin reading a new book. Begin playing a higher level on a video game.)

3. *How can we make a new start when God forgives us for the wrong things we have done?* (We can know that our sins are forgiven. We can ask God to help us love and obey Him.)

Art Center: *Shofar* Sounds

Materials

Brown wrapping paper or grocery bags, scissors, ruler, a paper party horn for each student, glue, craft sticks.

Prepare the Activity

For yourself and each student, cut a 12-inch (30-cm) square of brown wrapping paper or grocery bag. Make a sample *shofar* following the directions below.

Lead the Activity

1. Give each student a party horn and a square of brown paper. Students put several drops of glue on paper, using craft sticks to spread glue into a thin layer that covers the paper.

2. Students place party horn at one corner of glue-covered paper and roll the paper around the party horn (see sketch a), trimming off extra paper at the end where horn is blown.

3. Students bend up extra paper at other end of horn and hold for a few minutes while glue dries (see sketch b).

Options

1. Use half a paper-towel tube or a toilet-paper tube instead of a party horn. Cut slit at one end of the tube and wrap tape around ends, shaping it like the mouthpiece.

2. Lead students to blow their horns, following this traditional pattern: one blast followed by a long pause, three blasts, nine fast and short blasts, one blast.

> **Shofars are horns or trumpets made from ram's horns. In the Old Testament, the priests blew the horns to remind the people to listen to and obey God and to remember their need for God's forgiveness. Let's make our own shofars to remember that God's forgiveness helps us make a new start.**

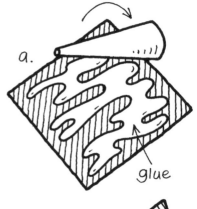

glue

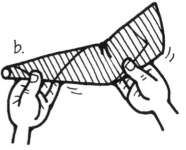

· ·

Discussion Questions

1. ***What does it mean to say that God's forgiveness helps you make a new start?*** (You don't have to feel guilty for the wrong things you have done. You can have a new chance to obey God and do right things without worrying about the wrong you did.)

2. ***When are some times that kids your age need to ask forgiveness?***

3. ***How do we know God forgives us?*** (He sent Jesus to take the punishment for our sin. God promises to forgive us when we are sorry for what we have done and ask for His forgiveness.)

"Therefore, if anyone is in Christ, he is a new creation." 2 Corinthians 5:17

BUTTERFLY KISSES!

2 Corinthians 5:17

The Challenge

As you know, some caterpillars change into butterflies, just as if they were new creations. The caterpillars below are changing into butterflies. Find the hidden number on each butterfly and caterpillar and then write the words of the verse in order. Just for fun, circle the one caterpillar who hasn't changed into a matching butterfly!

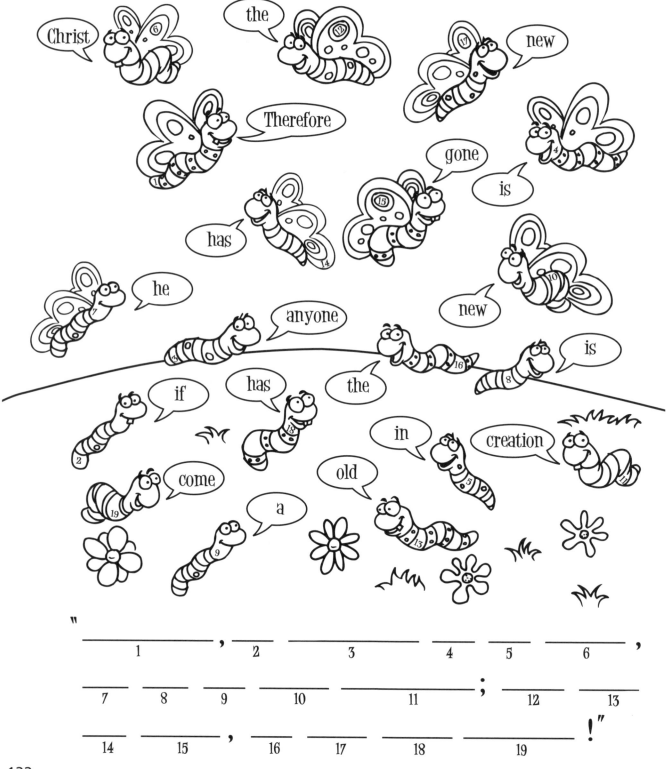

" ___ ___ ___ ___ ___ ___ ___ ,
    1   2   3   4   5   6

___ ___ ___ ___ ___ ; ___ ___
7   8   9   10   11   12   13

___ ___ , ___ ___ ___ ___ !"
14   15   16   17   18   19

Joseph Forgives His Brothers

Bible Verse

Be kind and compassionate to one another, forgiving each other, just as in Christ God forgave you. Ephesians 4:32

Bible Story Reference

Genesis 37; 39; 41:41—45

Teacher's Devotional

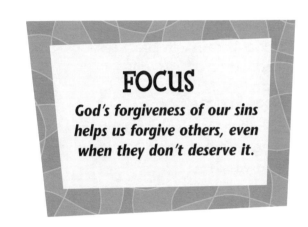

FOCUS

God's forgiveness of our sins helps us forgive others, even when they don't deserve it.

Joseph, son of Israel, lived and died long before God mandated a spiritual new year or a day of atonement. But Joseph certainly lived out the forgiveness and reconciliation that God asks from all who claim identification with Him. Had any of us been so horribly treated by our own family and endured such trouble because of their actions, would we have responded with such mercy and forgiveness? Joseph, however, saw the big picture of God's plan and trusted the dreams God had given him, in spite of years of evidence to the contrary! This is why he could say to his frightened brothers, "You intended to harm me, but God meant it for good" (see Genesis 50:20).

Forgiveness of others is a recurring theme throughout God's Word. The Old Testament tells of a special time for personal examination and repentance. During this time, now referred to as the Days of Awe, old grievances are to be forgiven and the sins of the past year are to be repented. The Days of Awe, which last 10 days, begin with the Feast of Trumpets (Rosh Hashanah) and culminate in a day of fasting and prayer on the Day of Atonement, or Yom Kippur (YAHM kih-POOR). On this final day of the Days of Awe, the Old Testament high priest offered sacrifices for the sins of the people.

Now we are living in the fullness of forgiveness of God through Jesus Christ. We no longer have to wait in fear for our salvation, but we can come boldly to God Himself, confident in the sacrifice of Jesus Christ (see Ephesians 1:7). How much more, then, are we not only expected but also enabled to forgive those who have hurt us! When we were hating God, doing our best to ignore or hurt Him, He was loving us and offering forgiveness to us in Jesus. If we have accepted His forgiveness, we have at our disposal the fullness of His ability to forgive! Celebrate God's forgiveness and His ability to help us forgive others, gently helping your students understand that forgiveness is not only Christlike but also possible!

Story Center

Materials
Bible.

Before the Story
Guide students to briefly practice signs for underlined words.

Tell the Story
As you tell the story, lead students in responding as shown when you say the underlined words.

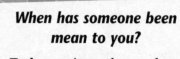

When has someone been mean to you?

Today we're going to hear about a boy whose brothers were VERY mean and hurt him. We'll find out how he treated his brothers!

1. Long ago, there was a man named Jacob. He had 12 sons, but he loved one son more than all the rest. That son was named Joseph. Because Jacob loved Joseph so much, he gave Joseph a beautiful <u>coat</u>. Joseph's brothers didn't like that one bit! Besides that, Joseph had some unusual dreams. Joseph told his family he dreamed that they would bow down to him one day. His brothers began to HATE him!

2. Not long after his dreams, Joseph went to meet his <u>brothers</u>. When they saw him coming, they decided, "We'll take his coat and throw him in a pit. We'll tear the coat up and tell our father that a wild animal KILLED Joseph!" And that's just what they did! Soon, some traders came by on their way to Egypt. Joseph's <u>brothers</u> took him from the pit and SOLD him to the traders!

3. Now Joseph was a <u>SLAVE</u>! He was bought by a man named Potiphar, one of the officials who worked for Pharaoh, the ruler of Egypt. Even while Joseph was a <u>slave</u>, God helped him in everything he did! Things looked pretty good for a while. But then, Potiphar's wife told LIES about Joseph, and her husband believed her lies.

4. Because of the lies, Joseph was put in <u>JAIL</u>! He was in the <u>jail</u> where the pharaoh's prisoners were kept. But even there, God kept right on helping him. The jail keeper trusted Joseph and put him in charge. And while Joseph was in <u>jail</u>, he helped two of Pharaoh's servants. He told them what their dreams meant.

1. Coat: Move fists down either side of chest.

2. Brother: Extend thumbs and index fingers; move right hand from forehead to top of left hand.

3. Slave: Face palms up, moving back and forth alternately; move hands down sides.

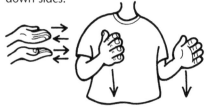

4. Jail: Face palms in, spread fingers crossing.

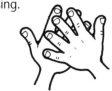

5. Two years later, Pharaoh himself had a <u>dream</u>. He knew it was an IMPORTANT <u>dream</u>. So he called his wise men, but they couldn't tell him what his <u>dream</u> meant. Finally, one of the servants who had been in jail with Joseph remembered him! He told Pharaoh that Joseph could tell Pharaoh what his <u>dream</u> meant!

5. Dream: Right index finger at forehead; move up and out while repeatedly bending finger.

6. Pharaoh called for Joseph right away! When Pharaoh told Joseph about his dream, Joseph knew it meant there would be a long time without rain. He told Pharaoh that Egypt needed to save lots of <u>food</u> for the next seven years so that when the famine came (a time when no <u>food</u> would grow), Egypt would have plenty of <u>food</u>. Pharaoh thought this was a wonderful idea and put Joseph IN CHARGE again! Now Joseph was second ruler in the country of Egypt!

6. Food: Fingertips touching, move right hand to mouth a few times.

7. Just as Joseph had told Pharaoh, after seven years of saving food, there were seven years with no rain. It wasn't long before people from other countries came to Egypt to buy food. Among those people were Joseph's own brothers! And they <u>BOWED</u> to Joseph as the dream so long ago had told they would! They didn't recognize Joseph. And Joseph pretended not to know them. But he filled their sacks with grain and returned the money they had given him, too.

7. Bowed: Palms out, left hand higher, move hands down in two moves.

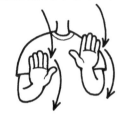

8. The NEXT time his brothers came to buy food, Joseph told them who he was. And his brothers were TERRIFIED! What would Joseph DO to them? Joseph told them NOT to be afraid. He <u>FORGAVE</u> his brothers who had been so mean! Joseph told them God had sent him to Egypt so that he could help his family now. And he invited his brothers and all their families to come and live in Egypt, so they would have food. HOORAY! They were <u>forgiven</u>!

8. Forgive: Stroke edge of left palm with right fingertips.

• •

Discussion Questions

What are some reasons Joseph might not have forgiven his brothers? (They were mean to him. They sold him.) **What did Joseph tell his brothers when he forgave them?** (God had sent him to Egypt, so he could help his family.) **God helped Joseph through all these hard times he faced. God even helped Joseph forgive his brothers for what they had done.**

   God has forgiven us for many things, too. His love and forgiveness help us forgive others, even when we think they don't deserve it.

Object Talk

Scripture Background
Psalm 139:23,24

Materials
Bible with bookmarks at Psalm 139:23,24 and Ephesians 4:32; large sheet of paper; marker.

Prepare the Activity
Print several misspelled words and incorrect math problems on large sheet of paper, adjusting the difficulty of the spelling and math according to the age of your students.

Because God forgives us when we ask, we can forgive others, even when they don't ask! In Old Testament times, there were 10 days during which God especially wanted His people to carefully think about the sins for which they needed to be forgiven. Let's find out about these 10 days and what it means to carefully look for something wrong.

Lead the Activity

1. **The 10 days between the Feast of Trumpets and the Day of Atonement are now called the Days of Awe. What do you think of when you hear the word "awe"?** (Awesome. Things that are very good or beautiful.) **The word "awe" means those things, but it also means respect, admiration and amazement. During the Days of Awe, as God's people thought about how wonderful and perfect God is, they also thought about their own lives and realized the wrong things they had said and done.**

2. Show paper you prepared. Invite volunteers to correct the spelling and math. **In order to find what was wrong with these words and problems, we looked carefully for what was wrong. In the same way, during the Days of Awe, people examined their actions so that they knew what sins to ask forgiveness for.**

3. **When we believe in Jesus and become members of God's family, we are forgiven once and for all—forever! But the Bible says we should still look carefully at our lives and make sure they are pleasing to God.** Read or ask a student to read Psalm 139:23,24.

Pictrue thrugh kicthen

$$\begin{array}{ccc} 6 & 21 & 14 \\ \times 3 & -4 & +12 \\ \hline 15 & 16 & 25 \end{array}$$

Conclude
Knowing we are forgiven should make us want to please God more and more. There's something else that being forgiven makes us want to do. Read Ephesians 4:32 aloud. **What does God's forgiveness help us want to do?** (Forgive others.) Pray, thanking God that when we ask, He forgives our sins and helps us want to forgive others.

• •

Discussion Questions

1. *When can kids your age forgive others?* (When others cheat you or lie to you.)

2. *What can we do to show forgiveness?* (Say I forgive you. Smile. Be friendly.)

Active Game Center: Balloon Challenge

Materials

Large balloons (at least two for each student).

Lead the Game

1. Give each student a balloon to partially inflate and tie. Students sit close to each other to form circles of no more than six students. Students sit on inflated balloons. Give each group an additional inflated and tied balloon.

2. Students in each circle try to tap the balloon 10 times, tapping it to each other in random order without popping the balloons on which they are sitting. Lead students in counting aloud the number of times the balloon is tapped. If balloon touches the floor or if a balloon pops, distribute new balloons as needed and students begin again.

> We can celebrate the fact that God will always forgive us when we ask Him. His forgiveness helps us want to forgive others. In Bible times God asked His people to think about their wrong actions during the 10 days now called the Days of Awe. We'll play a game by trying to tap a balloon 10 times in a row.

3. After several rounds of play, circles compete to see which circle can keep the balloon in the air the longest. Winning circle earns a letter in the word "forgive." Continue until one circle has earned all the letters or time is up.

Options

1. Some students may prefer to sit directly on the floor.

2. To add interest and increase the challenge, try these ideas: give each group an additional balloon to keep in the air; students say the words of Ephesians 4:32 as they tap the balloon, continuing to tap balloon until entire verse is quoted; students hold each other's wrists while trying to tap balloon with hands (or other body parts—elbows, heads, knees).

3. Put a masking-tape line on the floor and play a game like volleyball. Students form two teams and sit on balloons on opposite sides of masking-tape line. Teams hit balloon back and forth across masking-tape line. Teams follow volleyball rules, serving the balloon and hitting it over the line on the third hit.

• •

Discussion Questions

1. **When has someone forgiven you for doing wrong?** Tell your answer before asking students to answer.

2. **Why does God's forgiveness help us forgive others, even if they don't deserve it?** (God forgives us, even when we don't deserve it. To show our thankfulness to God, we show His love to others by forgiving them.)

3. **When might you need to forgive a friend or family member?** Volunteers tell ideas.

Art Center: What's Inside?

Materials

Construction paper in a variety of colors including one 12x18-inch (30x45-cm) sheet of light-colored construction paper for each student, markers, scissors, glue; optional—tape.

Prepare the Activity

Make a sample card following directions below.

> God's forgiveness of our sin helps us forgive others, even when we don't feel like they deserve it. Let's make cards to help us celebrate God's forgiveness. We'll draw pictures of ourselves on the outside of the cards, and we'll write prayers about forgiveness on the inside.

Lead the Activity

1. Students fold light-colored construction paper in half. Each student draws the shape of a person on the folded paper, making sure that the person's right hand is against the fold of the paper (see sketch a).

2. Students use markers to decorate the drawing to look like themselves. Students may draw clothes or cut clothes and other details from colored construction paper and glue the clothes to the shapes.

3. Students cut around the shapes, cutting through both layers of folded paper and leaving the fold uncut. (Hint: Repair cutting mistakes with tape.)

4. **People can't always tell by looking at us what we are thinking. Our thoughts are on the "inside" of us. Open up your cards. When we pray, we tell God our thoughts and feelings.** On the insides of their cards, students write prayers asking or thanking God for His forgiveness, or asking God to help them forgive others (see sketch b).

Options

1. For younger students, provide several cardboard person patterns for students to trace around. Younger students may also wish to dictate their prayers to you.

2. Provide a variety of additional materials for students to use in decorating person shapes: rick rack, chenille wire, buttons, etc.

3. In addition to making cards, bring gingerbread people to decorate with frosting.

Discussion Questions

1. *What can people tell about you from the outside?* (How I look. If I feel sad or mad.)

2. *Why might you feel that others don't deserve to be forgiven?* (They've done something very wrong. They keep doing wrong things over and over.)

3. *Why does God forgive us, even when we don't deserve it?* (He loves us so much that He sent Jesus to take the punishment we deserve for our sins.)

"Forgive each other, just as in Christ God forgave you." Ephesians 4:32

GOD'S GOT YOUR NUMBER!

The Challenge

Ephesians 4:32

Use the number code below to discover the words of the verse.

A=1   B=2   C=3   D=4   E=5   F=6
G=7   H=8   I=9   J=10   K=11   L=12
M=13   N=14   O=15   P=16   Q=17
R=18   S=19   T=20   U=21   V=22
W=23   X=24   Y=25   Z=26

" 2.5 / 11.9.14.4 / 1.14.4 /

— —   — — — —   — — —

3.15.13.16.1.19.19.9.15.14.1.20.5 /

— — — — — — — — — — — — —

20.15 / 15.14.5 / 1 14.15.20.8.5.18 /

— —   — — —   — — — — — — — ,

6.15.18.7.9.22.9.14.7 /

— — — — — — — — —

5.1.3.8 / 15.20.8.5.18 /

— — — —   — — — — — ,

10.21.19.20 / 1.19 / 9.14 /

— — — —   — —   — —

3.8.18.9.19.20 / 7.15.4 /

— — — — — — —   — — —

6.15.18.7.1.22.5 / 25.15.21 /

— — — — — — —   — — —

— — — — — — . "

140   © 2005 Gospel Light. Permission to photocopy granted. *The Big Book of Holiday and Bible Celebrations*

Jonah Preaches to Nineveh

Bible Verse

God our Savior . . . wants all men to be saved and to come to a knowledge of the truth.
1 Timothy 2:3,4

Bible Story Reference

Jonah

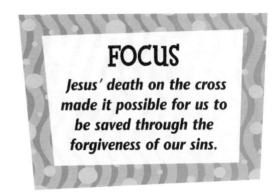

FOCUS

Jesus' death on the cross made it possible for us to be saved through the forgiveness of our sins.

Teacher's Devotional

The Day of Atonement, now called by its Hebrew name Yom Kippur (YAHM kih-POOR), was mandated in detail by God in Leviticus 16. Read this chapter to gain a better understanding of the great meaning of the day as God originally gave it to Moses. The high priest of Israel was required to make a series of particular washings and sacrifices before coming into the Holy of Holies (the innermost room of the Tabernacle). He had to choose by lot one goat to be sacrificed and one to be released into the wilderness to symbolically bear away the sins of Israel. Then, having sprinkled blood from a bull as atonement for himself and his family, he sprinkled the sacrificed goat's blood on the lid of the Ark of the Covenant to atone for the sin of the people of Israel. This ceremony could only be done once a year and only in the strictest order. To disregard God's holy order would mean death for the high priest. And assurance of forgiveness could only come once a year!

A feature added over the years to the solemn celebration of Yom Kippur has been the reading aloud of the book of Jonah. This reading emphasizes, first, the fact that God is the God of all nations, not only of Israel. Second, it is a dramatic example of a man who repented, accepted responsibility for his actions and obeyed God, even in a thing he didn't want to do. (Jonah wanted judgment for the Ninevite oppressors and chafed at the thought that God chose to have mercy on them!)

What may we as Christians celebrate? That we (mostly Gentiles) have come under the mercy of the Almighty! While Jonah became a conduit of God's grace to some Gentiles, Jesus became the final and full conduit of God's grace to both Jews and Gentiles by His complete and perfect obedience! Christ's atonement (that which brought us together to be "at one" with God) is offered to all who trust in Him. Tell your students how God's wonderful grace and Jesus' atonement have changed your life! Is there any better reason to celebrate?

Story Center

Materials
Bible.

Before the Story
Guide students to briefly practice signs for underlined words.

Tell the Story
As you tell the story, lead students in responding as shown when you say the underlined words.

When have you not wanted to listen to your parents or your teacher? What did you want to do instead?

Today we'll meet a person who decided to say no to God! And we'll find out how God helped that person change and obey Him!

1. There was once a man named Jonah who was a prophet of God; he <u>told</u> people messages from God. One day, God <u>said</u> to Jonah, "Go to Nineveh right away! Tell the people there to stop their wickedness or I will have to punish them!" But Jonah didn't like the people of Nineveh and didn't WANT to warn them. He wanted God to DESTROY them.

2. So Jonah got up and went, but instead of going to Nineveh, he got on board a ship that was going the OTHER way. Jonah thought he could <u>hide</u> from God! He went down into the bottom of the ship and fell asleep.

3. While Jonah slept, God sent a storm! The wind began to blow and the <u>ship</u> began to rock back and forth! The waves got higher and HIGHER! And soon the sailors were praying to their false gods to help them. Then they remembered Jonah, asleep in the bottom of the rocking <u>ship</u>.

4. The sailors didn't waste any time! They hurried to Jonah and shook him awake. "Help us!" they said. Jonah knew GOD had sent the storm because of Jonah's disobedience. "You'll have to <u>throw</u> me overboard," he said. "Then the storm will stop."

   So the sailors took Jonah and <u>THREW</u> him over the side. SPLASH!

1. Told, said: With right index finger, make circular movement from mouth.

2. Hide: Touch lips with right fist; move right fist under cupped left hand.

3. Ship: Right hand with first three fingers extended on left palm; move both hands in a forward wavy motion.

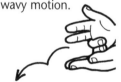

4. Throw: Raise right fist beside head; move hand forward while opening.

5. Jonah went down, down, down—sinking like a stone. But then, a HUGE <u>fish</u> came by. The <u>fish</u> opened wide and swallowed Jonah whole! Jonah was in the smelly belly of the great big <u>fish</u>.

5. Fish: Place left fingertips on right wrist; swing right hand from wrist.

6. Soon Jonah began to think about how he had disobeyed God. And he began to <u>pray</u>. He asked God to give him another chance to obey by going to warn the people of Nineveh. He <u>prayed</u> some more. And he waited. And the great big fish kept right on swimming!

6. Pray: Touch palms in front; move hands to body and bow head.

7. Can you guess what happened? God sent that fish close to the shore. And he coughed Jonah right out onto the beach—not too far from the city! Then God called to Jonah AGAIN, "Go to Nineveh! Warn those people like I told you to do!" And this time Jonah <u>obeyed</u>.

7. Obeyed: Hold fists near forehead; bring down and palms up.

8. Jonah marched right into Nineveh. He must have looked very strange after three days in the big fish's belly. He may have smelled funny, too! But Jonah was going to tell these people God's message, no matter what! He began to warn everyone he saw. "Change your ways," he called out, "or God will destroy this city in 40 days!"

8. Forgave, forgiveness: Stroke edge of left palm with right fingertips.

And the people of Nineveh listened! They didn't want to keep on with their wicked ways! And God <u>forgave</u> them and did not punish them. Because Jonah obeyed God, the Ninevites heard God's message and had the opportunity to ask His <u>forgiveness</u>.

• •

Discussion Questions

What did Jonah do when God told him to warn the people of Nineveh? Why? (He wanted God to punish the Ninevites.) **How did God help Jonah to change his mind and obey?** (Sent a storm.) **Jonah learned that God loves all people!**

God will forgive anyone who asks. He will make us part of His family when we are sorry for our sin and we believe that Jesus died on the cross to pay for our sin. That's a BIG reason to celebrate!

Object Talk

Scripture Background
Leviticus 16; 23:26-32; Numbers 29:7-11

Materials
Bible with bookmark at 1 Timothy 2:3,4; variety of objects used to cover things (tablecloths, blankets, slipcovers, hats, coats, canopy, box or pan lids, umbrellas, etc.).

God loves us so much that He planned a way for our sins to be forgiven. In Bible times, on a special day called the Day of Atonement, the priests followed God's instructions for forgiveness. Let's find out what happened on the Day of Atonement and how we can be sure that our sins are forgiven.

Lead the Activity

1. Show each object you brought. **What is this object used for?** After all objects have been shown, ask, **What do all of these objects have in common?** (They are all used to cover something.) Ask students to name other coverings.

2. **The Hebrew name for the Day of Atonement is Yom Kippur (YAHM kih-POOR) which means "day of covering." When something is completely covered up, you can't see it. It's like the object doesn't exist. That's how it can be with our sins—the wrong things we have done. Even though the first people who celebrated the Day of Atonement didn't know about Jesus, today we can believe that Jesus is God's Son and that He died on the cross to take the punishment for our sins. Then we become members of God's family. When God looks at us, He doesn't see our sins— they are not only covered up by Jesus' death, but our sins are also removed. God forgives us and our sins are gone! God promises that He will NEVER remember them again!**

Conclude
Because Jesus took the punishment for our sins by dying on the cross, we say that Jesus atoned for our sins. Instead of being separated from God by our sins, our sins are removed. Now we can be "at one" with Him. So no matter what name you call this holiday, Day of Atonement or Yom Kippur, the good news for everyone everywhere is that our sins are forgiven. Read 1 Timothy 2:3,4 aloud. Pray, thanking God for sending Jesus to die on the cross so that our sins can be forgiven.

• •

Additional Information for Older Students
A scapegoat is something or someone blamed when things go wrong. That word comes from something that happened on the Day of Atonement. Ask a student to read Leviticus 16:10. **On the Day of Atonement the high priest would ask God to put all the blame for everyone's sins onto a goat. Then the goat was chased away into the desert never to be seen again to show that God had removed the guilt of the people's sins for another year.**

Active Game Center: Jonah's Journey

Materials

Length of butcher paper, markers, masking tape, small index cards cut in half, scissors, blindfold.

Prepare the Game

Draw outlines of a whale and Nineveh on butcher paper (see sketch). Then tape butcher paper on classroom wall.

Lead the Game

1. Invite volunteer(s) to tell the story of Jonah's journey to Nineveh. On an index card half, each student draws a stick figure to represent Jonah and attaches a masking-tape loop to the back of the card.

2. Students line up approximately 5 feet (1.5 m) from butcher paper. Blindfold first student and spin him or her three times. Student walks to butcher paper and tapes card to the paper. Continue until all students have had a turn. Student who placed his or her card closest to Nineveh answers one of the Discussion Questions below or repeats the words of 1 Timothy 2:3,4.

> *We can celebrate the fact that when we believe that Jesus died to take the punishment for our sin and ask God for forgiveness, all our sins are forgiven. In the Old Testament, Jonah went on an unusual journey and as a result people learned about God's forgiveness. Let's play a game to remind us of his journey.*

Option

If you have more than six to eight students, make additional papers. Students play game in small groups.

• •

Discussion Questions

1. ***How can we stop doing wrong things?*** (Ask God to forgive our sin and to help us do what's right.)

2. ***How do we know that our sin is forgiven?*** (The Bible tells us that if we ask God for forgiveness for the wrong things we have done, we will be forgiven.)

3. ***What are some ways we can learn the right things God wants us to do?*** (Read God's Word. Follow the instructions of people who love God. Pray.)

Art Center: Party Plates

Materials

Two clear plastic plates (available at party supply stores) for each student, clear-drying glue, scissors, materials for decorating plates (permanent markers, wrapping paper, party napkins, confetti, glitter, etc.).

Lead the Activity

1. Give each student a plastic plate. On plates, students use permanent markers to write short phrases celebrating God's forgiveness of sin. Ask the Discussion Questions below to help students think of phrases ("God's forgiveness is great!" "Thank God for forgiveness!").

2. Students add decorations around phrases, cutting shapes from wrapping paper or party napkins and sprinkling confetti and glitter onto plates.

3. Student applies a thin line of clear glue to edge of his or her decorated plate. Give student a second plastic plate to place on top of decorated plate. Allow glue to dry before using plate.

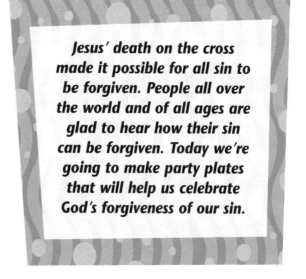

Jesus' death on the cross made it possible for all sin to be forgiven. People all over the world and of all ages are glad to hear how their sin can be forgiven. Today we're going to make party plates that will help us celebrate God's forgiveness of our sin.

Options

1. Invite students to participate in a party celebrating God's forgiveness of sin. Students decorate classroom with streamers and balloons and use their party plates for snacks. Serve party finger foods or sweet foods such as *challah* with jam (traditionally eaten to celebrate the holiday called the Day of Atonement, or Yom Kippur, when God's people followed His instructions to receive forgiveness of sin).

2. Instead of using clear plastic plates, students glue slogans and decorations onto solid-colored paper or plastic plates.

3. Younger students may dictate their slogans to you.

• •

Discussion Questions

1. ***How does God show His love for us?*** (Sent Jesus to take the punishment for our sin. Forgives our sin. Helps us obey Him.)

2. ***What did Jesus do to make God's forgiveness possible?***

3. ***Why is knowing about God's forgiveness such good news?***

4. ***What are some ways to celebrate this good news?*** (Sing songs of praise. Thank God in prayer.)

"God...wants all men to be SAVED and to come to a knowledge of the TRUTH"

1 Timothy 2:4

JONAH'S ALL WASHED UP!

The Challenge → Jonah

Break the code to discover what Jonah said in Jonah 1:9 about God.

The Super Challenge → You know what happened to Jonah. There's something fishy about all the stuff washed up on the beach. Eyeball the picture for a minute; then turn over the page to see how many items from the picture you can write down.

Jubilee

The Forgiving King

Bible Verse

Forgive, and you will be forgiven. Luke 6:37

Bible Story Reference

Matthew 18:21-35

Teacher's Devotional

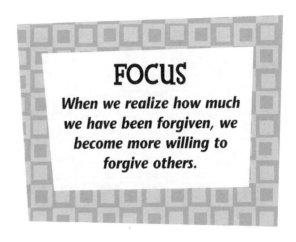

FOCUS

When we realize how much we have been forgiven, we become more willing to forgive others.

"Jubilee!" The word paints a picture of a special event marked by joy and celebration. In Leviticus 25, God decreed that every seven years Israel was to release slaves and not plant any crops so that the land would rest. He also commanded that after 49 years (seven sevens), every piece of land was to be returned to its original owner, every slave was to be freed and every debt was to be canceled. This Year of Jubilee was to begin with the same blast of the *shofar* that announced God's forgiveness at the end of the Day of Atonement!

While historians agree that these requirements were probably not put into practice, the shofar was sounded as a reminder of God's forgiving care and concern for others in need. If you had been standing among the Israelites, hungry from fasting and waiting to hear if the sacrifice of the Day of Atonement had been accepted, how would you have reacted as you heard the blast of the *shofar*? At such a time of joyful relief, would you quietly head for home? It certainly seems that such great joy and relief would need to be expressed! And how better could you express it than to forgive any and all wrongs and draw into loving embrace even those who had wronged you?

This picture illustrates what God expects of His forgiven people—both then and now. His forgiveness of us is so astounding and powerful that we are no longer able to hold any grudge or deprive anyone of forgiveness. More than that, in His introduction to the story of the forgiving king, Jesus made it very clear the high priority He places on forgiveness of others (see Matthew 18:21,22).

So both by reason of our being forgiven and by reason of our needing forgiveness, we must become people who live in forgiveness! As you share the importance of forgiving others with your students, remind them that we don't have to work at drumming up enthusiasm to forgive others; we need only to admit our grudges and repent of our inability to forgive. Then as we ask God to make us able to forgive, we find that His Spirit enables us to forgive as we have been forgiven. And that is yet another reason to celebrate!

Story Center

Materials
Bible.

Before the Story
Guide students to briefly practice signs for underlined words.

Tell the Story
As you tell the story, lead students in responding as shown when you say the underlined words.

> *When have you forgiven someone for something wrong that was done?*
>
> *Today we're going to hear a story Jesus told about two men who had to choose whether or not to forgive.*

1. Jesus wanted to teach His friends something very important. So He told them this story:

Once there was a <u>king</u> who had many servants. One of those servants had borrowed a lot of money from the <u>king</u>. One day the <u>king</u> noticed that this servant had never repaid ANY of the money. The <u>king</u> called for his servant to come to him.

1. King: Right thumb between index and middle fingers; move from shoulder to waist.

2. The king said, "You must pay me what you owe!" Now this <u>servant</u> owed the king 10,000 talents. It was like owing millions of dollars! There was no way the <u>servant</u> could pay back so much money! So the king ordered that the <u>servant</u> and his family be sold as slaves. Everything they owned would be sold to repay the <u>servant's</u> debt.

2. Servant: Face palms up, moving back and forth alternately; move hands down sides.

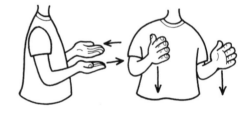

3. "Oh, PLEASE, your majesty," the servant cried. "PLEASE be patient. I will pay back EVERYTHING I owe."

The king felt sorry for his servant, so the king said, "I will <u>forgive</u> and forget about your debt. You no longer owe me ANY money!" The servant must have been VERY happy. The king had <u>forgiven</u> him his whole ENORMOUS debt!

3. Forgive: Stroke edge of left palm with right fingertips.

4. But that wasn't the end of the story. As the servant was walking home, he saw a <u>friend</u>. This <u>friend</u> had borrowed a small amount of money from him. He had borrowed a hundred denarii, which was like a few dollars. The servant grabbed his <u>friend</u>. "You owe me money," he growled. "Pay it NOW!"

4. Friend: Interlock index fingers; repeat in reverse.

150

5. "I'm sorry," said the friend. "I don't have the money. Please be patient. I will pay back what I owe you."

But the servant would NOT be patient. He had his friend thrown in <u>jail</u> because the friend could not pay what he owed.

5. Jail: Face palms in, spread fingers crossing.

6. Other people saw what this servant did to his friend. They ran to the king. They reminded the king of ALL the <u>money</u> the king had forgiven. They told the king that the very same servant had put his friend in jail because the friend couldn't pay back a LITTLE bit of <u>money</u> he owed that mean servant!

6. Money: Touching, right fingertips strike left palm a few times.

7. "What?!" roared the <u>king</u>. "Bring that servant here IMME-DIATELY!"

The servant was brought to the <u>king</u>.

"I forgave you a LARGE amount of money. In the same way, you should have forgiven your friend for a small amount!" the <u>king</u> said. "Now YOU will be put in prison!"

7. King: Right thumb between index and middle fingers; move from shoulder to waist.

8. Then Jesus explained His story. "<u>God</u> is like the king. He will forgive you for all the wrong and unkind things you do, if you ask Him. You do not have to pay for your sins. In fact, you CANNOT pay for them. Your debt is TOO BIG to pay. But because <u>God</u> has forgiven you such a BIG debt, He wants you to forgive others when they do wrong things to you. In the same kind way <u>God</u> has forgiven you, you should forgive others."

8. God: Point right index finger; lower and open hand at chest.

. . . .

Discussion Questions

Why didn't the servant have to pay back the large amount of money he owed? (The king forgave his debt.) **How did the forgiven servant treat his friend who owed him money?** (Had him thrown into jail.)

Jesus told this story so that we would know that because God has forgiven us such a big debt, He wants us to forgive people in the way He has forgiven us. When we experience forgiveness and forgive others, it makes us feel like celebrating!

Jubilee

Object Talk

Scripture Background

Leviticus 25:8-55; 27:17-24

Materials

Bible with bookmark at Luke 6:37, a variety of household bills.

Lead the Activity

1. Show students the bills you brought and make a comment such as, **When I get bills like these, it means I have to pay someone for the gasoline I've put in my car and for the electricity and water I've used in my house. Until I've paid these bills, I'm in debt, which means I owe money. How do you think I would feel if someone told me I didn't have to pay these bills?** (Excited. Happy. Glad.)

Because God has forgiven us, we are to forgive others, too! In Bible times, God's people celebrated a holiday that reminds us how important it is to forgive others. This holiday, called the Year of Jubilee, was celebrated once every 50 years! Let's find out what happened in this holiday.

2. **During the Year of Jubilee if you owed someone money, your debt was taken away, or forgiven. Slaves were set free! And if you had sold land to someone, that land would be returned to you. God wanted His people to celebrate the Year of Jubilee so that poor people would receive the help they needed. The word "jubilee" means liberty or freedom. This holiday was celebrated the whole year long!** (Optional: Older students read Leviticus 25:10; 27:24.)

Conclude

God thinks forgiving others is so important that He doesn't want us to do it only once every 50 years. Read Luke 6:37 aloud. **The Bible teaches us that because God has forgiven us, He wants us to forgive others every day.** Pray, thanking God for His forgiveness and asking His help in forgiving others.

. . . .

Discussion Questions

1. *In what ways do people today show that they forgive others?* (Treat the person kindly. Be friendly. Say "I forgive you.")

2. *When has someone forgiven you? How did you know you were forgiven?*

Jubilee

Active Game Center: Who's Forgiven?

Materials

An index card for each student, marker.

Prepare the Game

On one card print the word "forgiven." Hide all cards around classroom.

Lead the Game

At your signal, each student finds one of the hidden cards. Students with blank cards are debtors (people who owe money) and must do 10 jumping jacks to pay their debts. Student with the word "forgiven" on his or her card does not have to do jumping jacks. Repeat game as time permits, each time choosing a different way in which debts are to be paid (do 10 sit-ups, hop across the room, touch toes, pat head and rub tummy for 10 seconds, etc.).

When God forgives the wrong things we've done, it makes us want to forgive others, too. A long time ago, Jesus told a story about a king, and a servant who owed the king lots of money. We're going to play a game that reminds us of what the king did.

Option

If you are unable to hide cards in your room, give each student a card. At your signal, students begin trading their cards facedown with each other. When time is up, students determine who is forgiven and who are debtors by looking at their cards.

Discussion Questions

1. *How do you feel when someone tells you that you have done something wrong?*
2. *How do you feel when someone says you are forgiven for what you did?*
3. *Why does God's forgiveness of our sins make us want to forgive others?* (God has been kind to us, so we want to be kind to others.)
4. *When might it be hard for a kid your age to forgive someone? Who helps us forgive?*

Jubilee

Art Center: Confetti Cards

Materials

Colored paper, an assortment of gift wrap, scissors, glue, markers, several hole punches, envelopes; optional—shape punchers.

Lead the Activity

1. Give each student a sheet of colored paper. Students fold paper in half or in fourths to make cards. Students cut a variety of shapes from gift wrap and glue shapes to front of cards, making collages.

2. Inside the cards, students write messages about ways to celebrate God's forgiveness. Ask the Discussion Questions below to help students think of messages.

3. Students cut colored paper and gift wrap into small pieces of confetti or use a hole punch to create confetti. (Optional: Students make confetti with shape punchers.) Students carefully put confetti into card against folded edge and insert card into envelope, putting folded edge in first. Invite students to tell to whom they plan to give their cards.

> *Because God's forgiveness of the wrong things we have done is so great, it makes us want to forgive other people for the wrong things they have done to us! Let's make cards to celebrate and share God's forgiveness with others.*

Options

1. Buy a package of A4 envelopes at a paper supply store. These envelopes will fit cards that have been made by folding 8½ x11-inch (21.5x27.5-cm) paper in half vertically and then in half horizontally.

2. Bring a variety of colors and types of paper to make into confetti: neon, metallic, wallpaper, etc.

3. Younger students may dictate their messages to you.

• •

Discussion Questions

1. When are some other times people use confetti? How? What are they celebrating?

2. What are some ways we can show that we are celebrating God's forgiveness? (Forgive others. Sing a song to praise Him. Tell others about God's forgiveness.)

3. What should everyone know about God's forgiveness? (God forgives everyone who believes in Jesus and confesses their sin. God forgives any sin. God's forgiveness lasts forever.)

God Provides for His People

Bible Verse

My God will meet all your needs according to his glorious riches in Christ Jesus. Philippians 4:19

Bible Story Reference

Exodus 16—17:7

FOCUS
God gives us everything we need.

Teacher's Devotional

We often find it difficult to build time into our hurried lives for rest and recreation. But consider God's ordered balancing of time in the lives of the Israelites: not only were they to rest on every seventh day, but also they were to rest (and let the land rest) during every seventh year and for up to two years every fiftieth year. However, rest was only half of this balance: taking time for celebration was also commanded! God told the Israelites to come together to celebrate Passover in the spring as well as the Day of Atonement and the Feast of Tabernacles in the fall. Once the Day of Atonement was over, the Feast of Tabernacles began (see Leviticus 23:33-36).

Called Sukkot (suh-KOHT), which means "tabernacles" in Hebrew, God established the Feast of Tabernacles as a hands-on recreational learning experience designed to remind His people of His care for them in the 40 years of desert wandering after escaping slavery in Egypt. Every family built a wooden booth called a *sukkah* (SOO-kah) and lived in it for seven days. Traditionally, stars were to be visible through its leafy roof, and fruit of the harvest was to be both hung as a decoration and waved before the Lord in praise. Rest, worship, feasting and rejoicing before the Lord of the harvest were the order of the week-long celebration.

A traditional feature of the final day of the festival was the rejoicing over water. The high priest poured water over the altar as prayer was made for a good rainy season, amidst a crowd waving branches and shouting with joy. It was at this point during one Feast of Tabernacles that Jesus interrupted the proceedings to declare, "If anyone is thirsty, let him come to me and drink" (John 7:37).

More than the need for rest, for celebration, for hands-on education or even for water, we need Jesus! Just as God provided every need for His people in those desert years, so also He provides all our needs today, according to His riches in Christ Jesus. Consider what that means in your own life. If you have Jesus, you have (right now!) everything you need! That is reason to celebrate!

Story Center

Materials
Bible.

Before the Story
Guide students to briefly practice signs for underlined words.

Tell the Story
As you tell the story, lead students in responding as shown when you say the underlined words.

When you really need something, who do you ask to help you?

Today we're going to find out about some people who thought they would die if they didn't get what they needed!

1. God's people, the Israelites, had been slaves in a country called Egypt. They had prayed to God for help, and He had sent a man named <u>Moses</u> to lead them away from Egypt. God had even parted the waters of the Red Sea, so His people could escape from the Egyptian army. After all the ways God had helped them, you would think the Israelites would have been happy. But they were UNHAPPY.

2. One day, the Israelites gathered around Moses. They <u>grumbled</u>, "When we left Egypt, you said we would go to a new home where we could be happy. Well, Moses, we're NOT happy. We don't have houses to live in! We're stuck out here in the desert, and our food is all GONE. We're HUNGRY. We're going to starve to death and it's ALL YOUR FAULT!"

3. Moses turned and walked away from the people. He was TIRED of all this complaining! He sat down on a rock and sighed. But he knew what to do. He talked to <u>God</u> about this grumbling. <u>God</u> told Moses, "I have heard the people. I will send you all the food you need. There will be so much that you will think the sky has opened up and rained food!"

4. Just as God had promised, the food came! Later that day, thousands and thousands of small <u>birds</u> called <u>quail</u> came flying over the camp. The <u>quail</u> flew so low that the people could just reach out and grab as many as they wanted! There were <u>quail</u> EVERYWHERE! Soon everyone was eating roasted <u>quail</u>. They ate and ate until they were FULL.

1. Moses: Extend thumb and index finger of both hands at temples; close fingers as you move hands to sides.

2. Grumbled: With right hand curved, strike chest with fingertips a few times.

3. God: Point right index finger; lower and open hand at chest.

4. Birds, quail: Right thumb and index finger at mouth; open and close fingers a few times.

5. But that wasn't ALL God did! The next morning the people woke to find something on the ground they had never seen before. It looked like little seeds. Moses told the people, "This is <u>bread</u> God has given you to eat." It was delicious! It tasted like little cakes made with honey. The Israelites called it manna.

5. Bread: Move edge of right hand down back of left a few times.

6. God told the people to gather only as much manna as they needed for each day. Before the <u>Sabbath</u>, they were to gather enough for two days. That way, they could rest on the <u>Sabbath</u>. When people gathered too much manna or kept it from the day before, it smelled awful and got worms in it!

6. Sabbath: Fists with thumbs facing out; move in opposite-direction circles.

7. Every single day, God sent food to feed all those people. But now the Israelites were THIRSTY. NOW all they wanted was cool, clear water. So what did they do? They grumbled to Moses AGAIN. Moses couldn't wait to get away from them and pray to God. After all, God had <u>taken care of</u> them so well up to now! Moses knew that God would <u>take care of</u> them here. Moses asked God what to do. And sure enough, God had a plan! He had a way to give them water, right there in that dry desert!

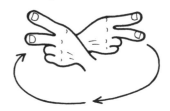

7. Take care of: Cross hands, right over left, each with two fingers extended; move in outward circle.

8. As soon as he got back to camp, Moses called the leaders of each family. Moses and the leaders walked and walked until they came to a big rock. Before anyone else could open his mouth to complain, Moses did what God had told him. Moses lifted his walking stick high over his head and swung it toward the rock. CRACK!!! Something AMAZING happened! <u>Water</u> came out of the rock! And guess what? Those Israelites quit complaining! God gave them <u>water</u> right out of a rock in the middle of a desert! Once again, God gave them EVERYTHING they needed!

8. Water: Extend three fingers of right hand; touch mouth a few times.

• •

Discussion Questions

Why were the Israelites unhappy? (They were hungry. They were out of food.) **What did God do to give them food?** (Sent quail. Sent manna.) **What else made the people complain?** (They had no water. They were thirsty.) **How did God give them water?** (Moses hit a rock in the desert.)

What kinds of things do kids your age need? (Food. Water. Loving family.) **What does God promise to do?** (Give us the things we need.) **Because God loves us, He gives us everything we need. That's a big reason to celebrate!**

Object Talk

Scripture Background

Exodus 23:16; Leviticus 23:33-36,39-43

Materials

Bible with bookmark at Philippians 4:19, several tree branches; optional—one or more objects used at sporting events (pom-pom, pennant, foam hand, etc.).

It's important to remember all that God has done for us. In the Old Testament God's people celebrated the Feast of Tabernacles to help them remember how God took care of them when they left Egypt. Let's find out some of the things they used in this celebration and how the celebration got its name.

Lead the Activity

1. Show branches. **At the Feast of Tabernacles, called Sukkot (suh-KOHT) in Hebrew, God told His people to gather different types of tree branches and fruit.** (Optional: Read Leviticus 23:40 aloud.) **The branches and fruit were used in several ways. One way was to decorate small booths the people built. Traditionally, the people lived in these booths for the seven days of the celebration. Living in the booths reminded them of the time after they escaped from Egypt when they had no houses to live in. The word "sukkot" means booths or tabernacles, and that's why this celebration was called the Feast of Tabernacles.** (Optional: Read Leviticus 23:42 aloud.) **Even today Jewish people build and decorate booths as part of this holiday.**

2. **Besides being used to decorate the booths, the branches were used to show praise to God. What kind of objects do people use to cheer for or praise a sports team?** Volunteers tell. (Optional: Display objects used at sporting events.) Invite volunteers to wave branches (or hands) in the following traditional pattern for Sukkot: to the front, sides, back, up and down. **The branches were waved in all directions to show that God is ruler over all the earth.**

Conclude

We can praise God, too, not just at the Feast of Tabernacles, but all year long. Read Philippians 4:19 aloud. **What does this verse tell us about God?** Volunteers answer. **This verse tells us a good reason to celebrate!** Pray, thanking God for giving us all that we need.

• •

Additional Information for Older Students

Traditionally, branches from three trees—myrtle, willow and palm—were collected at the Feast of Tabernacles. (Optional: Show one or more of the named branches.) **The branches were braided together and then waved in the air as a way of praising God. A fruit—called a citron—was also held and waved. A citron looks like a lemon.** (Optional: Show lemon.) **In Hebrew, the branches were called a *lulav* (LOO-lahv) and the fruit was called the *etrog* (EH-trog).**

Active Game Center: Frisbee Bowling

Materials

Paper cups, markers, Frisbee.

Lead the Game

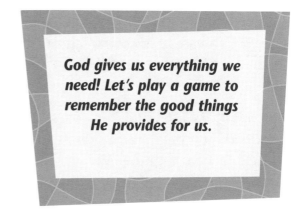

God gives us everything we need! Let's play a game to remember the good things He provides for us.

1. **What are some of the needs people have?** (Family. Friends. Clothes. Help. Shelter. Food. Transportation.) Print each category on a separate paper cup. On one side of the classroom, set cups up like bowling pins (see sketch).

2. Students stand in a line at least 6 feet (1.8 m) from cups. Students take turns rolling the Frisbee on its edge toward cups. When a student knocks over a cup, student names one specific thing God has given him or her from category on that cup (Family: mom, grandpa, sister), and then places cup back in correct position. Repeat play as time allows.

Options

1. Instead of paper cups, collect empty soda cans or plastic liter bottles. Print categories on separate index cards and tape cards to cans or bottles. Set up cans or bottles as above.

2. Make one set of cups for every six to eight students. Set up bowling areas for each group of students.

3. Adjust distance from which students roll Frisbee according to age of students. Older students may stand further back than younger students.

4. If students continually knock down all the cups, spread cups further apart or let students choose one of the cups which have been knocked down.

5. Add a cup with the reference Philippians 4:19 printed on it. Students recite verse when they knock over that cup.

• •

Discussion Questions

1. *What are some times in the Bible when God gave people what they needed?* (Manna and water to the Israelites in the desert. A dry sea for the Israelites to get away from Pharaoh. Instructions for Noah to build an ark, so he could be safe during the flood.)

2. *With the things God has given us, how can He use us to help provide for other people's needs?* (Share what you have with people who need it. Help serve food to people at a homeless shelter. Give offering at church, so the church can use the money to help people with their needs.)

Art Center: Booth Building

Materials

Materials for booth of your choice, construction paper in a variety of colors, scissors, tape; optional—tree branches, artificial fruit and greens.

Lead the Activity

1. Indoors or outdoors, lead students to construct one of the booths below.

2. Students decorate booth by cutting construction paper fruit and leaves and taping them to booth. (Optional: Place branches and/or artificial fruit and greens on roof.)

Build-a-Booth

Use wood or PVC pipe to build booth frame. Place wood pieces or lattice across top of booth. Attach lattice or hang blankets on three sides of booth (see sketch a).

Improvise-a-Booth

Make a booth using available materials. For example, (*a*) set up a canopy and attach lattice to the sides; (*b*) securely fasten a tarp or blanket across two shelves (see sketch b); (*c*) drape a blanket or butcher paper over a table turned on its side.

> *In Bible times, God's people celebrated His care for them at the Feast of Tabernacles, sometimes called the Feast of Booths. As part of this celebration the people built booths, which reminded them of the time they lived in tents or booths on their journey to the Promised Land. Let's build our own booth and decorate it with things that remind us of God's care.*

Options

1. Add booth decorations such as paper stars on ceiling, paper chains and artwork of things God has given us. Punch holes in paper fruit and string with yarn. Tape yarn ends to booth.

2. Make small, individual booths with strawberry baskets. Student cuts off one side of basket to make three-sided booth. Students weave green chenille wires through basket roofs and sides to represent branches. Students cut out magazine pictures of leaves and fruit and glue to roofs and sides of booth (see sketch c).

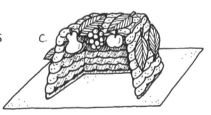

Discussion Questions

1. *What else could we add to our booth(s) to show what God has given us?* (Pictures of Jesus. People in our families. A Bible. A cross.)

2. *In what ways can you thank God for giving you everything you need?* (Pray. Tell others about His gifts. Sing songs of praise to God.)

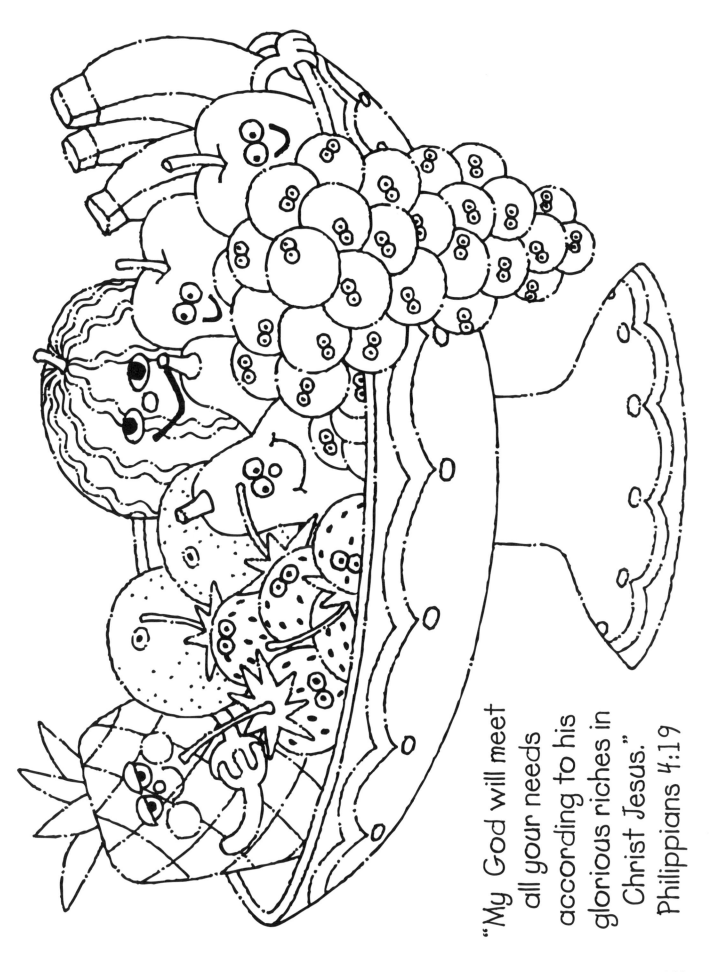

"My God will meet all your needs according to his glorious riches in Christ Jesus." Philippians 4:19

GOD FEEDS NEEDS!

Philippians 4:19

The Challenge → These papers have gotten all mixed up, but if you write the words from each paper in order on the numbered lines below, you will find the Bible verse.

Return# Return from Exile

Return from Exile

Bible Verse

We know that in all things God works for the good of those who love him. Romans 8:28

Bible Story Reference

Nehemiah 8

Teacher's Devotional

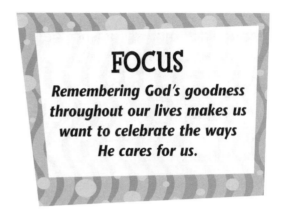

FOCUS

Remembering God's goodness throughout our lives makes us want to celebrate the ways He cares for us.

Water is the essence of life. This is sometimes easy to take for granted because safe drinking water is so readily available to us, even in areas where life would not be possible without tremendous irrigation efforts. Yet periodically, a drought or some other natural disaster reminds us that we are vulnerable, completely dependent on God's care for us. This thought is the essence of the Feast of Tabernacles (see Deuteronomy 16:13-15).

In Jesus' day, the Feast of Tabernacles traditionally culminated in a joyous ceremony to celebrate God's gift of water and to fervently ask for good rains during the next growing season. This is why, when Jesus stood up on the last day of the feast to invite anyone who is thirsty to come to Him to drink, He declared Himself to be the source of all that keeps us living, the essence of our spiritual survival, now and forever (see John 7:37,38). On the night following the water ceremony, huge oil lamps were lit in the Temple's Court of Women. Men took torches and danced, sang and played instruments as they rejoiced before the Lord. The light was so great that the whole city was illumined. It may have been at this point or soon after that Jesus spoke these words: "I am the light of the world" (John 8:12). Just as Jesus is the water of life who gives us life worth living, so also He is the light whose illumination reaches far beyond anything seen before.

Take some time this week to look back at the ways Jesus has been like both water and light to you in the time you have known Him. Read the story in Nehemiah 8 of how God's people were reminded of God's care for them. Then list those ways and times in which He quenched your thirst for something more than the world offered, or where He gave you light when you were in darkness. Making such a "looking back" list is a great way to recount reasons to celebrate, beginning right now in the temple of your own heart!

Story Center

Materials
Bible.

Before the Story
Guide students to briefly practice signs for underlined words.

Tell the Story
As you tell the story, lead students in responding as shown when you say the underlined words.

When have you been in a really big crowd? What was the crowd doing?

Today we're going to find out how God's people worshiped God when they were all crowded together.

1. For many years, God's people did not live the way God had wanted them to. They <u>didn't remember</u> God's Word. Because of their disobedience, God let them be taken from their homes and forced to live in another country. But God had told them that He would bring them back to Israel. And He did! By the time of today's story, many people had returned to Israel. But they still <u>didn't remember</u> God's Word.

2. Nehemiah and Ezra were two leaders of the people who had come back to Israel. These men loved God and wanted to <u>obey</u> Him. But they had a problem because the people they had led back to Israel did not know much about God anymore. And since they did not know God's Word, they could not <u>obey</u> God.

3. Nehemiah and Ezra had an idea. They sent word to everyone to come <u>together</u>. They were going to read God's Word out loud, so everyone could HEAR it! Soon, grandpas, grandmas, parents and children came to Jerusalem. Hundreds and hundreds of people crowded <u>together</u> in the big square and sat down.

4. Ezra climbed up to the high platform that had been built, so everyone could hear him. He unrolled a scroll of God's words. As he did, ALL the people stood up to <u>worship</u> God. Here was the book of God's words! Ezra and all the people praised the Lord. The people shouted, "Amen! Amen!" Then they bowed down and <u>worshiped</u> the Lord.

1. Didn't remember: Right fist under chin, move forward; move right fist from brow to left fist and thumbs touch.

2. Obey: Hold fists near forehead; bring down and palms up.

3. Together: Place fists together; move in circle to the left.

4. Worship: Left hand over right fist; move hands to body and bow head.

5. The people stood for hours and hours, <u>listening</u> to Ezra and his helpers. They heard how God had cared for their people through years and years and YEARS. The speakers explained the words to the people and helped them understand what God's Word said. The people learned that they had not been obeying Him and many cried as they <u>listened</u>. They had been disobeying God and hadn't even known it!

5. Listening, listened: Cup right ear; turn head to left.

6. When Ezra and his helpers were through reading God's words, Ezra said, "Don't cry! This is not a sad day but a day to <u>celebrate</u>! NOW you know what God says to you. You understand what He wants you to do! Be happy. Have a party. Share your food with people who don't have enough. Show God you love Him." So the people stopped crying. Instead, they began to <u>celebrate</u>!

6. Celebrate: Right index finger and thumb touching, make small circles.

7. The next day the people gathered again to hear more of God's Word. It was then that they heard God's command to celebrate the Feast of Tabernacles by building little <u>houses.</u> The little <u>houses</u>, called <u>booths</u>, would remind the people of God's care for their ancestors as they traveled to the Promised Land. Everyone went out into the countryside and gathered branches to build the <u>booths</u>.

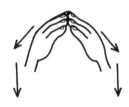

7. Houses, booths: Hands outline roof and sides of house.

8. The people lived in their leafy booths and celebrated for a whole week of <u>joy</u>! They ate special foods and prayed to God. The Bible says that there had never been such a big celebration for hundreds and hundreds of years! Everyone was full of <u>joy</u>!

8. Joy: Move hands in forward circles, palms touching chest.

• •

Discussion Questions

Why did the Israelites need to hear God's Word? (They had forgotten God's Word.) **What did the people do as they listened?** (They cried with sadness.) **What holiday did they celebrate?** (Feast of Tabernacles.) **Why?** (Because they heard God's Word and remembered God's goodness.)

God's people celebrated when they heard God's Word and remembered His goodness in keeping His promises. When we look back to see how God has cared for us, even in hard times, it makes us want to celebrate, too!

Object Talk

Scripture Background

Exodus 23:16; Leviticus 23:33-36,39-43;
Deuteronomy 16:13-15

Materials

Bible with bookmark at Romans 8:28, several
types of fruits and vegetables, large bag, one or
more blindfolds, knife.

Prepare the Activity

Place fruits and vegetables in large bag.

> *When we remember God's goodness
> throughout our lives, we want to cele-
> brate His care. During Old Testament
> times God's people celebrated the Feast
> of Tabernacles, called Sukkot (suh-
> KOHT) in Hebrew, as a reminder of the
> good things God provides for His peo-
> ple. Let's discover some of the things
> they used in their celebration.*

Lead the Activity

1. **What did the people build during the Feast of Tabernacles? Why?** (God's people built booths to remind them of God's care for their ancestors while they traveled in the
desert on their way to the Promised Land.) **Try to discover what items people in our
city might use to decorate a booth during the Feast of Tabernacles.**

2. Blindfold one or more volunteers. Take out one fruit or vegetable from
bag. Volunteer(s) tries to identify the food only by touching it. If volun-
teer(s) cannot identify food by touching it, suggest volunteer(s) smell and
then taste bite-size pieces of the food. As time allows, repeat with new
volunteers for each fruit and vegetable. **During Sukkot, the booths
are decorated with fruits and vegetables as a reminder of
the good things God provides for His people.** (Optional:
Read Deuteronomy 16:13-15 aloud.)

Conclude

**Fruits and vegetables are only a few of the good things God has given
to His people.** Read Romans 8:28 aloud. **This verse tells us that God always cares
for us no matter what happens. What are some of the ways God has cared for
you?** Pray, thanking God for the things mentioned in student responses. Close prayer by
praising God for His goodness to us.

. . . .

Additional Information for Older Students

**The Feast of Tabernacles was one of three important holidays God instructed
His people to celebrate. In Bible times, God's people (called Hebrews, or Israelites) traveled to Jerusalem for these three celebrations. As they traveled, they
sang songs from the book of Psalms. Psalms 120—134 are called the Psalms
of Ascent. The word "ascent" means to be rising or climbing up toward something.** Invite volunteers to read aloud the first verse of Psalms 120, 121, 122 and 123.

Active Game Center: Fruit Basket Upset

Materials

None.

Lead the Game

1. Play Fruit Basket Upset with your students. Students sit in a circle. One student is selected to be the Farmer and stands in the middle of the circle. Assign each student the name of a fruit (banana, apple, grape, peach, nectarine, etc.), making sure to assign more than one student the name of each fruit.

2. The Farmer calls out the name of a fruit. Students with those fruit names jump up to trade places in the circle before the Farmer can take one of the places.

3. The student left without a place becomes the Farmer. Repeat play as above. If the Farmer calls out "Fruit Basket Upset!" all students must change places. Game continues as time allows or until all students have had a chance to be the Farmer.

Option

Each new Farmer answers one of the questions below before calling out a fruit name.

Remembering the good ways God helps us in our lives makes us want to celebrate His care. The Israelites celebrated God's goodness and care for them during the Feast of the Tabernacles. As part of their celebration, they brought fruit from their fields as an offering to God. Let's play a game with fruit to celebrate God's goodness, too!

Discussion Questions

1. *How has God cared for you? for people in your family? for a friend?* (Given family to love and care for us. Gives us food and clothing. Sent Jesus to die for all people's sins.)

2. *What are some ways to celebrate God's goodness?* (Thank Him when you pray. Treat others with the same goodness God shows to you. Tell people about God's goodness. Sing songs of praise to Him.)

3. *What are some other ways God has shown His love to you?*

Art Center: Fruit Prints

Materials

Newspaper, fruits or vegetables, knife, tempera paint, clean Styrofoam bakery trays or pie tins, construction paper, markers.

Prepare the Activity

Cover tables with newspaper. Cut fruits and vegetables in half or into slices which are large enough to easily handle. Pour a shallow layer of paint into bakery trays or pie tins.

Lead the Activity

Give each student a sheet of construction paper. Students take turns dipping cut side of each fruit into paint and pressing it onto paper to make fruit prints. Students repeat with additional sheets of paper as time allows.

Options

1. If possible, add the prints to the decorations on the booth made in Feast of Tabernacles Story 1. Allow time for prints to dry. Students cut around prints and tape pieces of string to the backs of the prints, taping or tying opposite end of strings to ceiling of booth.

2. Older students find Galatians 5:22,23 in Bible and read verses aloud. Students write the fruit of the Spirit around their fruit prints. Students may also write prayers thanking God that He cares for our physical needs, as well as giving us the Holy Spirit to help us live in ways that are pleasing to Him.

3. Provide old T-shirts or smocks for students to wear while making prints.

There are many ways we can celebrate the good ways in which God cares for us. In Bible times as part of the Feast of Tabernacles, God's people remembered God's care by gathering fruit. Let's make fruit prints to remember the ways God cared for the Israelites and His goodness to us.

Discussion Questions

1. *What does God show us about Himself by caring for us?* (He loves us. He is good.)

2. *How does God show His goodness to us in hard times?* (Keeps His promises to us.)

3. *What are some of the ways people today celebrate God's care?* (Thank Him in prayer. Make banners or write prayers about God's care.)

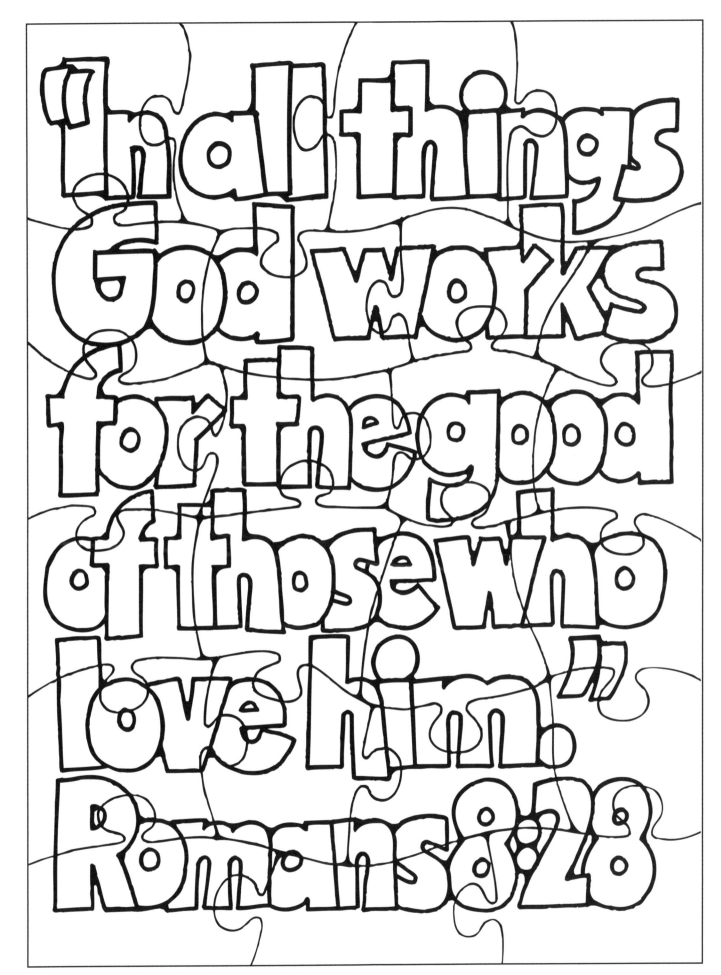

"In all things God works for the good of those who love him." Romans 8:28

FEAST ON THIS!

 **The Challenge**

Nehemiah 8

God commanded the children of Israel to take some special time off to celebrate! Cool, huh? Unscramble the letters on the flags to find out what the Israelites said about God's command to feast and rest.

K T A H N   U Y O   D G O

_____ _____ _____, _____

The Super Challenge

All the town is ready to celebrate the Feast of Tabernacles. See if you can figure out who owns which booth in the marketplace and what he's providing for the feast. Write each food name in the top of the booth and each man's name in his booth's oval.

Clue 1: Micah has the round-topped booth, to the right of the meat man.

Clue 2: David and Joel's booths are next to each other.

Clue 3: David's booth is right next to Micah's. David sells drinks.

Clue 4: The veggie man's booth is not next to Micah's.

Clue 5: The bread man's booth has a round top.

Clue 6: Simeon's booth is the biggest.

Old Testament Offerings
Cain and Abel

Bible Verse

Ascribe to the Lord the glory due his name. Bring an offering and come before him; worship the Lord. 1 Chronicles 16:29

Bible Story Reference

Genesis 4:1-16

Teacher's Devotional

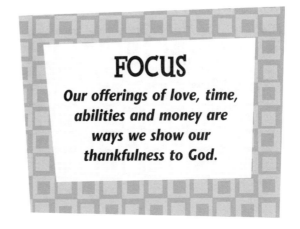

FOCUS

Our offerings of love, time, abilities and money are ways we show our thankfulness to God.

This lesson helps us focus on a different kind of celebration: the offerings that were part of religious life in Israel. Such acts of worship and celebration were made whenever the Israelites worshiped at the Tabernacle or Temple. Though the offerings prescribed in Leviticus 1—7 may seem strange to us today, they were—and are—a powerful teaching tool to help us understand our relationship with God.

Several kinds of offerings might express one's heart of love and thankfulness to God. Burnt offerings, in which animals were consumed by fire, pictured complete dedication to God. Fellowship offerings, in which animals were also sacrificed, declared one's relationship with God and other believers. Thank offerings, peace offerings, freewill offerings and vow offerings were usually animals; but they were not sacrificed in their entirety: a part of the animal was offered; then the rest became a celebratory meal for the one who offered it, and family and friends. Grain offerings, usually along with another offering, were waved over or burned on the altar to recognize God's goodness and provision.

As important as the sacrifices and offerings were, God declared throughout Scripture that obedience and love are more important; one's heart attitude was and is what makes an offering truly acceptable (see Micah 6:6-8). This emphasis on attitude is illustrated in the story of Cain and Abel. While we are not told in the Bible what made Cain's offering displeasing to the Lord, Cain's angry response to God's rejection of his offering seemingly indicates his lack of both a love for God and a desire to obey Him. This, then, is the kind of offering that God wants from us: a gift of our best given in a true spirit of love, thankfulness and obedience.

Of course, Jesus became our final offering. And for this reason, we are told to bring an offering or sacrifice of praise to God continually, for Jesus opened the way for fellowship at any time! Give Him your best as you celebrate!

Story Center

Materials

Bible.

Before the Story

Guide students to briefly practice signs for underlined words.

Tell the Story

As you tell the story, lead students in responding as shown when you say the underlined words.

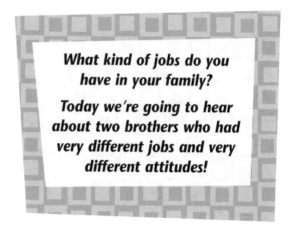

What kind of jobs do you have in your family?

Today we're going to hear about two brothers who had very different jobs and very different attitudes!

1. The very first <u>baby</u> born to the very first people was named Cain. Adam and Eve were thankful to God for their son. Later, they had a second son. They named this <u>baby</u> Abel. As the boys grew up, they learned how to work and help provide their family with food.

1. Baby: Rock crossed arms.

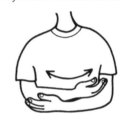

2. As the two brothers <u>grew</u>, they learned how to do different kinds of jobs. Cain, the older brother, became a farmer. He worked with plants and <u>grew</u> food for his family to eat. Abel, the younger brother, <u>grew</u> up to be a shepherd. He took care of the animals that his family used for milk, meat, wool and skins.

2. Grew: Palms face each other; hands flip positions.

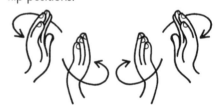

3. It came time to give an <u>offering</u> of thanks to the Lord for all the good things He had given Adam and Eve's family. Since the brothers were grown up now, they brought their own <u>offerings</u> to God. Since he was a farmer, Cain brought an <u>offering</u> of some vegetables he had grown.

3. Offering: With palms up, move hands forward.

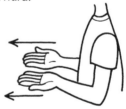

4. Abel also brought an offering to God. Since he was a shepherd, he selected from the first animals that had been born in his flocks. Abel gave his <u>thanks</u> to God by giving Him the best gift he could.

4. Thanks: Place fingertips of both hands against mouth and throw forward and down.

5. God was happy with the offering Abel brought. But God was not pleased with Cain's offering. And here's where the big trouble started. Cain got very <u>angry</u>. God said to Cain, "Why are you <u>angry</u>? If you do what is right, your offering will please Me. But if you do not do what is right, more trouble will come."

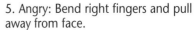
5. Angry: Bend right fingers and pull away from face.

6. And more trouble DID come. Not long after this, Cain and Abel were out in the fields together. And while they were far from home, Cain attacked his brother and <u>killed</u> him. Then God called to Cain, "Where is your brother, Abel?" Cain angrily said to the Lord, "I don't know where he is. Do I have to take care of my brother ALL the time?" Cain didn't want to admit that he had <u>killed</u> Abel.

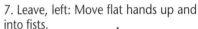
6. Killed: Point right finger; twist and move under left hand.

7. The Lord replied, "What have you done? I know you have killed your brother in anger. You are not going to be a farmer any longer. If you work in the soil, it will not grow anything for you ever again. You will have to <u>leave</u> home and travel from place to place." And that's what Cain did. He <u>left</u> home and traveled to another place.

7. Leave, left: Move flat hands up and into fists.

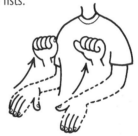

8. Cain was VERY <u>sad</u>. He thought he was being punished too much! But Cain's trouble came because of his own anger and his unwillingness to worship, love and obey God! What a <u>sad</u> end to this family's life together!

8. Sad: Palms in, drop hands down face.

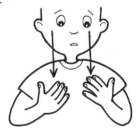

• •

Discussion Questions

How were Cain and Abel different? What did they give in their offerings to God? (Cain gave vegetables. Abel gave from his flock of animals.)

What are some offerings we can give to God? (Our obedience by helping others. Our money. Our praise.) **When we want to show God our love and thankfulness, we use the things He has given us—our time, our abilities and our money—in good ways.**

Object Talk

Scripture Background
Leviticus 1:1,2; 2:1,2; 3:1

Materials
Bible with bookmark at 1 Chronicles 16:29, objects used by your church to collect offerings (boxes, bags, plates, tithe envelopes, banks, etc.), large bag, blindfold.

Prepare the Activity
Place in bag objects used to collect offerings.

> *An offering is anything we give to show love for God. We can give offerings of love, time, abilities and money to show our thankfulness to God. In the Old Testament, people gave many different types of offerings to God, too. Let's look at different ways to give to God.*

Lead the Activity

1. Invite a volunteer to wear a blindfold. Then take one object from the bag, hand it to blindfolded volunteer and ask him or her to identify the object. **What is this object used for?** Volunteer responds. Repeat, using a different volunteer for each object.

2. **We use all these objects in our church to collect offerings.** Explain use of objects to students as needed. **What are some other ways people give to show their love and thankfulness to God?** (Bring canned foods. Give used clothes. Volunteer time to help or teach others at church. Sing in the choir.)

3. **In Old Testament times, people gave different kinds of offerings, too. They gave animals, grains, oil, fruit and vegetables. God's people brought their offerings to the Tabernacle and later to the Temple—the places where the people gathered to worship God. The offerings were burned at a special place called an altar. These offerings were called sacrifices.** (Optional: Read Leviticus 1:1,2; 2:1,2; 3:1 aloud.) **Some of the offerings showed God that the people were sorry for sinning; others showed that they wanted to love and obey God and were thankful for His good gifts to them.**

Conclude
The Bible tells us to give offerings to God. Read 1 Chronicles 16:29 aloud. **Unlike people in Old Testament times, we don't have to make offerings because of sin. Jesus died and rose again for ALL our sins. His sacrifice was the most important offering ever. Now we bring offerings to show our praise to God.** Pray, thanking God for the good things He gives us.

• •

Additional Information for Older Students
Provide several children's Bible dictionaries or encyclopedias. Invite students to read information about the different types of offerings described in the Old Testament: burnt offerings, grain offerings, fellowship offerings, sin offerings and guilt offerings.

Active Game Center: Balloon Trolley

Materials

Balloons, garbage bag, chairs.

Prepare the Game

Inflate one balloon for every pair of students, plus several extras. Transport inflated balloons to class in garbage bag. Place several chairs about 3 feet (.9 m) from the edge of one side of the playing area, making sure chairs are at least 4 feet (1.2 m) from each other and that there are approximately two chairs for every eight students.

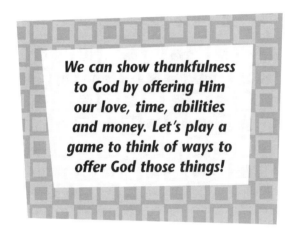

We can show thankfulness to God by offering Him our love, time, abilities and money. Let's play a game to think of ways to offer God those things!

Lead the Game

1. Students form pairs. Give each pair a balloon. Students in pairs decide the best way to hold balloon between themselves without touching it with their hands (between hips, between upper arms, between back and stomach). Pairs practice moving around room in manner chosen.

2. Invite pairs to stand opposite chairs. Pairs position balloon in manner chosen. At your signal, all pairs move toward chairs, walk around one chair and return to starting position without dropping balloons. First pair back to the starting side names one way to show thankfulness to God. Repeat play as time allows, with first pair finished telling a way to give God their time, a way to give God their money or answering one of the questions below.

Options

1. If a pair drops or pops balloon, pair must return to starting place and begin again.

2. If you have a large group, pairs form teams and complete game as in a relay.

3. Older students may play the game by forming groups of four to six students each. Each group creates a "balloon trolley" by standing in a single-file line and placing a balloon between each student. Groups take turns to see who can cross the playing area and move around chair the fastest.

• •

Discussion Questions

1. *How can kids your age give their time as an offering to God?* (Play fairly with a brother or sister. Help clean up trash in their neighborhood.)

2. *When have you or your family given money or other things you own to show thankfulness to God?* (Given books to a missionary family. Given money to church to help other people learn about God.)

3. *Why is it important to give offerings to God?* (Helps us remember God's gifts to us.)

Art Center: Offering Banks

Materials

Bible, materials for bank of your choice.

Prepare the Activity

Make a sample bank following directions below.

Lead the Activity

Lead students in making offering banks. Students take home finished offering banks to collect change, allowance or money they earn. Students bring collected money to church at a designated time and give offering to a church project.

> *We can show our thankfulness to God with our offerings of love, time, abilities and money. Let's use our time today to make personal banks for saving offering money.*

Can Bank

Give each student a clean can with plastic lid (potato chip, nuts, baking powder, etc.) in which you have cut a slit large enough to insert money. Students measure and cut sheets of construction paper to wrap around cans. Students draw on papers ways to offer love, time, abilities and money to God and then wrap papers around cans, securing with tape. Students may also tie ribbon around cans.

Box Bank

Give each student a small box (check box, small gift box, etc.) in which you have cut a slit large enough to insert money. Students cover boxes with wrapping paper and then use markers to write slogans about giving to God.

Options

1. Photocopy and send home a note for parents explaining the collection project. If there is no special giving project at your church, send the money to a church missionary, buy a plant for an elderly shut-in or purchase a children's and/or adult book for your church library.

2. Write a note of love to God and put it in your offering bank. Have an older student read the note aloud. Students write notes of love and thankfulness to God and place in banks.

Discussion Questions

1. *What kinds of offerings can you give to God?* (Money. Time helping others.)

2. *How can we give an offering of praise to God?* Read Hebrews 13:15,16 aloud.

3. *What attitude should we have when we give offerings to God?* (An attitude of thankfulness. A happy and willing attitude that shows we are glad to give to God because we love Him and want to help the people He loves.)

"Come before him; worship the Lord." 1 Chronicles 16:29

PINBALL PARLOR!

1 Chronicles 16:29

"Ascribe to the Lord the glory due his name. Bring an offering and come before him; worship the Lord."

Follow the arrows to find the path that goes through all the words of the verse.

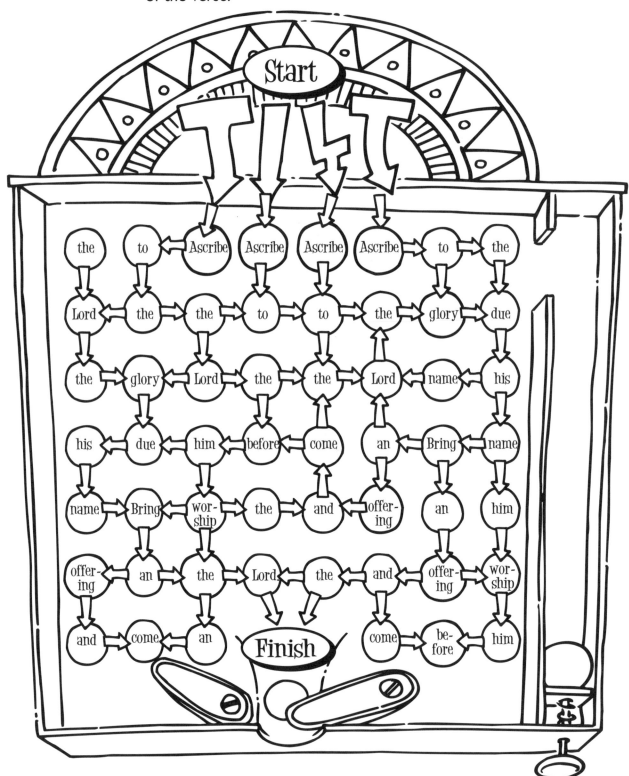

Building of the Temple

Bible Verse

The Lord is my rock, my fortress and my deliverer; my God is my rock, in whom I take refuge. He is my shield and the horn of my salvation, my stronghold. Psalm 18:2

Bible Story Reference

1 Kings 5—8

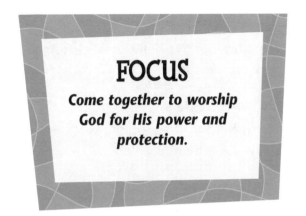

FOCUS

Come together to worship God for His power and protection.

Teacher's Devotional

The building of the Temple by King Solomon was quite an occasion for celebration! In his prayer of dedication, Solomon leads the people in recalling the Lord's power and protection throughout the years. After this time of worship, the people returned home "joyful and glad in heart for all the good things the Lord had done" (1 Kings 8:66). The Temple was revered among the Hebrew nation as a holy place. This is the setting for the focus of celebration in this lesson.

The Feast of Dedication is mentioned in the New Testament when Jesus was in the Temple in Jerusalem at the time of its celebration (see John 10:22,23). The Feast of Dedication, or Hanukkah (HAH-nih-kah) in Hebrew, was a major Jewish celebration in New Testament times and continues as such today. It provides us a rich opportunity to celebrate God's power and protection. (The story of this feast is recorded in the apocryphal book of First Maccabees, which is considered a reliable historical source.)

Between the events of the Old and New Testaments, a Greek general moved to control Israel. He forbade all Jewish religious practices and turned the Temple into a pagan shrine. The Israelites could either save their lives and become pagans or fight for freedom to worship God. The sons of Mattathias the priest began the revolt; they became known as the Maccabees. The Jews routed the Greeks and regained control of the Temple in 165 B.C.

Their first order of business was to dedicate the Temple to God again. The menorah was lit and the priests led God's people in a great celebration of worship. The Temple was once again a holy place where love for God and gratitude for His power and protection could be expressed. God's power is seen in the lives of His people both then and now. Consider the ways He has given light to your life. Then celebrate God's power!

Story Center

Materials
Bible.

Before the Story
Guide students to briefly practice signs for underlined words.

Tell the Story
Lead students in responding as shown when you say the underlined words.

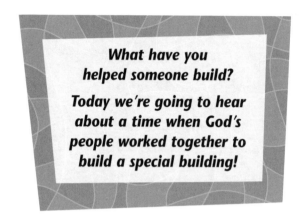

What have you helped someone build?

Today we're going to hear about a time when God's people worked together to build a special building!

1. When David the king of Israel died, his son Solomon became king. Solomon asked God for <u>wisdom</u> so that he could rule the people well. God was so pleased with Solomon's request that He gave Solomon not only <u>wisdom</u> but also wealth. Because Solomon loved God very much, Solomon decided to use his riches to build a beautiful Temple where the Israelites could come to worship God.

1. Wisdom: Bend right index finger; move up and down on forehead.

2. Solomon gathered many good workers to build the <u>Temple</u>. Some of them dug and cut huge white stones for the <u>Temple</u> walls. Solomon arranged to get strong cedar wood from his friend, King Hiram. Every log was cut to the right size and then taken, along with the stones, to the place where the <u>Temple</u> was being built.

2. Temple: Place heel of right hand on back of left fist.

3. Artist: Trace wavy line over left palm with right little finger; move hands down sides to waist.

3. Solomon also gathered wonderful <u>artists</u>. Some of the <u>artists</u> made gold lamp stands and tables. Still others carved flowers, palm trees and angels in the doors and on the walls of the Temple. It was beautiful!

4. Beautiful: Right hand opens and then closes as it moves around face.

4. It took seven years for Solomon's workers to build the Temple. Even though it was not a very big building, it took a long time to build because it was so <u>beautiful</u>! The Temple was built on a hill, so everyone could see it. The white stones of its walls sparkled in the sunlight. Much of the inside was covered with gold.

5. The Ark of the Covenant, the box where God had told Moses to place the stone tablets of the <u>Law</u>, was put in a special room called the Most Holy Place. Great statues of angels with gold wings that reminded people of God's power stood guard on either side of the Ark of the Covenant.

5. Law: Extend right thumb and index finger; move down left palm.

6. After the Ark was placed in the Most Holy Place, an amazing thing happened. The whole Temple filled with a beautiful <u>cloud</u>. By this <u>cloud</u>, God showed He was there with His people and that He was very pleased with this Temple Solomon had built. Now God's people could come together to worship Him in a special place.

6. Cloud: Curve raised hands; make circular movements to side.

7. Solomon stood in front of the Temple. He spoke to the people who had come to worship <u>God</u>. He praised <u>God</u> and told the people the story of how the Temple had been built. He reminded the people of the ways <u>God</u> had used His power to protect them over the years, rescuing them from Egypt, keeping His promises and forgiving their sins. Then Solomon prayed. Solomon asked <u>God</u> to take care of His people forever.

7. God: Point right index finger; lower and open hand at chest.

8. The people listening had come from all over the kingdom. Some were from very far away. They were so happy to be <u>worshiping</u> God at the beautiful Temple that they all stayed and celebrated for 14 days, twice as long as they usually came for any feast! The Temple stood for many, many years. The people of Israel were glad to <u>worship</u> God in the Temple.

8. Worship: Left hand over right fist; move hands to body and bow head.

• •

Discussion Questions

Why did Solomon want to build a Temple? (He loved God. He was thankful to God.) **How did God show He was pleased with the Temple?** (Came in a cloud.) **What did Solomon do to worship God at the Temple?** (Praised God with all the other Israelites. Prayed.)

When we come together to worship God, we can thank Him, just as the Israelites did, for His power, for keeping His promises and for caring for us!

Object Talk

Scripture Background
John 10:22,23

Materials
Bible with bookmark at Psalm 18:2, a variety of candles (birthday cake candles, decorative candles, votive candles, etc.), menorah (or nine candles and candlesticks), matches.

Lead the Activity

1. Show different candles one at a time. (Optional: Light candles.) **How is this type of candle used?** Volunteers answer.

2. Show menorah (or nine candles and candlesticks). **This is called a Hanukkah menorah. Many years ago, God's people used a menorah in the Temple in Jerusalem. The Temple was where God's people came to worship Him. But in between the time of the Old Testament and the coming of Jesus in the New Testament, a Greek ruler who hated God did many wrong things in the Temple. The menorah was not lit for many years.**

After a group of Israelites defeated the army of this general, the religious leaders of the Israelites wanted to dedicate the Temple so that they could worship God in the Temple again. To dedicate something means to set it apart for a special purpose. The menorah was lit as part of the dedication of the Temple.

3. **To remember God's power, Hanukkah, which is the Hebrew word for dedication, is celebrated for eight days. The Hanukkah menorah is a symbol of that celebration. Each day one candle is lit.** Light the candles, using the middle candle to light them from left to right. **When Jesus lived on earth, this holiday was celebrated by the Jews as a reminder of God's power in helping His people defeat their enemies.** (Optional: Read John 10:22,23 aloud.)

> *God's power and protection are great reasons to come together and worship Him. In New Testament times God's people worshiped Him at a holiday called the Feast of Dedication. Today we call this holiday Hanukkah (HAH-nih-kah). Let's find out how this holiday started and what was done to celebrate it.*

Conclude
Read Psalm 18:2. **What does this verse say about God's power?** Pray, thanking God for His power to help and His protection from harm.

• •

Additional Information for Older Students
Hanukkah is sometimes called the Festival of Lights. This name not only reminds people of the lighted candles on the menorah but also of a story that was told about the relighting of the menorah. In Bible times, the branches of the menorah held oil, not candles. The story is told that there was found only enough oil for the menorah to burn for one day. However, the menorah continued to burn for eight days until more oil was made. God's people said that it was God's power that kept the menorah burning.

Active Game Center: Dreidel, Dreidel, Dreidel

Materials

A dreidel for every four to six students, game pieces (small candies, nuts, paper squares or pennies); optional—large sheet of paper, marker.

Lead the Game

1. Students form groups of four to six. Give each group a dreidel and give each student at least six game pieces.

2. Groups sit in circles. Each student puts one game piece into the center of the circle. Students take turns spinning the dreidel and following the directions for the letter the dreidel lands on: *gimel* (GIH-mel)—take all pieces from the center; *hei* (HEH)—take half of the pieces; *shin* (SHIHN)—add one; *nun* (NOON)—do nothing. (Optional: Print game instructions on paper for students to refer to.) **The letters on the dreidel are the first letters from the Hebrew words for "a great miracle happened there." God's people believed God had done a miracle when during the Temple's rededication a one-day supply of oil for the menorah lights lasted for eight days.** If all game pieces are taken, each student puts in one game piece. The game ends when one player has all the game pieces or when time is called.

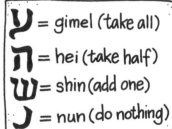

ע = gimel (take all)
ה = hei (take half)
ש = shin (add one)
נ = nun (do nothing)

We can worship God for His great power and protection. In New Testament times, the Hebrew people worshiped God at the Temple during a holiday called the Feast of Dedication, now called Hanukkah. This holiday reminded God's people of God's power. Let's play a game that is played by people today to celebrate Hanukkah.

Options

1. Buy or borrow dreidels. Dreidels are available at craft or party stores throughout the holiday season.

2. Play dreidel as part of a Hanukkah party. Decorate room with blue and white streamers, play Hebrew songs, serve a holiday snack such as *latkes* (potato pancakes) or powdered donuts and use chocolate foil-wrapped coins as game pieces for the dreidel game.

• •

Discussion Questions

1. *What stories about God's power have you read in the Bible?* (The parting of the Red Sea. Elijah being fed by ravens. Jesus healing the blind man.)

2. *When have you been helped by God's power? How has God cared for you?*

3. *How do you need God's help and care today?*

Art Center: Clay Menorahs

Materials

Fist-sized lump of modeling clay or play dough and nine birthday candles for each student, paper, sturdy paper plates; optional—plastic forks or toothpicks.

Lead the Activity

1. Students roll clay into logs long enough to hold candles and make an elevated lump in the center of the logs. (Optional: Students form logs into shapes or use forks or toothpicks to make designs in the logs as shown in sketch a.)

2. Students place candles in clay as shown in sketch b. **Lighting the candles reminds us of the menorah that was lit in the Temple to celebrate its rededication.** Students take menorahs home on paper plates.

We can think of many reasons to worship God. In the New Testament there was a celebration to remember God's power called the Feast of Dedication, now called Hanukkah. At Hanukkah people light candles in a special candlestick called a menorah. Today you can make a menorah as a reminder of God's power.

Options

1. Make your own clay with this recipe: Mix together 1½ cups of flour, 1 cup of cornstarch, 1 cup of salt and 1 cup of warm water. If dough is sticky, dust with flour. Add powdered tempera paint or food coloring if desired. Store clay in an airtight container.

2. If your class is participating in a Hanukkah party (see suggestions in this lesson's Active Game Center), students make menorahs as part of the party.

3. Send brief notes to parents explaining the Feast of Dedication, or Hanukkah, celebration. Use the information in the Teacher's Devotional for this lesson.

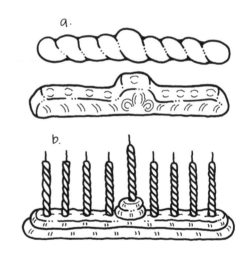

Discussion Questions

1. *How does God show His power and protection to kids your age?* (Gives families to help and take care of them. Answers prayers.)

2. *Why is it good to know about God's power?* (We can be sure of His help when we need it. We know we can depend on Him.)

3. *When can you celebrate God's power and protection?*

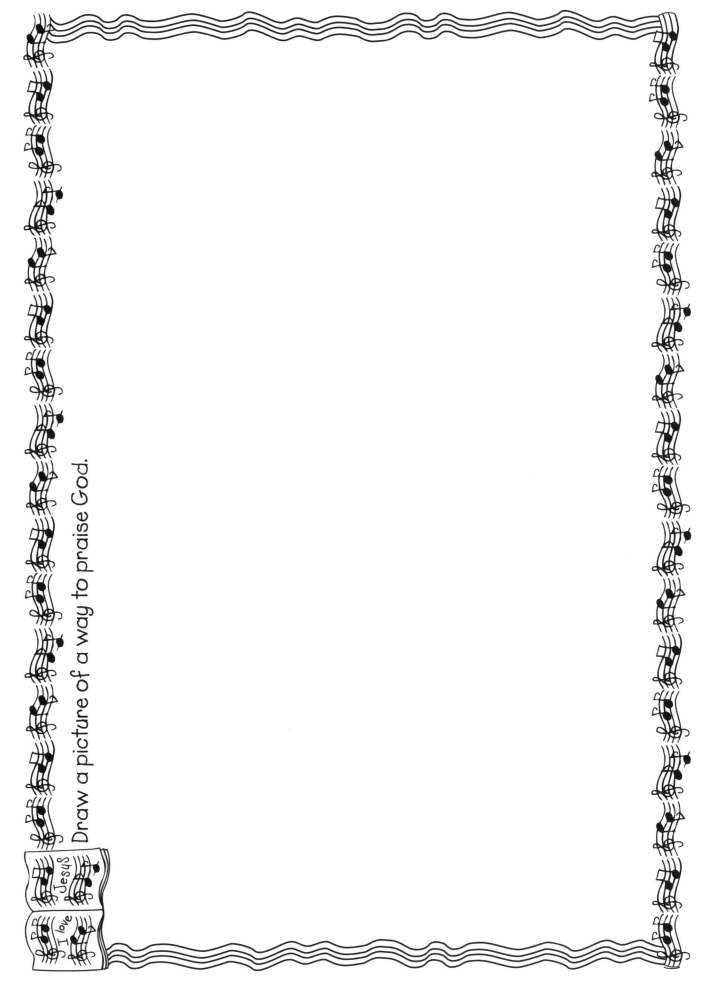

Draw a picture of a way to praise God.

PICK-UP STICKS!

1 Kings 5—8

The Challenge ➤ The builders of the Temple used a lot of logs to build the Temple. To solve this puzzle, pretend you're playing Pick-up Sticks. "Pick" up the log that's on top of the pile. Write the word on it in the first blank below. If you pick up the logs in the correct order, you'll spell out why we can worship God. (The first one is done for you.)

God _____ _____

_____ _____ _____

_____ _____ _____

_____ _____ _____

_____ _____ _____

The Super Challenge ➤ How many squares can you find on the Temple? _____

Purim

Esther Helps Her People

Bible Verse

The plans of the Lord stand firm forever, the purposes of his heart through all generations.
Psalm 33:11

Bible Story Reference

Esther

FOCUS
God's power helps us accomplish His plans.

Teacher's Devotional

When we think of biblical holidays, we generally think of the ones described in Exodus and Leviticus. Purim (POO-rihm), another Old Testament holiday, originated from the time of Queen Esther. Purim (the plural for the Hebrew word *pur)* means "lots." The word refers to Haman's casting of lots to establish the day the Jews would be destroyed. However, after Esther's dramatic intervention on behalf of her people and Haman's subsequent destruction, King Xerxes signed an edict allowing the Jews to protect and avenge themselves on the day that had been designated for their annihilation. The Jews in Persia were kept safe, and the holiday has been celebrated ever since (see Esther 9:24-28).

The celebration has always included feasting and sending gifts of food to others (see Esther 9:22). Traditionally, Jewish people dress in costume for the holiday, representing the characters in Esther's story. The entire book of Esther is read in the synagogue with loud and enthusiastic responses from the audience. Whenever Haman's name is read, noisemakers are shaken and booing ensues as ways to blot out the memory of him. Parades and costume parties are often held, and children dressed in costume take treats to others. Purim is celebrated in February or March.

Take the opportunity of this lesson to help your students understand that even when they are in frightening situations, God can be trusted to help them. Like Esther, it is never easy to do the brave or right thing. However, God's power is always available to His children to help us do the good things He wants us to do. We are His expression to the world of what He is like (see Ephesians 2:10). God is ready, willing and able to help us express our love and obedience in doing difficult things—if we will let Him! That's a wonderful reason to celebrate His power!

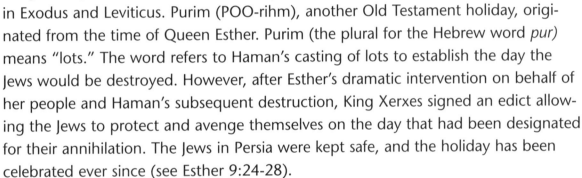

Story Center

Materials
Bible.

Before the Story
Guide students to briefly practice signs for underlined words.

Tell the Story
As you tell the story, lead students in responding as shown when you say the underlined words.

> Have you ever had to do something you were afraid to do? What happened?
>
> Today we're going to meet a queen who had to do something she was afraid to do. And we'll find out how God's power helped her!

1. Esther was a Jewish girl who lived in Persia. Her <u>family</u> was one of many Jewish <u>families</u> that had been taken from Israel many years before. Her parents had died and her only <u>family</u> was her cousin Mordecai who had taken care of her until she was grown. Because the king was looking for a new queen, Esther was one of many young women who had been chosen to come to the palace and prepare themselves to meet the king.

2. For a whole year, the young women prepared themselves. Then, one by one, the king met each of these young women so that he could choose the one who <u>pleased</u> him most. When Esther finally had her turn to meet the king, he was so <u>pleased</u> with her that he chose Esther to be the next queen!

3. Now about this time, the king put a man named Haman in charge of the other government officials. Haman was so proud of his new job, he wanted everyone to <u>bow</u> down to him! Esther's cousin Mordecai also worked for the king. But Mordecai would not <u>bow</u> to Haman—only to God. This made Haman SO angry that he planned to DESTROY not just Mordecai but ALL the Jewish people!

4. Haman told the king <u>lies</u> about the Jewish people in the kingdom. He didn't tell the king WHO these people were. But his <u>lies</u> made them sound SO dangerous that the king gave Haman permission to KILL them! Soon, the orders to kill the Jewish people were sent all over the country!

1. Family: With thumbs and index fingers touching, make outward circle until hands touch.

2. Pleased: Circle right hand.

3. Bow: Palms out, left hand higher, move hands down in two moves.

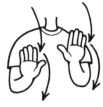

4. Lies: Move right index finger left across lips.

5. Esther's cousin Mordecai heard about Haman's horrible <u>plan</u>. He sent a message to Queen Esther and asked her to beg the king for help. After all, if Haman's <u>plan</u> succeeded, ALL the Jews would be killed—even Esther! But Esther's problem was this: The king didn't know she was Jewish. And he didn't know that it was the JEWS whom Haman planned to kill!

6. On top of that, the king hadn't invited Esther to come and see him for a full month. Anyone who came to the king without being invited could be KILLED! Mordecai reminded Esther that she might have been made queen just so she could <u>help</u> to save her people. So Esther and Mordecai and all the Jews in the city fasted for three days. They went without food and spent time in prayer. These three days <u>helped</u> Esther get ready to go to talk to the king. According to the law, unless the king held out his scepter to her, Esther would be killed!

7. Soon Esther stood in the palace court. *Would the king hold out his scepter?* She must have held her breath. The king saw her—and held out his scepter! He asked Esther to tell him what she <u>wanted</u>. Esther didn't tell the king what she <u>wanted</u> just yet. Instead, she invited him and Haman to a banquet. At the banquet, the king asked again what Esther <u>wanted</u>. Once more, Queen Esther asked the king and Haman to another banquet the next day.

8. When the king and Haman came to the second banquet, <u>Queen</u> Esther told the king about the orders to kill her people. She asked the king to please help. The king wanted to know who was threatening to kill his <u>queen</u>! He was VERY angry when Esther told him it was HAMAN. He ordered that Haman be killed. Then the king gave <u>Queen</u> Esther and Mordecai permission to write a new law to protect the Jews. Finally, <u>Queen</u> Esther ruled that the Jewish people celebrate! Even now, Jewish people remember Esther's actions and God's power by celebrating the Feast of Purim.

5. Plan: Move hands left to right, bouncing slightly.

6. Help: Raise right fist with left palm.

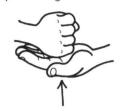

7. Want: Palms up, move curved hands toward self a few times.

8. Queen: With thumb and index finger extended, move right hand from left shoulder to waist.

Discussion Questions

Why did Haman want to kill the Jews? (To get back at Mordecai who wouldn't bow to him.) **What would have happened to Esther if the king had not held out his scepter to her?** (She would have been killed.) **How did Esther help her people?** (Fasted and prayed to God. Went to the king. Asked for his help.)

God tells us we can ask for His help, especially when we have hard things to do. He uses His power to help us do the good things He wants us to do. That's a good reason to celebrate!

Purim

Object Talk

Scripture Background
Esther 9:18-32

Materials
Bible with bookmarks at Esther 9 and Psalm 33:11, basket; optional—canned foods.

Lead the Activity

1. Display the basket you brought. **If you were to fill this basket with food for a friend, what would you put in it?** Volunteers answer. Repeat with gifts for a neighbor, a teacher and a grandparent. (Optional: Put canned foods in basket to make a gift for a needy person.) **Giving gifts to others, especially those in need, is one of the ways Purim is celebrated.**

> God has many good things He wants us to do and with His power, He helps us to do them. Queen Esther, who lived long ago in Old Testament times, rescued her people to keep them safe as God had planned. Her brave and good actions are remembered with a special holiday called Purim (POO-rihm). Let's find out how this holiday is celebrated.

2. **Purim is also celebrated by reading aloud the whole book of Esther. As the story is read, children in costumes act out the story of how God's people were saved. The audience cheers the good characters and boos the bad characters in the story. Purim is a day for celebrating God's power and doing good things to help others. The custom of giving gifts to friends and to the poor is written about in the book of Esther.** Read Esther 9:22 aloud. **This custom is called *Shalach Manot* (shah-LAHK muh-NOHT).** (In English *Shalach Manot* means "sending portions.")

Conclude

When we do things that show our love and obedience to God, we are following God's plans for us. Read Psalm 33:11 aloud. **This verse helps us learn that God's power is so strong that nothing can keep His plans from taking place. What are some of the good things God wants us to do?** (Receive His love. Become a member of God's family. Talk to God in prayer.) Pray, asking for God's help to do the good things He wants us to do.

• •

Additional Information for Older Students

The word "Purim" is the plural form of a Hebrew word that means "lots." The name refers to the way in which the evil Haman decided which day to destroy the Jews. Haman cast lots, a phrase that means to choose something by chance—like drawing straws or participating in a lottery. Another way in which Purim is celebrated is by eating a special pastry called *hamantaschen*. This pastry is shaped like a triangle to remind people of the shape of Haman's hat.

Purim

Active Game Center: Gamefest

Materials

Materials needed for one or both of the games.

Lead the Game

Lead students in one or both of the games.

Beanbag Toss

Before class, draw a large face on a 4-foot (1.2-m) or larger cardboard square. Cut out a mouth and two eye shapes large enough for a beanbag to fit through. Add a triangle-shaped hat to represent Haman (see sketch a). Place target on one side of the playing area, propped up against a table or chairs. During class, students line up about 5 feet (1.5 m) from the target and take turns tossing beanbags through the target. Have a volunteer collect the beanbags for the students.

Ring Toss

Set up six to eight water bottles, filled and capped, in any type of geometric shape (circle, square, triangle, etc.). Students stand about 3 feet (.9 m) from the bottles and take turns tossing rings made from paper plates onto the bottles as shown in sketch b.

Options

1. Adjust distance students stand from targets according to age and skill level.

2. Add these additional games if you have space and helpers: guess the number of jelly beans in a jar, throw a Nerf ball into a trash can, participate in an outdoor egg toss, toss coins into a variety of containers, etc. Distribute individually wrapped candy as prizes.

3. Older students make signs to display in room: "Hooray for Esther!" or "Celebrate God's Power!"

> Long ago in Old Testament times, Queen Esther rescued her people to keep them safe as God had planned. God's power and Esther's brave actions are celebrated with a holiday called Purim (POO-rihm). Children today often celebrate this holiday by playing games. Let's play some games to remind us of this holiday.

a.

b.

Discussion Questions

1. ***What did Esther and her people celebrate on Purim?*** (Esther's brave actions. The defeat of Haman. God's power and care for them.)

2. ***What are some of the good things God has helped you do?*** (Be kind to a brother or sister. Tell others about Him. Help someone who was in danger.)

3. ***What are some ways to learn more of the good things God has planned for you to do?*** (Read God's commands in the Bible. Ask teachers or older Christians. Pray to God.)

Art Center: Purim Fest

Materials

Materials for one or more of the activities below.

Lead the Activity

Lead students in making masks and/or groggers.

Masks

To celebrate Purim, some people wear masks and act out the story of Esther.
Give each student half of a 9-inch (22.5-cm) paper plate. With a friend's help, student places plate half over upper face and makes pencil marks where eyes and nose should be. Students draw eye shapes and nose triangles, carefully cut out the shapes and then punch holes on sides and attach string pieces (see sketch a). Students decorate the plates with markers and/or add other materials for different masks (construction paper crown for the king, sequin earrings for Esther; yarn hair for Mordecai or Haman).

Groggers

When the story of Esther is read during Purim, people make loud noises whenever Haman's name is mentioned. The noisemakers they use are called groggers.
Give each student a 9-inch (22.5-cm) paper plate. Students fold paper plate in half, fill it with a small amount of dry beans and staple it closed. Students insert a tongue depressor into one side of the shaker and glue in place (see sketch b). Students use markers to draw designs on the groggers, attaching crepe paper streamers, feathers and sequins as desired.

> *Let's celebrate that God uses His power to help us do the good things He has planned for us, just like He helped Queen Esther save the Jewish people. A holiday called Purim (POO-rihm) celebrates this time when the Jews were saved. We'll make (masks) to celebrate Purim.*

a.

b.

Options

1. Have a *Purimspiel* (Purim play). Four students wear their masks and act out the main parts as you tell a brief version of the story of Esther. Other students shake their groggers and boo or hiss every time Haman's name is mentioned.

2. Serve store-bought or homemade *hamantaschen* (three-cornered pastries representing the shape of Haman's hat). For a quick version, put a small spoonful of jam in the center of a slice of premade sugar cookie dough, pinch up the edges around jam and bake.

• •

Discussion Questions

1. ***What are some of the good things God has planned for all people to do?*** (Love God. Love your neighbor. Share with needy people. Tell others about God.)

2. ***In what ways does God help us do the good things He has planned for us?*** (Gives us the Bible to help us learn what good things we should do. Provides money and possessions, like clothes, books and toys, that we can share with others. Gives us teachers for an education to help us grow up and get jobs with which we can help others.)

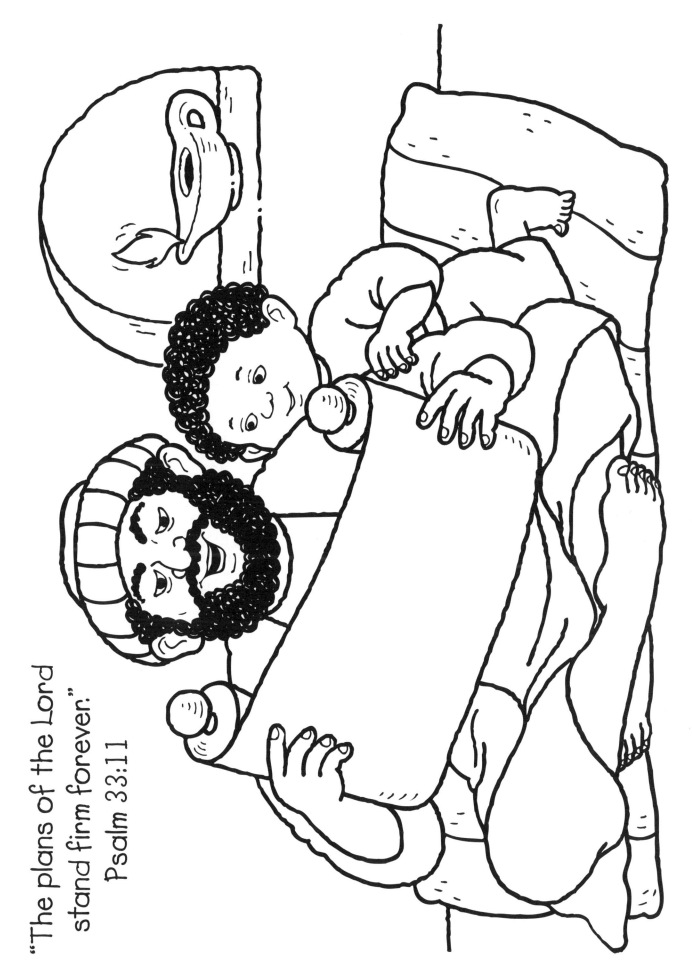

"The plans of the Lord stand firm forever." Psalm 33:11

MUSIC TO YOUR EARS!

Psalm 33:11

The Challenge The word of God is music to your ears. If you follow the instructions, you'll have something to sing about.

Step 1: Cross off the jobs.

Step 2: Cross out all the words with a double *z* in them.

Step 3: Everyone loves animals, but we don't need them here.

Step 4: You didn't eat your vegetables, so cross off all the desserts!

Step 5: Cross off the places to go.

Step 6: Finally, lose all the round things.

Step 7: Write the remaining words on the blank lines.

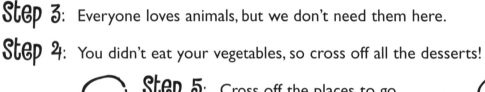

mouse	The	artist	beach	plans
of	ring	the	pudding	ice cream
fizzy	Lord	muzzle	stand	moon
firm	movies	duck	kangaroo	forever
cake	the	wheel	purposes	jazz
of	gardener	his	mall	bubble
ball	heart	pie	cat	through
all	park	generations	teacher	vet

"

"

Passover Story 1
Israel Escapes from Egypt

Bible Verse

God is our refuge and strength, an ever-present help in trouble. Psalm 46:1

Bible Story Reference

Exodus 1:6-14; 2:23-25; 3:1-10; 5—12

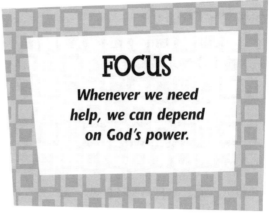

FOCUS

Whenever we need help, we can depend on God's power.

Teacher's Devotional

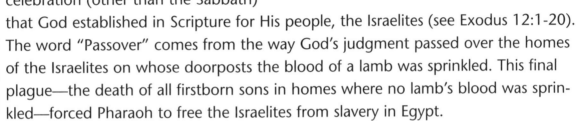

Passover is the first recorded celebration (other than the Sabbath) that God established in Scripture for His people, the Israelites (see Exodus 12:1-20). The word "Passover" comes from the way God's judgment passed over the homes of the Israelites on whose doorposts the blood of a lamb was sprinkled. This final plague—the death of all firstborn sons in homes where no lamb's blood was sprinkled—forced Pharaoh to free the Israelites from slavery in Egypt.

Even while God instructed Moses in the preparations for leaving Egypt, He instructed the Israelites to yearly eat the Passover meal as a way of remembering their great deliverance from slavery. During the Israelites' travel in the wilderness, a second celebration, the Feast of Unleavened Bread, also began. Unleavened bread symbolized complete purity; leaven (yeast) symbolized sin (see 1 Corinthians 5:8). So as a way of showing their rejection of sin in their lives, God's people were to eat only unleavened bread for seven days after Passover. After the Temple was built in Jerusalem, the Passover and Feast of Unleavened Bread merged into one holiday (which is the reason we are not treating them separately). Passover is one of the three pilgrimage feasts for which all Jewish men (usually accompanied by their families) were supposed to travel to Jerusalem.

Although over the years there have been many changes made to the Passover tradition, the *seder* (meaning "order"), or Passover meal, is a wonderful tool and a learning experience for all ages. Not only does the Passover celebration remember the great deliverance from Egypt, but it also motivates us to consider anew the greatest deliverance made by the greatest deliverer, Jesus Christ, the final Passover Lamb!

God is as powerful today as He was in Moses' day. This lesson has the ingredients to stir up trust in God and prepare us, and our students, for difficult times in life. It is important for us and those we teach to reaffirm the truth that God is always with us, always available, an ever-present help in trouble. That's an awesome reason to celebrate!

Story Center

Materials
Bible.

Before the Story
Guide students to briefly practice signs for underlined words.

Tell the Story
As you tell the story, lead students in responding as shown when you say the underlined words.

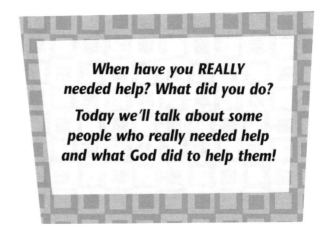

When have you REALLY needed help? What did you do?

Today we'll talk about some people who really needed help and what God did to help them!

1. The king of Egypt was afraid. He was the Pharaoh, ruler of the land, but he was afraid of the THOUSANDS of Israelites living in his country. He was afraid these people might try to take over his kingdom. Many, many years before this story begins, Joseph's <u>family</u> had come from Canaan to live with Joseph in Egypt. Joseph had helped the people of Egypt during a time when there was no rain or food. Now many years had passed. The <u>families</u> of Joseph and his brothers had become HUGE! Pharaoh was so afraid, he made them slaves.

2. The Israelites were very <u>sad</u>. They prayed to God to help them out of this horrible slavery! And of course, God knew they were <u>sad</u>. And God had a plan. Many years before, an Israelite baby named Moses had been rescued by Pharaoh's daughter and had grown up in Pharaoh's palace. Now Moses was living way out in the desert, herding sheep. But God knew right where he was!

3. One day while Moses was out with his sheep, he saw a bush that was on fire! As he came closer to see this bush, he heard a voice calling his name! WOW! God told Moses He was going to <u>rescue</u> the Israelites from Egypt and lead them back to the land they had come from! God wanted Moses to tell Pharaoh to let them leave! Now Moses didn't want to talk or <u>rescue</u> or lead anyone! But God told Moses that He would help him.

4. Soon Moses and his brother Aaron went to see Pharaoh. They <u>told</u> him that GOD wanted Pharaoh to let the Israelites leave! Pharaoh <u>told</u> them he didn't care. He wasn't about to let his SLAVES leave! He even made the Israelites work harder!

1. Family: With thumbs and index fingers touching, make outward circle until hands touch.

2. Sad: Palms in, drop hands down face.

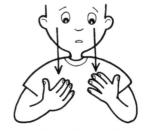

3. Rescue: Cross first two fingers; then cross and uncross hands.

4. Told: With right index finger, make circular movement from mouth.

5. Well, GOD had a way to convince Pharaoh to change his mind. God sent 10 terrible troubles, or plagues. First, the great Nile <u>River</u> turned to BLOOD and all the fish died! Then millions and millions of FROGS came up from the <u>river</u>. They were EVERYWHERE! Then other plagues of gnats and flies, hailstones and locusts (like grasshoppers) came, filling the land with trouble!

5. River: Extend three fingers; touch mouth a few times; flow fingers horizontally.

6. But no matter what happened, Pharaoh did NOT change his mind. He would NOT let the Israelites leave! He got more and more angry and more and more stubborn. But of course, God had MORE ways to convince the stubborn ruler! Next came a very strange plague: It was simply <u>DARK</u>, night and day! It was SO <u>dark</u>, the Egyptians couldn't see at all! But in the houses of all the Israelites, there was LIGHT!

6. Dark: Cross palms downward in front of face.

7. Then God told Moses, "One more plague will come. Then Pharaoh will let you go. So get ready. Follow My instructions: Every family must take a <u>lamb</u> and kill it at sunset. Paint lamb's blood across the tops and down the sides of your doorways. Roast the <u>lamb</u> that night. Eat it with bitter herbs, and bread made without yeast. There won't be time to let regular bread rise."

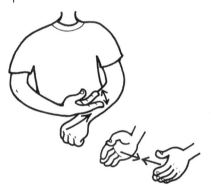

7. Lamb: Open and close right fingers, moving up left arm. Bring together open hands for "small."

8. God had more instructions. "<u>Eat</u> the meal dressed to travel. <u>Eat</u> quickly and don't leave any food for the morning. I am going to pass through Egypt with a plague of death. Every firstborn animal and person will die. But when I see the blood on the doorposts of your houses, I will pass over you. No one in your houses will be hurt." And that's just what happened! After death came to the Egyptian homes, Pharaoh ordered the Israelites to leave. They were free! And every year they <u>eat</u> the Passover meal as a celebration and a way to remember the time that the Lord brought them out of Egypt. It was a celebration to be remembered forever!

8. Eat: Fingertips touching, move right hand to mouth a few times.

Discussion Questions

Why did Pharaoh make the Israelites slaves? (He was afraid because there were so many of them.) **Whom did God choose to lead them?** (Moses.) **How did God convince Pharaoh to let the Israelites go?** (He sent 10 plagues.)

God helped the Israelites when they were slaves. And whenever we need help, God's power can help us, too. His promise of power is a great reason to celebrate!

Object Talk

Scripture Background

Exodus 12:1-27; Deuteronomy 16:1-8

Materials

Bible with bookmark at Exodus 12:24-27 and Psalm 46:1, bite-size pieces of unleavened bread (or *matzo* crackers) and bread prepared with yeast, two paper plates.

Prepare the Activity

Put each type of bread on a different plate.

> *We can depend on God's power whenever we need help. Long ago in Old Testament times, God helped the Israelites escape from slavery in Egypt. Let's find out how God told His people to remember and celebrate His great power and help.*

Lead the Activity

1. **As part of this celebration God told His people to eat a special kind of bread.** Students eat samples of each type of bread. **What are the differences you can find by touching and tasting the two different kinds of bread?** Volunteers respond. Identify which is unleavened bread. **Because unleavened bread does not have yeast in it, it doesn't rise or puff up into a loaf shape when it is baked, and it can be made very quickly. Why do you think the Israelites only had time to make unleavened bread?** (They were in a hurry to escape from Egypt.)

2. **What else do you remember about the Israelites' escape from Egypt?** (God sent 10 plagues to convince Pharaoh, the Egyptian ruler, to let the people leave.) **The name of this holiday, Passover, comes from the last plague. God had given the Israelites special instructions to paint on their doorposts the blood of a lamb. On the night the Israelites escaped from Egypt, in any house that did not have the lamb's blood painted on its doorposts, the oldest son would die. Because death passed over the Israelite homes, the holiday is called Passover. The lamb killed at this celebration was called the Passover Lamb. Jesus is called our Passover Lamb because He gave His life to rescue us from sin.**

3. **The Passover celebration helps people remember God's power.** Read, or ask an older student to read, Exodus 12:24-27.

Conclude

God's power helps us today, too. Read Psalm 46:1 aloud. **What do you learn about God from Psalm 46:1?** Pray, thanking God that we can depend on His power.

● ●

Additional Information for Older Students

Yeast spreads through dough and causes the bread to rise, or get bigger. How does yeast remind us of sin? (When a person sins, it can spread through his or her life.) **Throughout Scripture, yeast is compared to sin. Read 1 Corinthians 5:6-8 to find what the apostle Paul wrote about sin and how Jesus' death on the cross takes away our sin.**

Active Game Center: Exodus Relay

Materials

Bible, two bathrobes with ties, two pairs of adult-size sandals, two walking sticks or canes, two paper plates, crackers (*matzos* or saltines).

Prepare the Game

On one side of the playing area make two piles, placing one bathrobe, a pair of sandals and a walking stick or cane in each pile. On the other side of the playing area, put a paper plate across from each pile and place half the crackers on each paper plate.

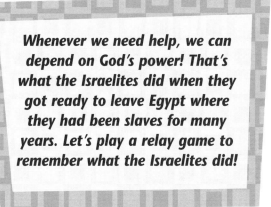

Whenever we need help, we can depend on God's power! That's what the Israelites did when they got ready to leave Egypt where they had been slaves for many years. Let's play a relay game to remember what the Israelites did!

Lead the Game

1. **Guess where we're going to find the directions for today's game—in the Bible! Let's listen to the command God gave the Israelites when they were getting ready to leave Egypt.** Read, or have a volunteer read, Exodus 12:11. **For our relay, we're going to put on this cloak (bathrobe), put on the sandals and carry the staff across the room to get a cracker from the plate. Then we eat the cracker and return to our team for the next player to have a turn.** (Optional: Volunteer demonstrates how to wear the clothing as you explain.)

2. Have students form two teams. Each team lines up by one pile of clothing. At your signal, students begin relay. Continue until all students have had a turn.

Options

1. Use sandals big enough for students to slip their feet into with their shoes on, or have all students remove their shoes before the game begins.

2. If you have more than 16 students, form additional teams and bring additional game supplies.

Discussion Questions

1. ***When are some times kids your age need God's help?***

2. ***When are some times God has helped you?*** Tell your own answer before volunteers respond.

3. ***What can we do to receive God's help?*** (Pray to God and ask for His help. Read what God tells us to do in the Bible.)

Art Center: Freedom Walk

Materials

Dark-colored butcher paper, tape, chalk.

Prepare the Activity

Tape paper all the way along the bottom of one or two walls of your room. Print "Egypt" on one end of the paper and "To the Promised Land" on the other end of the paper.

> Whenever we need help, we can depend on God's power. The Israelites needed God's help and depended on His power when they escaped from Egypt and traveled to the Promised Land. Let's make a mural about their escape from Egypt!

Lead the Activity

Students form pairs. Each student takes a turn to stand alongside the butcher paper, posing as though walking toward the Promised Land. Student's partner uses chalk to carefully trace the student's legs and feet. Encourage students to pose in a variety of ways (running, marching, tiptoeing, big steps, etc.). (Optional: Instead of tracing, students may draw legs and feet.) As time permits, students fill the paper with outlines of feet and legs. Students may also draw cloaks hanging down to cover some of the legs, sandals on feet, smaller kids' and bigger adults' legs and feet, outlines of walking sticks and outlines of sheep and cattle legs and hooves.

Options

1. Instead of placing the dark paper against the walls, lay a long sheet of it on the floor. Students trace their feet, filling the paper with footprints. Students may also draw outlines of sheep and cattle hoofprints.

2. Bring in pictures of sheep and cattle for students to refer to.

3. Students dip chalk into water for brighter chalk outlines.

• •

Discussion Questions

1. How did God show His power and help the Israelites when they were leaving Egypt? (Sent punishments called plagues to Egypt so that Pharaoh said they could leave.)

2. How does God show His power and help us today? (Gives us people to care for us. Protects us when we travel. Provides food for us. Helps us when we are sick.)

3. Why can we depend on God's power and help? (He loves us. He keeps His promises.)

"God is our refuge and strength, an ever-present help in trouble." Psalm 46:1

I'LL PASS ON THAT!

The Challenge

Exodus 12

Lead Moses to the Hebrew family. Make sure you pass by all the sheep. Avoid the homes of the Egyptians marked by the pharaoh.

The Super Challenge

Write down the words as you pass them, and find what Moses wanted to tell the Hebrew family about God.

_____

Josiah Celebrates the Passover

Bible Verse

I will meditate on all your works and consider all your mighty deeds. Your ways, O God, are holy. What god is so great as our God? Psalm 77:12,13

Bible Story Reference

2 Chronicles 34; 35

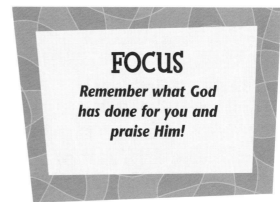

FOCUS

Remember what God has done for you and praise Him!

Teacher's Devotional

The first Passover meal was fairly simple: a young male lamb or kid, roasted whole, eaten with bitter herbs and unleavened bread. The meal was originally eaten with the people dressed to travel. The *seder* (meaning "order") grew into an elaborate meal as time went on. One custom that developed is for the youngest person at the *seder* table to ask four questions about the Passover. Answering these questions gives the adult conducting the *seder* a chance to expand on the meaning of Passover.

The overarching question is, "Why is this night different from all other nights?" The answers to the succeeding questions give explanations for the basic elements of the Passover celebration. The first succeeding question asks, "Why do we eat only unleavened bread on this night?" The *matzos* commemorate the Jews' hasty departure from Egypt. The second question asks about the bitter herbs eaten as part of the Passover meal; these reflect the bitterness of slavery. The third question asks why the bitter herbs are dipped into *haroset* and why parsley is dipped into salt water. *Haroset* (a mixture of chopped apple, nuts and honey) symbolizes the mortar between the bricks with which the slaves were forced to build. Salt water represents the tears of the enslaved Israelites. This last answer goes on to explain that the meal is now eaten in a comfortable position, instead of standing dressed to travel, because God has given His people rest. They no longer have to be ready to run.

As you celebrate more of this wonderful holiday with your students, help them see how each symbolic food on the *seder* plate points to the great things God has done. His love is shown not only to His chosen people but also to everyone whom He has invited into His family, Jew and Gentile, through Jesus, our Passover Lamb.

Story Center

Materials
Bible.

Before the Story
Guide students to briefly practice signs for underlined words.

Tell the Story
As you tell the story, lead students in responding as shown when you say the underlined words.

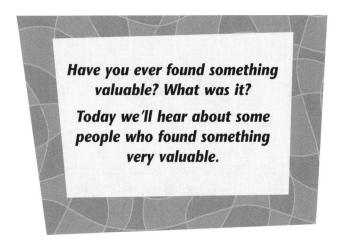

Have you ever found something valuable? What was it?

Today we'll hear about some people who found something very valuable.

1. God's Temple stood empty and dirty. It was many years after God led His people out of slavery in Egypt, and no one <u>remembered</u> God's Law or came to the Temple at all. But then Josiah became king. Josiah was only eight years old, but he did NOT want to be evil like his father, a wicked king who didn't love God! Josiah wanted his people to <u>remember</u> God's love and power and worship Him.

2. Right away Josiah prayed to the one true God. Then Josiah planned to make God's Temple <u>beautiful</u> again. He hired men to repair the Temple. They began to fix broken walls, clean the floors, shine the candlesticks and sew <u>beautiful</u> new curtains.

3. While the workers cleaned, Hilkiah the high priest was <u>looking</u> around. He saw something lying in a corner and picked it up. It was a scroll, a rolled-up book made from animal skin. Hilkiah began to read and got very excited. Hilkiah showed the scroll to King Josiah's servant. He said, "<u>Look</u>! It's a scroll of God's Law! This is IMPORTANT. Show it to King Josiah!"

4. King Josiah's servant didn't waste any time. He RAN to show King Josiah the scroll of God's Law! King Josiah knew this scroll had not been <u>read</u> in a long, LONG time. So Josiah asked his servant to please <u>read</u> the scroll aloud.

1. Remember: Move right fist from forehead to top of left fist, thumbs touching.

2. Beautiful: Right hand opens and then closes as it moves around face.

3. Look: Move right two fingers away from eyes.

4. Read: Move index and middle fingers down left palm.

5. As the servant read, Josiah listened carefully to the laws God had given to the Israelites. What he heard made him feel so sad! He and his people had NOT been <u>obeying</u> God! Because they had not read God's Word, they had not even KNOWN what God wanted them to do. Josiah said, "We must read God's words to all the people, so EVERYONE can <u>obey</u> God."

5. Obey: Hold fists near forehead; bring down and palms up.

6. King Josiah sent messengers to tell everyone to come to the Temple. Mothers, fathers, grandmothers, grandfathers, boys and girls came to hear God's words. When King Josiah finished reading, he said, "I am going to follow the Lord and obey His words. And I want all of you to <u>promise</u> God that we ALL will obey His words." All the people <u>promised</u> to obey and worship the God of Israel.

6. Promise: Right index finger on lips; move to open hand on left fist.

7. Josiah led the people in obeying God by destroying the idols—the false gods the people had been worshiping. THEN Josiah was ready to open the Temple. It was time to <u>CELEBRATE</u> and praise God for the great things He had done! The time for the Passover feast was coming, when everyone was supposed to remember how God brought the Israelites out of slavery in Egypt. Josiah called the priests and the singers and the Temple workers together. They got themselves and everything in the Temple ready for the best <u>celebration</u> ever!

7. Celebrate: Right index finger and thumb touching, make small circles.

8. The people were <u>glad</u> to come to Jerusalem as God's Law said to do! King Josiah had made sure everything was prepared: the animals, the musicians, the priests—it was the BIGGEST celebration of Passover in many, many years! The people sang and <u>rejoiced</u> and worshiped the one true God. King Josiah remembered what God had done for his people and he did EVERYTHING he could to obey God.

8. Glad, rejoice: Move hands in forward circles, palms touching chest.

• •

Discussion Questions

How was King Josiah different from his father? (Wanted to obey God. Repaired the Temple.) **What did Hilkiah the high priest discover?** (A scroll of God's Law.) **What did the people promise when they heard God's Word?** (That they would obey God.) **What did the people celebrate at the Passover?** (Their rescue from Egypt.)

   When we remember what God has done, we want to praise Him. When we look back at the great things God has done for us, we want to celebrate, too!

Object Talk

Scripture Background

Exodus 12:1-14

Materials

Bible with bookmarks at Exodus 12:14 and Psalm 77:12,13; plate; several of these foods—parsley, salt water, horseradish, *matzo* crackers, *haroset* (chopped apples and nuts mixed with honey), lamb or other clean bone, hard-boiled egg; optional—*seder* plate or picture of *seder* plate.

> *It's important to praise God and remember all that He has done for us. After God rescued His people from slavery in Egypt, He told them to eat a special meal to help them remember and celebrate His help and protection. Let's find out what foods are eaten at this special meal.*

Lead the Activity

1. **What is the name of the celebration at which God's rescue of His people from slavery is remembered?** (Passover.) **Another name for the Passover meal is** *seder* **(SAY-dehr).** *Seder* **means "order." As the foods are eaten in order, questions are asked and answered to tell the story of the escape from Egypt.**

2. Show and discuss each food item you brought. (Optional: Place food items on *seder* plate. Invite volunteers to taste items.) **The Hebrew word for green plants is** *karpas* **(CAHR-pahs). This green parsley reminds us that everything that grows is a gift from God.** Dip parsley in salt water. **The salt water reminds us of the tears of the Hebrew slaves in Egypt.** Place horseradish on a piece of *matzo*. **The horseradish tastes bitter and reminds us of the terrible years of slavery in Egypt.** *Haroset*, **made with apples, nuts and honey, reminds us of the mortar between the bricks that the Hebrew slaves used to build in Egypt. The bone reminds us of the lamb that was sacrificed at the first Passover. The hard-boiled egg is another reminder of the sacrifices made by God's people in Bible times. The** *matzo* **crackers (***matzo* **is bread made quickly without yeast) remind us how fast the Hebrews left Egypt.**

3. **Why did God want His people to celebrate the Passover?** You or older student read Exodus 12:14 aloud. **The Passover celebration reminds us all of God's power.**

Conclude

Read Psalm 77:12,13 aloud. **What does Psalm 77:12,13 tell us about God?** (God is holy. He is the greatest.) Pray, asking for God's help to remember all the great things He has done and thanking Him for His love and power.

• •

Additional Information for Older Students

During the *seder* **meal, a large cup is placed in the center of the table for the Old Testament prophet Elijah. In Old Testament times, people believed that Elijah would appear to announce the coming of the Messiah. Placing a cup on the table showed that the people were ready for the Messiah. Now we know that the Messiah, Jesus, has already come!**

Active Game Center: Leaven Hunt

Materials

Construction paper in two colors, ruler, pencil, scissors or paper cutter, clock or watch with second hand; optional—bite-size candy or crackers.

Prepare the Game

Cut construction paper into 1-inch (2.5-cm) squares, making approximately 40 squares of each color. Hide squares in your classroom.

Every day we see things that remind us to praise God for the great things He has done! During the Passover celebration, God's people remember the way He rescued them from slavery in Egypt. Today we are going to play a game that reminds us how fast the Hebrews left Egypt.

Lead the Game

1. **The Hebrews left Egypt in such a hurry that God told them to make their bread without yeast because it wouldn't have time to rise. Another name for yeast is "leaven." The yeast, or leaven, is what makes bread rise, or get bigger. To get ready to celebrate Passover, it's a custom to look all over your house to remove anything made with leaven.** Divide class into two teams and explain that each team will have 30 seconds to collect paper squares representing leaven. Assign each team one of the two colors.

2. At your signal, students begin looking for paper squares. Call time after 30 seconds. Each team counts the total number of squares they were able to find. (Optional: Give candy or crackers to the team that found the most squares.) If time permits, students close eyes or briefly leave room while you, or older student, hide squares again. Repeat activity.

Options

1. Limit the number of students on each team to seven or eight, preparing paper squares of other colors if needed.

2. Explain to older students that yeast, or leaven, is a symbol for sin. When God's people remove anything made with leaven from their homes, it shows their rejection of sin in their lives.

Discussion Questions

1. *What are some of the great things God has done that you have read about in the Bible?* (Helped the Israelites escape from Pharaoh's army. Helped the Hebrew people get to the Promised Land. Healed people. Sent Jesus to die for our sins.)

2. *What are some of the great things God has done for you and your family?* Tell your own answer as well as inviting volunteers to respond.

3. *When can you praise God for the ways He helps you?*

Art Center: *Seder* Plates

Materials

A paper plate and six 2-inch (5-cm) construction paper circles in a variety of colors for each student; markers; glue sticks; a sample of the following food items: parsley, horseradish, *haroset* (see recipe in option 1 below), bone, boiled egg, matzo cracker; optional—a traditional *seder* plate.

Lead the Activity

1. Give each student a paper plate and six construction paper circles.

2. **We are going to make *seder* plates used at a Passover meal.** Show and identify the food items you have prepared, briefly explaining each one. **This green parsley reminds us that everything that grows is a gift from God. The horseradish tastes bitter and reminds us of the terrible years of slavery in Egypt. *Haroset* (made with apples, nuts and honey) reminds us of the mortar between the bricks which the Hebrew slaves used to build in Egypt. The bone reminds us of the lamb that was sacrificed at the first Passover. The hard-boiled egg is another reminder of the sacrifices made by God's people in Bible times. The *matzo* crackers (*matzo* is bread made quickly without yeast) remind us of how fast the Hebrews left Egypt.**

3. Students draw pictures of the food items on circles and then use glue sticks to glue the circles onto their plates. Students may also draw on the plates designs or pictures of the Hebrews escaping from Egypt, or write Psalm 77:12,13 in fancy writing. (Optional: Show *seder* plate.) Students take plates home.

> *When we remember the good things God has done for us, we want to praise Him! God's people remembered God's help by celebrating the time He rescued them from slavery in Egypt. This celebration is called Passover. We're going to make some special plates called seder plates, like the ones people use today when celebrating Passover.*

Options

1. Students follow this recipe to make *haroset*: Core and then use plastic knives to cut three or four large apples into small pieces. Mix apples with 1 cup chopped walnuts or almonds and 1 tablespoon of honey to make a paste. (Optional: Add 1 teaspoon of cinnamon and ¼ cup of grape juice.)

2. If someone in your church has led a *seder* dinner in the past, invite him or her to lead students in this traditional meal. Send home an explanation of the dinner to parents.

Discussion Questions

1. *What kinds of special plates do your families use? What do they look like? What kinds of celebrations do you use them for?*

2. *What can we remember to praise God for when we look at our seder plates?* (Saving the Israelites from the Egyptians. Always caring for His people. His power and greatness.)

"I will meditate on all your works and consider all your mighty deeds. Your ways, O God, are holy. What god is so great as our God?" Psalm 77:12,13

STORY TIME!

The Challenge

2 Chronicles 34—35

The kids have written the story of their time at the Passover feast, but they mixed up some of the words. Figure it out to read the story.

I [remember] when we went to the verPasso feast near the pleTem. [What] a day! The estpri
——————— ———— ———— ————

was excited about the goodness of [God.] He wore long elegant esrob of plepur and ldgo.
——————— ———— ————

After ingpray at the taral, he [has]tily came out and proclaimed the tionbracele. When he was
———— ———— ————————

[done,] everyone chedeer and started to isepra God. At the feast, I ate lots of tableveges.
———— ———— ————————

After eating, we ceddan be[for]e the Lord. Later we ate the Passover mbla. My father was one
———— ————

of the erssing. It was a eatgr day. It was the rstfi time the Passover had been celebrated since
———— ———— ————

Samuel the phetpro was alive. [You] should have seen it! I still had vense days of fun [and] the
———— ————

astFe of Unleavened eadBr to enjoy. [Praise] God. I love [Him] !
———— ————

The Super Challenge

If you read the words in the boxes from left to right, you will discover a very important thing to do to please God.

————————————————————————

The Ten Commandments

Bible Verse

Teach me knowledge and good judgment, for I believe in your commands. Psalm 119:66

Bible Story Reference

Exodus 19—20:21

Teacher's Devotional

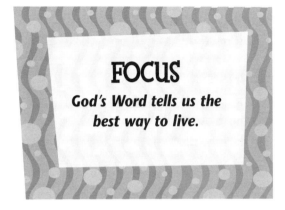

FOCUS
God's Word tells us the best way to live.

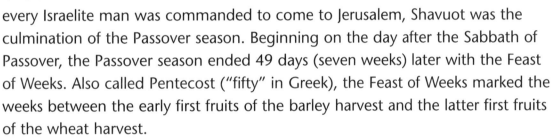

This lesson will focus on Shavuot (shah-voo-OHT), the Feast of Weeks. One of the three celebrations for which every Israelite man was commanded to come to Jerusalem, Shavuot was the culmination of the Passover season. Beginning on the day after the Sabbath of Passover, the Passover season ended 49 days (seven weeks) later with the Feast of Weeks. Also called Pentecost ("fifty" in Greek), the Feast of Weeks marked the weeks between the early first fruits of the barley harvest and the latter first fruits of the wheat harvest.

As the people of Israel became more urbanized, the agricultural significance of this holiday began to change. When third-century rabbis realized that the giving of the Law on Mount Sinai had taken place at this very time of year, the tradition of reading the Ten Commandments became part of the holiday. Connecting the holiday with a historical event probably helped to keep it alive among Jews who were largely no longer farmers.

As we commemorate this aspect of the holiday, let's remember that God spoke these laws out of compassion. He knows how we are made. He understands what makes us crumble and what builds us up. And these laws simply explain to us what we don't want to do lest we destroy ourselves, those we love, and our relationship with our Creator. God wants His creatures to live in wholeness as we live in right relationship with Him.

The Law shows us how to gain wholeness. But since the Law also shows up our inability to obey God fully, it brings us to a wonderful place—the place where we see how badly we need Jesus. That's a good reason to celebrate!

Story Center

Materials
Bible.

Before the Story
Guide students to briefly practice signs for the underlined words.

Tell the Story
As you tell the story, lead students in responding as shown when you say the underlined words.

> *What kinds of rules do you have to follow at school or when playing a game?*
>
> *Today we'll hear about a time when God gave His people some rules to follow.*

1. For three months after the Israelites escaped from Egypt, they walked through the desert. They were on their way to the land God had promised to give them. God guided them with a cloud during the day and a fire by night. One day, the cloud that guided them stopped at the base of steep, rocky Mount Sinai. As the Israelites set up their tents and put their sheep out to graze, they had no idea that an important event was about to take place!

2. Moses climbed the mountain to talk to God. Somewhere, WAY UP among the rocks and boulders, the Lord told Moses how He wanted the Israelites to be His special people, a nation that belonged to Him. Moses listened carefully and then climbed back down the mountain to the Israelite camp. He told all the leaders what God had said. The people all responded, "We will do everything the Lord has said!"

3. For the second time, Moses climbed up Mount Sinai and told the Lord that the people wanted to obey. God answered, "I am going to visit the people. When I speak with you, everyone will hear the sound of My voice. Then they will always believe you. Have the people get ready," the Lord continued. And once again Moses listened carefully to God's instructions and then hurried down the mountain to call the people together.

4. "The day after tomorrow the Lord is going to visit us in a special way," Moses said. "Get ready for His visit!" So the people did the things God had told them to do to get ready for His visit—including washing all their clothes. Moses also told the people to set up a boundary around the mountain. NO ONE was to go up on the mountain—or even touch it!

1. Cloud: Curve raised hands; make circular movements to side.

2. Climb: Curve index and middle fingers; alternately move up in small arcs.

3. Hear, listen: Cup right ear; turn head to left.

4. Ready: Facing hands bounce left to right.

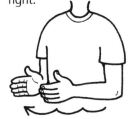

5. Everyone got busy and prepared for the visit. Finally, the day of the Lord's visit arrived. <u>Thunder</u> and lightning came over the mountain and a LOUD trumpet blast rang out. The people trembled as it <u>thundered</u> and billows of smoke rose from the mountain. The Lord CERTAINLY had their attention now! And that was just what He wanted, for God had some VERY important things for Moses to tell them!

5. Thunder: Point to ear; move fists alternately back and forth.

6. God called Moses up to the top of the mountain and began to speak. He gave Moses 10 commandments written on two stone tablets. The first four commandments that God gave were about how to <u>worship</u> and respect Him. He said the people were not to make or <u>worship</u> any idols (false gods) as the people around them did. They were not to mis-use God's name in any way. And they were to keep the Sabbath (the seventh day of the week) holy and special by resting on that day and not doing any work.

6. Worship: Left hand over right fist; move hands to body and bow head.

7. Then God gave six <u>commandments</u> about how people should treat each other. God said children should treat parents with respect. God told Moses that the people should never murder, take each other's wives or husbands or steal anything from each other. God also <u>commanded</u> not to give false testimony against a neighbor, which means we should not lie about others. Finally, God warned against wanting what others have.

7. Command: From lips, move index finger out and down with emphasis.

8. Then God was quiet. But the smoke rose and the thunder and trumpeting continued. The people stayed far away. They were all <u>terrified</u>! They said to Moses, "YOU listen to God and then tell us God's message! Don't let God speak to us or we will die!"

"Don't be <u>afraid</u>," Moses told them. "God has shown you His mighty power so that you will have respect for Him and won't sin against Him." But the people stayed at a distance while Moses returned to the mountain to talk with God. Moses listened carefully as God gave him more instructions for the Israelites.

8. Terrified, afraid: Fingertips touching, open hands and cover chest.

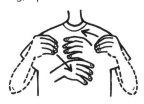

● ●

Discussion Questions

How did the Israelites know God had come to the mountain to talk with Moses? (They saw and heard smoke, thunder, lightning and trumpet sounds.) **What are some of the things God commanded the people? Why did God show the people His power?** (So that they would not sin against Him.)

We don't have to figure out the very best way to live all by ourselves. God's commands teach us the best way to live. That's a GOOD reason to celebrate!

Object Talk

Scripture Background

Leviticus 23:15-21

Materials

Bible with bookmarks at Leviticus 23:17 and Psalm 119:66, two loaves of bread, honey, softened cream cheese (8 oz.), small bowl, plastic knives, napkins.

> *We can learn the best way to live by studying God's Word. People in the Old Testament celebrated a holiday which reminded them of the time when God gave His Law to Moses. They called this holiday the Feast of Weeks. Let's find out how the holiday was named and what the people did to celebrate it.*

Lead the Activity

1. **The Feast of Weeks is celebrated seven weeks plus one day after the Passover celebration. Another name for this holiday is Shavuot (shah-voo-OHT) which is the Hebrew word for "weeks."**

2. **At this celebration, God told His people that two loaves of bread were to be waved as an offering, or gift, to God.** Wave loaves of bread in the air as a demonstration. Read, or ask an older student to read, Leviticus 23:17. **At this time of the year, the harvest of wheat used to make bread had just been completed, and the people were glad to thank God for the food they would make from the grains.**

3. **Today the two loaves of bread remind us of the two tablets on which God wrote the Ten Commandments He gave to Moses. God gave the Ten Commandments so that His people would have His Word to help them. During the Feast of Weeks, Jewish people read the Ten Commandments aloud.**

4. **During the Feast of Weeks, it is also traditional to eat dairy products as reminders of God's Word, which is "sweet" because it gives us what we need to grow in our knowledge of God.** Mix small amounts of honey with cream cheese to form a spread. Spread mixture on bread. Cut bread into quarters and serve.

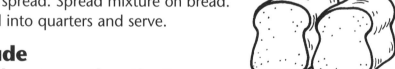

Conclude

Now we have more than the Ten Commandments to help us learn the best way to live. We have the whole Bible to help us! Read Psalm 119:66 aloud. **To have good judgment means to be wise and know the right things to do and say. We know that we can depend on God to help us be wise and make good choices.** Pray, asking God's help in doing what's right.

● ●

Additional Information for Older Students

The Bible uses word pictures to describe God's Word and the ways in which it helps us. Students find and read these verses in their Bibles: Psalms 12:6; 19:9,10; 119:103,105.

Active Game Center: Balloon Burst

Materials

Bibles, slips of paper, pen, balloons, whistle; optional—children's music CD and player.

Prepare the Game

Print the following verse references on separate slips of paper: Exodus 20:7; 20:12; 20:15; Matthew 22:37,38; Luke 6:27,28; 6:31; John 15:12; Ephesians 4:29; 4:32; Colossians 3:13. Blow up balloons, inserting a verse reference paper in each balloon before tying balloon.

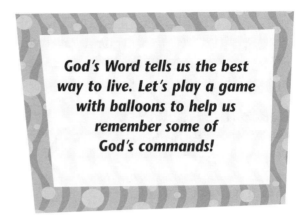

God's Word tells us the best way to live. Let's play a game with balloons to help us remember some of God's commands!

Lead the Game

1. Students stand in a circle and pass one balloon around the circle (first student passes balloon over his or her head; second student passes it between his or her legs and so on) until you blow the whistle. (Optional: Play children's music CD as students pass balloons.)

2. Student holding the balloon when the whistle is blown moves to the center of the circle and pops the balloon by stomping on it. Student finds verse in the Bible and reads it aloud. Ask the group one or more of the Discussion Questions below to discuss the verse. Repeat play with other balloons as time allows. (Optional: Students find and read verses after all balloons are popped.)

Options

1. Print the words of the verse on the slip of paper. Students read verse from paper.

2. If you have a large number of students, create more than one circle, or pass more than one balloon around the circle at a time.

3. In addition to the verse papers, put a variety of items in balloons, such as stickers, small individually wrapped candies, slips of paper that tell other instructions to follow ("do three jumping jacks," etc.).

• •

Discussion Questions

1. *What does this command tell us to do? How might following this command help you at home? at school?*

2. *Why is it important to follow God's commands?* (God made us and loves us, so He knows what's best for us. Following His commands helps us show we love Him.)

3. *When can a kid your age obey this command?*

Art Center: 3-D Mural

Materials

Length of butcher paper for each group of six to eight students, markers, chenille wire, tape, construction paper in a variety of colors including green, scissors, pebbles, glue.

Prepare the Activity

Draw a wide path on butcher paper (see sketch a).

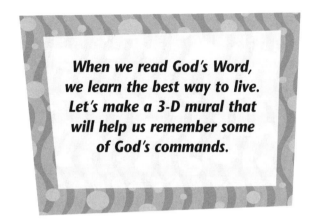

When we read God's Word, we learn the best way to live. Let's make a 3-D mural that will help us remember some of God's commands.

Lead the Activity

1. Place butcher paper on table or floor. **Psalm 119:105 says that God's Word helps us know the right path on which to walk, which means that as we obey God's commands, we learn the best way to live.** Invite volunteers to tell Bible commands. As commands are suggested, print them on path, spacing them out along the path. Supplement student responses with these Bible commands: "Honor your father and your mother" (Exodus 20:12), "Love each other" (John 15:17), "Do not repay anyone evil for evil" (Romans 12:17), "Let us do good to all people" (Galatians 6:10), "Give thanks in all circumstances" (1 Thessalonians 5:18).

2. Each student forms a figure from two chenille wires (see sketch b) and tapes it standing on the path near a Bible command he or she plans to obey. As students tape figures onto mural, invite students to tell one or more ways in which they can obey the commands.

3. As time permits, students draw and cut items such as buildings or trees from construction paper, fold tabs at the bottom of items and tape items to mural around the path. Students make grass by fringing a strip of green construction paper. Students may also glue pebbles to path.

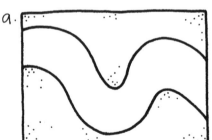

Discussion Questions

1. **What are some of the commands God gives us in the Bible?** (Love God more than anything. Love your neighbor. Forgive each other. Do not lie. Do not steal. Honor your parents. Treat others fairly. Say kind words.)

2. **What is one way you can follow these commands this week?** Volunteers respond.

3. **When you need help following God's commands, what can you do?** (Ask God for help to obey. Talk to your mom or dad about what to do.)

"I believe in your commands." Psalm 119:66

BOOK 'EM

The Challenge

Psalm 119:66

"Teach me knowledge and good judgment, for I believe in your commands."

Use the words of the verse to get from start to finish. Don't jump over any book or cross over any book. It can be tricky because the words are repeated on more than one book.

Parable of the Sower

Bible Verse

*I have hidden your word in my heart
that I might not sin against you.*
Psalm 119:11

Bible Story Reference

Mark 4:1-20

Teacher's Devotional

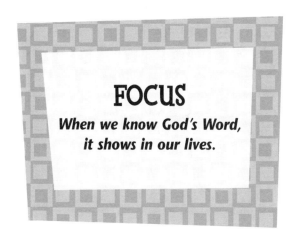

FOCUS

*When we know God's Word,
it shows in our lives.*

In this lesson we focus on a parable told by Jesus that helps us understand how the Word of God can guide one's life to a place of bearing fruit.

As Jesus explained to His disciples, "The seed is the Word of God." There is no fault in the seed. It is bursting with life-giving potential, ready to grow. In Jesus' story, there is no fault in the weather, either: the rains fall or the sun shines. The only variable factor in the parable is the quality of the soil. Unless the hardness of the soil is broken up, unless the soil is deep enough to support growth to maturity, unless the soil is sufficiently free of weeds to allow the plant to mature and bear fruit, a seed may sprout and a plant push up, but that plant never produces fruit. Fruit proves a growing life! It is the result God desires.

However, having a mere mental possession of the content of God's Word and having information held in our heads is a very different situation from *knowing* God's Word in a way that guides our thoughts and grows into spiritual fruit in our words and actions. God's Word produces this sort of knowing!

Jesus said that if our hearts are like the good soil, we will produce fruit and that our fruit will remain. A kind word, a nonjudgmental look, a gesture of loving acceptance in the right time and place can make a world of difference to a kid (or an adult) and be remembered forever. Lasting fruit is the goodness and patience and love lived out before another person that brings to him or her the realization that he or she can grow—and show—the same spiritual fruit. This is fruit that remains, that multiplies, that delights the heart of God. And as we apply His Word to every situation in our lives, we can grow this fruit. What a reason to celebrate!

Story Center

Materials
Bible.

Before the Story
Guide students to briefly practice signs for the underlined words.

Tell the Story
As you tell the story, lead students in responding as shown when you say the underlined words.

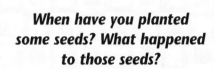

When have you planted some seeds? What happened to those seeds?

Today we're going to find out what happened to some seeds in a story Jesus told.

1. One day, a big crowd of people gathered to see <u>Jesus</u>. Shopkeepers closed their stores for the day; farmers left their fields, and women and children left their cooking and gardening and playing to come and hear <u>Jesus</u>. After all, <u>Jesus</u> healed sick people and made crippled people walk. Everyone wanted to see and hear <u>Jesus</u>! The people settled down and waited to hear <u>Jesus</u>' every word.

2. Jesus began His story: "A farmer went out to his field to plant a crop. He scattered handfuls of seeds from his seed pouch onto the ground. Some of the seeds fell on a pathway where the dirt was packed down as hard and smooth as <u>rock</u>. NO seed could put down roots and grow in such <u>rock</u>-hard soil!"

3. Jesus continued, "The seeds lay there until <u>birds</u> swooped down and snatched up the seeds."

   Everyone nodded. They had all planted gardens and sown seeds themselves. And they all knew that a seed on hard ground NEVER becomes a plant that produces grain! Those seeds just become food for hungry <u>birds</u>!

4. Jesus went on. "Other seeds fell in a spot where the <u>soil</u> was very shallow. The <u>soil</u> was soft on top, but there was hard rock under it. These seeds sprang up quickly because the <u>soil</u> was warm there. But as the plants grew, their roots hit the rock and could go no farther. The shallow <u>soil</u> didn't hold much water, either. Soon, the little plants dried up and died."

   Everyone had seen those kind of plants. They sprang up but soon dried out and died because the <u>soil</u> was shallow.

1. Jesus: Touch palms with opposite middle fingers.

2. Rock: Strike left fist with right; turn curved hands inward.

3. Bird: Right thumb and index finger at mouth; open and close fingers a few times.

4. Soil: Rub fingertips together.

5. Jesus said, "Some of the seeds that the farmer scattered landed in good soil, but the soil was full of weeds. At first, those thorny weeds shaded the young plants as they began to grow. But as the thorny weeds grew bigger, they took the water and light the young plants needed. Soon, the weeds had taken everything. The young plants had all the life choked out of them. They could never bear fruit."

6. Some people began to wonder if the farmer would have any crop at all! But Jesus wasn't finished.

He said, "The rest of the seeds fell on soft, rich soil. They grew into an ENORMOUS crop. Some plants had produced thirty times what the farmer had planted, some grew sixty times as much, and some produced even a HUNDRED times more! The farmer was delighted when he saw the crop!"

7. The disciples looked at each other, puzzled. "What does this story mean?" they asked Jesus.

He answered, "The seed is like the Word of God. Any person who hears God's Word is like one of those kinds of soil. Some people never believe the Word of God at all. They are like the hard dirt where the seeds were snatched up and eaten by birds. Other people are like the shallow soil. These people hear and gladly believe God's Word at first! But when it becomes too hard to do what God wants, they forget all about God and His Word. The truth they heard dries right up and dies. People like the soil full of weeds are people who become very, very busy with anything and everything," Jesus continued. "The truth they heard is choked by their busyness. They soon forget all about God."

8. Then Jesus probably smiled. He said, "But people who hear and believe God's Word are like the GOOD soil. They grow when they learn from it. And as they grow, their lives show what they've learned about God. More people learn about God's truth because they see the good things in these people's lives! That's how God's Word grows GOOD FRUIT in people. People who hear and believe are like GOOD soil!"

5. Take: Sweep open right hand to form a fist.

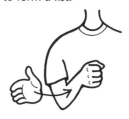

6. Grow: Right hand opens as it comes up through left.

7. Hear: Cup right ear; turn head to left.

8. Learn: Right fingertips on palm; fingers close as hand moves to forehead.

. . . .

Discussion Questions

What kinds of soil did Jesus talk about? (Hard. Shallow. Weedy. Good.) **What kinds of people are like the hard soil? like the shallow soil? like the weedy soil?** (Unbelieving. Quick to give up. Busy with other things. Forgetting God.) **What happened to the seeds in the good soil?** (They produced much fruit.)

When we know God's Word, it shows in our lives. When we read and obey God's Word, people can see our love for God and the ways we love Him. That's a great reason to celebrate!

Object Talk

Scripture Background
Leviticus 23:15-21

Materials
Bible with bookmark at Psalm 119:11, samples of different grains (barley, rice, rye, corn, rolled oats, wheat, wheat germ, cracked wheat flour, muesli cereal, puffed oat or rice cereal, etc.).

When we know God's Word, it shows in our lives by the good decisions we make and the right actions we take. One of the ways people in Bible times celebrated the Feast of Weeks was by bringing offerings of grains they had grown and harvested. Let's discover how these growing things remind us of obeying God's Word.

Lead the Activity

1. Show samples of different grains, passing samples around to students and allowing them to taste if desired. **Where do all these kinds of food come from?** (They are grown. You can make bread or cereal from them.) **These are grains. Unlike fruits or vegetables that also grow from the ground, grains are the seeds of plants, mostly different types of grass.**

2. **At the Feast of Weeks, also called Shavuot (shah-voo-OHT), the Hebrew word for "weeks," God's people celebrated and thanked God for the good things that grow from the earth. When we plant a seed and care for it by giving it light and water, the seed grows and produces grain. When we read and think about God's Word, it grows and produces good things in our lives. What are some of the good things that can grow out of our lives by studying God's Word?** (Courage to be honest. Kind ways to treat others. Patience. How to make good choices.)

Conclude

When we read God's Word and follow what it says, God helps us live the very best way. Read Psalm 119:11 aloud. **According to this verse, what should we do to keep from sinning? What do you think it means to hide God's Word in our hearts?** (Read God's Word and remember it.) **One important thing God's Word tells us about is how to become members of God's family.** Talk with students about becoming Christians (see "Leading a Child to Christ" on p. 253). Pray, thanking God for His Word and asking for His help in obeying it.

Additional Information for Older Students

The Feast of Weeks took place at the end of the barley harvest. Because the first sheaf of the barley harvest was to be dedicated, or given, to the Lord, the first day of the Feast of Weeks is called Firstfruits. Read Leviticus 23:9 aloud. **Until the dedication was made, no bread, grain or anything from the harvest could be eaten! The people wanted to give God the first and best part of their harvest.**

Active Game Center: Rhythm Relay

Materials

Bible, children's music CD and player.

Lead the Game

1. Group students into at least two even-numbered teams. Students form pairs within teams.

2. Demonstrate a grapevine step (moving sideways by bringing right foot behind left foot—see sketch). Students practice the step in pairs, holding their arm over their partners' shoulders as they try the step. After practice, students form teams again on one side of an open playing area.

3. Play children's music CD. At your signal, the first pair on each team takes grapevine steps to the opposite side of the playing area and back, tagging the next pair in line to repeat the action. When all students on a team have had a turn, volunteers from winning team answer one of the Discussion Questions below. Repeat relay as time permits.

When we know God's Word, it shows in our lives! The Hebrew people celebrated God's Word and His provision of food and crops for them during a harvest festival called the Feast of Weeks. For the Israelites, the Feast of Weeks was a time of joyous music and praising God.

Options

1. If you have space or can play this relay game outdoors, students form pairs and all pairs race each other at once.

2. Students may do steps as individuals rather than in pairs.

3. Play a cassette/CD of upbeat Hebrew music during the relay.

Discussion Questions

1. ***When might kids your age read and think about God's Word?*** (When hearing a Bible story at church. When reading a Bible story with parents.)

2. ***Who has helped you learn from God's Word?*** (Parents. Grandparents. Teachers.)

3. ***What do we learn from reading God's Word?*** (How to love and obey God. How to show His love to others. How to become members of God's family.)

Art Center: Grain Mosaics

Materials

Newspaper, grains and seeds, small containers, a square of cardboard or poster board and a pencil for each student, glue.

Prepare the Activity

Cover the work area with newspaper. Put grains and seeds into small containers.

Lead the Activity

1. Give each student a square of cardboard or poster board and a pencil. Students draw stick figures and objects showing ways they can obey God. Ask the Discussion Questions below to help students think of what to draw.

2. Students put glue over the stick figures and objects, placing seeds and grains on the glue. If time permits, students may fill in objects and backgrounds with additional seeds and grains.

Options

1. Provide a variety of colors of grains and seeds (popcorn, oats, barley, wheat berries, pinto or kidney beans, lentils, split peas, black beans, etc.), and if possible, use the grains brought in for this lesson's Celebration Object Talk.

2. Encourage students to fill in the background around their picture with contrasting colors of seeds and grains.

3. Instead of making pictures, younger students may simply glue grains and seeds in designs of their own choosing.

> *When we know God's Word, it shows in our lives. One of the ways it shows is when we obey God. Jesus said that God's Word is like a seed that grows to produce grain or fruit. Let's use seeds and grains to make pictures about ways we can obey God's Word.*

· ·

Discussion Questions

1. ***How might you obey the Bible command to help others?*** (Help parent with a task. Help a friend learn to play a sport better.)

2. ***When is a time you can obey God's Word by sharing with others?*** (Let a friend borrow a game. Give a snack to a brother or sister.)

3. ***When might you show love for God and His Word by obeying parents?*** (Turn off TV when asked. Do a chore without being reminded.)

"I have hidden your word in my heart that
I might not sin against you." Psalm 119:11

"I have hidden your word in my heart that

LIBRARY LOONIES!

The Challenge

Psalm 119:11

There are some very loony books at the library these days. Put the books in alphabetical order. (Hint: Number them in the circles on the spines.) Take the middle word from each title and write the words in order below to read the verse.

"

_____ _____ _____ _____ _____

_____ _____ _____ _____ _____ ."

Pentecost

God Sends the Holy Spirit

Bible Verse

Boldly and without hindrance he preached the kingdom of God and taught about the Lord Jesus Christ.
Acts 28:31

Bible Story Reference

Acts 2

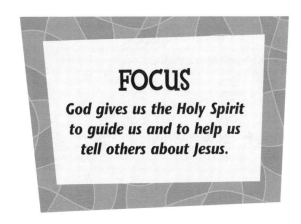

FOCUS
God gives us the Holy Spirit to guide us and to help us tell others about Jesus.

Teacher's Devotional

The Feast of Weeks was considered by ancient rabbis to be the official end of the Passover season; Passover had begun 50 days earlier. The Greek name for this holiday, Pentecost, means "fifty." But for us it is not an end at all. It is a continuation, a new reason to celebrate, for it is the day Jesus' promise of God's gift from heaven was fulfilled: The Holy Spirit came and the Church was born. That makes this day the Church's birthday!

Because the Holy Spirit was given at the end of the Feast of Weeks, the 120 followers of Jesus who were faithfully praying in an upstairs room had quite possibly made plans to make offerings at the Temple and participate in celebrations later that day. But what happened changed not only their religious and social schedules but also their whole lives!

The sound of a huge, violent wind came—not off the desert, not a hurricane from the ocean, but the sound of wind from heaven! The sound filled the room and certainly got everyone's attention! Then what looked like a flame separated into smaller flames. The flames indicated that the Holy Spirit had come; the power that accompanied the flames proved it!

As you celebrate the birthday of the Church with your students, take time to research the history of the ways God's Spirit has been active in the founding of your own church. Celebrate the fact that the book of Acts is still being written— right before your eyes in your own church!

Story Center

Materials
Bible.

Before the Story
Guide students to briefly practice signs for the underlined words.

Tell the Story
As you tell the story, lead students in responding as shown when you say the underlined words.

> **When have you heard a very big wind? How did it sound? What did the wind do?**
>
> **Today we'll hear about what happened when some people heard the sound of a HUGE wind.**

1. It had been 10 days since Jesus returned to heaven. His friends may have wondered, *What is going to happen now?* But then Jesus' friends <u>remembered</u> things Jesus had said to them. They <u>remembered</u> the instructions Jesus had given them.

2. "Do not leave Jerusalem," Jesus had told them. "<u>Wait</u> for the gift My Father promised you—the Holy Spirit. When the Holy Spirit comes, you will receive power so that you can tell people everywhere about Me."

   Jesus' friends remembered those words. Because they loved Jesus and wanted to obey Him, they stayed in Jerusalem together. They prayed and <u>waited</u>. And they prayed and <u>waited</u> some more!

3. Ten days later, the waiting was OVER. While Jesus' friends were all together praying, they heard a sound like a rushing, powerful <u>wind</u>. And even though it wasn't <u>windy</u> OUTSIDE, the sound of <u>wind</u> filled the whole house where they were! They looked up from their praying to see what was happening.

4. They looked at each other, amazed. What was THIS? Something that looked like fire was burning above each of their heads! The fire was a sign that God had sent His Holy Spirit, just as Jesus had said He would. This was too <u>WONDERFUL</u> to stay indoors! As Jesus' friends came outside, they saw a HUGE crowd of people coming toward them. These people had all heard the sound of the rushing wind, too.

1. Remember: Move right fist from forehead to top of left fist, thumbs touching.

2. Wait: Left hand in front of right, palms up, wiggle fingers.

3. Wind: Hold hands in front; move in unison along curved path.

4. Wonderful: Move open palms up and forward.

5. The HUGE crowd came together, following the sound to see what was going on! Then they heard another sound. They heard Jesus' friends <u>speaking</u> in many different languages! Many people in the crowd were visiting Jerusalem from other countries. They each heard Jesus' friends <u>speaking</u> the languages of their home countries. They stood there AMAZED. But other people just thought Jesus' friends were drunk.

5. Speak: Circular movement from mouth with right index finger.

6. Then Peter stood up. He began to <u>explain</u> the amazing things that were happening. He told the crowd that God was now keeping some of the promises He had made long ago in Old Testament times. Peter <u>explained</u> about Jesus and how He died to take the punishment for people's sins and had come back to life, so people didn't have to be afraid of dying anymore. They could become part of God's family.

6. Explain: With thumbs and index fingers touching, move hands alternately backward and forward.

7. Many people who were listening WANTED to be part of God's <u>family</u>. They asked Jesus' friends, "What shall we do?"

   Peter told them, "Turn away from doing wrong and be baptized in the name of Jesus Christ so that your sins will be forgiven. God will give you His gift of the Holy Spirit, too." And that day, about 3,000 people became part of God's <u>family</u>!

7. Family: With thumbs and index fingers touching, make outward circle until hands touch.

8. What a BIG family! And they loved each other in a BIG way! That love came from the Holy Spirit. God's Holy Spirit was God's birthday gift to His family to <u>give</u> them love, guide them and help them tell others about Jesus!

8. Give: Hands down and fingertips touching, flip hands forward and open, palms up.

• •

Discussion Questions

What were Jesus' friends doing when God sent the Holy Spirit? (Praying. Obeying Jesus.) **What did Jesus' friends hear? see?** (Sound of wind. What looked like fire.) **When Jesus' friends began to tell the people outside what had happened, what did the people notice?** (The words were in their own languages.)

   God's Holy Spirit is still with members of God's family. He guides us and gives us power to tell others about Jesus, just like He did when the Church was born. That's a great big reason to celebrate!

Object Talk

Scripture Background
Acts 2

Materials
Bible with bookmark at Acts 28:31, birthday candles; optional—small cake or cupcake, matches.

> The Holy Spirit was given to us by God in order to guide us and help us tell others about Jesus. Let's look at a way to remember the special day the Holy Spirit came to the disciples.

Lead the Activity

1. Display candles you brought. **How are candles used on birthdays? What do the number of candles on a birthday cake often show?** Volunteers tell. (Optional: Place candles in small cake or cupcake. Light candles and allow students to blow them out.)

2. **On one day every year, the birthday of God's Church is celebrated. This day is called Pentecost. The word "pentecost" means 50. Pentecost takes place 50 days after the Passover celebration. In Bible times, Jesus' disciples had come to Jerusalem after Jesus had gone to heaven. While they were there, God sent His Holy Spirit to the disciples. This day is celebrated as the beginning of God's Church.**

Conclude

The Holy Spirit is still with us, helping us to love and obey God. Read Acts 28:31 aloud. **What does it mean to do something "boldly and without hindrance"?** (Not to be afraid. To be brave and confident.) **This verse is talking about Paul. The Holy Spirit helped Paul tell others about Jesus. The Holy Spirit will help us, too! All we have to do is ask.** Pray, thanking God for His gift of the Holy Spirit and asking for His guidance and help as we tell others about Jesus.

• •

Additional Information for Older Students
The first Sunday after Pentecost is called Trinity Sunday. On this day, some churches celebrate the Holy Trinity, the fact that God is made up of three persons: God the Father, God the Son and God the Holy Spirit. One of the objects used to stand for the Holy Trinity is the candle, because a candle is made up of three parts: the wax, the wick and the flame. Students read Jesus' words about the Holy Spirit in John 15:26.

Active Game Center: Picture Hunt

Materials

Bible, old birthday cards, scissors, markers.

Prepare the Game

Cut the back off of each card, leaving only the front design.

Lead the Game

1. Ask volunteers to suggest sentences or phrases which describe the Holy Spirit ("Helps us" "Teaches us" "Guides us" "Sent from God" "Promised by Jesus"). As sentences or phrases are suggested, print them on separate birthday cards. Make enough cards so that there is a card for every two students. Repeat sentences or phrases as needed.

2. Students cut cards into two puzzle pieces.

3. Collect all puzzle pieces and mix them up. Then distribute puzzle pieces to students. At your signal, students race to match up their puzzle pieces. When students match pieces, they call out "Happy Birthday" and sit down. When all pieces have been matched, pair of students who first sat down read the message on their puzzle pieces aloud. Collect puzzle pieces and play again. Continue game as time permits.

> God gives us the Holy Spirit to guide us and to help us tell others about Jesus. When God first gave the Holy Spirit to Jesus' followers, the Church began as a place where people can learn about Jesus! Let's play a game to celebrate the birthday of the Church.

Options

1. Instead of using birthday cards, cut squares of a variety of styles of birthday wrapping paper.

2. After cards have been cut into puzzle pieces, keep one puzzle piece of each card and hide the other puzzle piece in your room. Give each student one puzzle piece. At your signal, each student hunts around the room to find the puzzle piece that fits his or her piece. After finding the piece, student calls out "Happy Birthday" and sits down.

• •

Discussion Questions

1. *Why did God send the Holy Spirit?* (To help members of His family love and obey Him.)

2. *What are some ways the Holy Spirit can help us?* (Guides us in knowing the right things to do. Reminds us of and helps us follow God's commands in the Bible. Helps us know the words to say when we tell others about Jesus.)

Art Center: Cupcake Art

Materials

Cupcakes, plastic knives, frosting, red sprinkles or candies, serving trays; optional—food coloring.

Prepare the Activity

Arrange to serve cupcakes to others in your church.

Lead the Activity

1. Students wash hands. **Pentecost is often celebrated with the color red! Let's see what kind of designs we can make on these cupcakes with red decorations. Then we'll serve the cupcakes to people in our church.**

> God gives us the Holy Spirit to guide us and to help us tell others about Jesus. The day when God first sent the Holy Spirit is called Pentecost and is also known as the time when the first church was formed. Today let's celebrate God's giving us the Holy Spirit and the birthday of the Church by decorating cupcakes!

2. Students use plastic knives to frost cupcakes and decorate them with red sprinkles or candies. (Optional: Students mix a few drops of food coloring into containers of frosting to make a variety of colors.) Students place completed cupcakes on serving trays and continue to frost and decorate as many cupcakes as time allows.

3. Students serve cupcakes to others in your church.

Options

1. Serve cupcakes to one or more adult or children's Sunday School classes or to the whole church. Students may also take home cupcakes to eat as a reminder of the birthday of the Church.

2. Bring a birthday candle to stick into each cupcake.

3. Frost sugar cookies instead of cupcakes.

• •

Discussion Questions

1. *What are some other red things that could help us celebrate the coming of the Holy Spirit?* (Balloons. Streamers. Flowers.)

2. *What happened when God first sent the Holy Spirit?* (The disciples spoke in different languages. Jesus' followers formed the first church.)

3. *Why did God send the Holy Spirit?* (To guide people and help them believe in Him. To help people remember what they know about God and to obey Him. To help people tell others about Jesus.)

"Boldly and without hindrance he preached the kingdom of God and taught about the Lord Jesus Christ." Acts 28:31

THE TALK OF THE TOWN!

Acts 28:31

The Challenge

"Boldly and without hindrance he preached the kingdom of God and taught about the Lord Jesus Christ."

All the words from the verse can be filled in the crossword grid. Are you up to the challenge?

2 Letters
he
of

3 Letters
and
and
God
the
the

4 Letters
Lord

5 Letters
about
~~Jesus~~

6 Letters
Boldly
Christ
taught

7 Letters
kingdom
without

8 Letters
preached

9 Letters
hindrance

Sabbath

God Creates the World

Bible Verse

Remember the Sabbath day by keeping it holy. Exodus 20:8

Bible Story Reference

Genesis 1—2:3

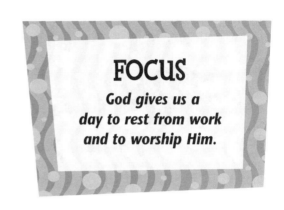

FOCUS

God gives us a day to rest from work and to worship Him.

Teacher's Devotional

All that God has made for us to live in and enjoy is certainly a gift worth celebrating, and today we focus on a gift that is closely linked to God's act of creation: the Sabbath. It's the first holiday in all of history, for it was a day of rest that God Himself took! He rested (or ceased from his work), not because He was tired, but because He wanted to enjoy what He had made.

He also did this as an example to His busy, busy creatures. He made us. He knows how we function and how easily we are buried in busyness, failing to see the beauty of what He has made and who He is. He gave us this day of rest, holiness and joy (as the Sabbath has traditionally been called) so that we would stop the work of the week and take time to think, wonder and contemplate the blessings that surround us and partake in loving worship of the One who has given all this to us. Jesus emphasized that the true purpose of the Sabbath was to benefit people (see Mark 2:27), not that people were to serve the needs of the Sabbath. It's a day meant for fellowship with Him as we worship and praise Him with others in our families and churches.

Before any other feast day or sacrifice was ever mentioned, God gave this holiday to Israel through Moses. Traditionally, the Sabbath begins Friday at sundown with the lighting of candles. A special meal and the speaking out of blessings of the members of one's family highlight the evening. The Sabbath ends at sundown on Saturday evening. While Jews celebrate the Sabbath on the seventh day of the week, Christians celebrate Sunday as their day of rest since Jesus' resurrection occurred on the first day of the week.

Take time this week to think about specific ways to incorporate God's gift of rest into your life. It's an often-neglected principle in our busy society. Our children would benefit from the extra time away from activity to enjoy time with God and with loved ones. It's a God-ordained time to celebrate. God knows we need it!

Story Center

Materials
Bible.

Before the Story
Guide students to briefly practice signs for underlined words.

Tell the Story
As you tell the story, lead students in responding as shown when you say the underlined words.

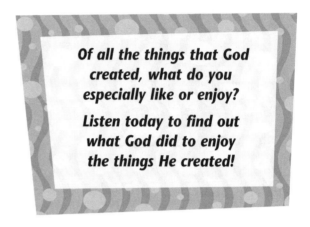

Of all the things that God created, what do you especially like or enjoy?

Listen today to find out what God did to enjoy the things He created!

1. Close your eyes and imagine what it might have been like before God made the world. There was nothing—no houses, no people, no animals, no sun or sky or land. Open your eyes. It was just <u>dark</u> and empty. But God was there! God decided to make something wonderful and beautiful in all that empty <u>darkness</u>.

2. So God said, "Let there be <u>light</u>!" What do you think happened then? <u>Light</u> shone all around! God called the <u>light</u> day and He divided the darkness from the <u>light</u> to make what He called night. That's what God did on the first day! God saw that it was GOOD.

   The next day, God said, "Let the sky and the water be made separate from each other." Now there was water below the sky and a sky that arched over the water. And that's what God did on the second day! What do you think God did next?

3. On the third day, God gathered the <u>water</u> together. He spoke, and the <u>water</u> moved around to form rivers and oceans. Once the <u>water</u> was moved around, the dry land appeared. Now there were mountains and hills, deep canyons and dry deserts. God had changed that empty darkness and shaped a beautiful world.

4. But God was not finished yet! There still was not anything on the earth that was ALIVE. The land and the sky and the waters were empty. Nothing was <u>growing</u> in all the earth.

   So God said, "Let there be all sorts of plants." Green grass <u>grew</u> and flowers bloomed! Trees of all shapes and sizes <u>grew</u>. Berry bushes and pumpkin vines <u>grew</u> fruit.

1. Dark: Cross palms downward in front of face.

2. Light: Open closed fists.

3. Water: Extend three fingers of right hand; touch mouth a few times.

4. Grow: Right hand opens as it comes up through left.

5. God saw all that He had done, and it was GOOD! Next, God made a bright light. He put it in the <u>sky</u> to shine during the day. We call that light the sun! He also made the moon and stars to shine in the <u>sky</u> at night. God did amazing things on the fourth day!

5. Sky: Right hand moves in arc over head.

On the fifth day, God filled the water and the <u>sky</u> with living creatures. He put fish and sharks and octopuses and whales into the oceans. Birds flew through the <u>sky</u>. Some birds were tiny; some birds were BIG. They were every color you can think of!

6. On the sixth day, God made land <u>animals</u>. He made little mice and middle-sized anteaters and laughing hyenas—and great big polar bears and water buffalo and even dinosaurs! Now the world was a hopping, buzzing, galloping, wiggling, lively place! This was all very wonderful, but the day was not over yet. The next thing God did was even more amazing than filling the earth with <u>animals</u>.

6. Animal: Keeping fingertips on chest, move hands back and forth.

7. God created a man. God called the man Adam. Then God made a woman called Eve. God made them different from the animals. They could think and they could make things; they could talk to each other and to God. God <u>loved</u> Adam and Eve. They were His special friends! Adam and Eve must have <u>loved</u> living in a beautiful garden that was full of the wonderful things God had made.

7. Love: Cross fists over heart.

8. Then God looked at the whole world He had created. It was exactly like He wanted it to be. What do you think God said about His world? He looked around at everything and said, "This is very <u>GOOD</u>!"

8. Good: Move right hand from mouth to palm up on left hand.

The wonderful work of creating the world was done. So God took time to enjoy the <u>good</u> things He had made! On the seventh day, He stopped His work. So that we can enjoy God and all that He has made for us, God later told humans that WE should rest one day out of every seven days, too!

• •

Discussion Questions

God used the word "good" to describe His creation. What words would you use to describe what God created? ("Wonderful." "Amazing." "Awesome.") **Why did God want people to rest?** (He made us and knows that we need rest and time to worship Him and the good things He made.)

God's love for us is so great, He gives us everything we need: a beautiful, wonderful world in which to live AND the time we need to enjoy it and to worship Him! What a celebration!

Sabbath

Object Talk

Scripture Background

Exodus 20:8-11; Leviticus 23:3; Deuteronomy 5:12-18

Materials

Bible with bookmarks at Exodus 20:8 and Leviticus 23:3, two white candles in candlesticks, matches or lighter.

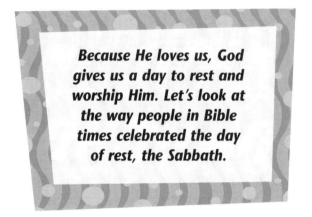

Because He loves us, God gives us a day to rest and worship Him. Let's look at the way people in Bible times celebrated the day of rest, the Sabbath.

Lead the Activity

1. **The Sabbath, the seventh day of the week, was the very first holiday God told His people to celebrate.** Read, or ask an older student to read, Leviticus 23:3. **In fact, God was the first to celebrate the Sabbath. What did God do on the seventh day after creating the world?** (He stopped His work and rested.) **The Hebrew word for the Sabbath is** *Shabbot* (shah-BAHT), **which means "to rest."**

2. **Traditionally, God's people worship God together and with their families by celebrating the Sabbath from Friday at sunset to Saturday at sunset.** Display candles in candlesticks and light the candles. **At every Sabbath celebration two candles are lit; and prayers, called blessings, are said. The blessings ask God to show His love and care to the people in the family. During the day-long Sabbath, God's people are to rest from all work and take time to celebrate God's love for them—especially shown by His creation of the world, His rescue of them from slavery in Egypt and all that He does for His people.**

Conclude

Read Exodus 20:8 aloud. **The Sabbath is called holy because it is a special day, a day that is set apart or different from all others. On the Sabbath, we honor and worship God and get the rest we need! Today, Christians all over the world celebrate this day of rest on Sunday, the first day of the week, as a way to joyfully remember that Jesus was raised from the dead on the first day of the week.** Pray, thanking God for His gift of the Sabbath to use to rest and worship Him. Blow out candles.

• •

Additional Information for Older Students

Traditionally, two loaves of a braided bread called *challah* (HAH-lah) **are eaten at the special Sabbath meal. These two loaves are reminders of the double amount of manna that God provided for the Israelites on the day before the Sabbath while they were traveling in the desert. God gave the extra manna so that the Israelites wouldn't have to work to gather manna on the Sabbath.** Students read Exodus 16:22,23. (Optional: Serve *challah* to students.)

Sabbath

Active Game Center: Toss and Rest

Materials

Masking tape, volleyball, stopwatch or watch with second hand; optional—inflatable beach ball or Nerf-type ball.

Prepare the Game

Make a masking-tape line across the center of the playing area.

Lead the Game

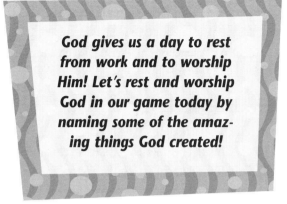

God gives us a day to rest from work and to worship Him! Let's rest and worship God in our game today by naming some of the amazing things God created!

1. Group students into two teams of varied ages and heights. Each team stands on one side of the masking-tape line, spreading out over the playing area.

2. **What are some of the things God created?** (Fish. Animals. Plants. Trees. Oceans.) **What did God do on the seventh day after He created everything?** (Rested.) **During our game today, we're going to name things God created for six rounds and then sit down and rest for the seventh round.**

3. Give volleyball to a student on one team. (Optional: Use inflatable beach ball or Nerf-type ball instead.) Student names a category of things God created (fish, animal, plant, water, etc.) and tosses the ball up in the air over the line to the other team. Student on the other team catches the ball and calls out an example of the category named (tuna, cow, lily, Atlantic Ocean, etc.). Student who caught the ball throws it back to the other team while naming a different category. After six tosses, students sit down and rest for 10 seconds. Repeat game as time allows. (Optional: While resting, students may pantomime God-created items for others to guess.)

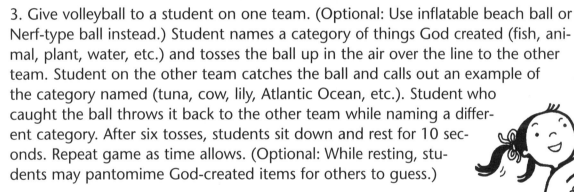

Options

1. For younger students, play with a balloon instead of a ball.

2. Play outside with a volleyball net.

3. For older students, list on paper what was created on each day of creation. Students name examples from categories in order for each round of the game.

• •

Discussion Questions

1. *What are some reasons to rest from work and to worship God?* (God knows that everyone needs to rest. To follow God's example of resting. To obey His command to remember the Sabbath.)

2. *What are some of the ways we rest and take time to worship God?* (Stay home from work and school. Go to church. Sing songs to praise God. Visit a sick or lonely person.)

3. *What's an example of a way your family rests and worships God?* (Read God's Word together. Pray together. Meet with other Christians.)

Sabbath

Art Center: Candleholders

Materials

Modeling clay, candles, nature items for decorating (small rocks, sticks, leaves or pine needles), paper plates; optional—play dough.

Lead the Activity

1. Give each student a fist-sized chunk of clay and a candle. (Optional: Distribute play dough instead.) Students form candleholders from clay (see sketches), pressing candles into the clay.

2. Students make prints in the clay with the nature items or stick items into the clay and leave them as decorative objects. Students place candleholders on paper plates in order to take candleholders home.

Options

1. Older students may use toothpicks to etch one of the phrases from the words of the traditional Hebrew Sabbath blessing into their candleholders: "Blessed are You, Lord our God, Ruler of the universe."

2. Send notes home to parents suggesting they light the candles as part of family prayer times at meals or bedtimes.

God gives us the Sabbath, a day to rest and worship Him. As part of their tradition, Jewish people light candles at their Sabbath celebration. Let's celebrate by making some candleholders.

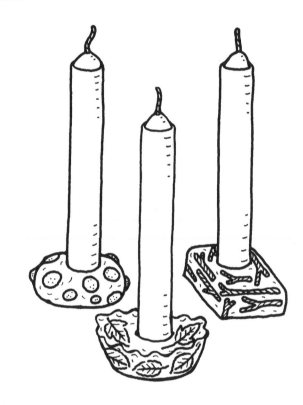

Discussion Questions

1. ***What work did God rest from on the very first Sabbath?*** (Creating the world.) ***What did God do on the Sabbath?*** (Enjoyed the creation He made.)

2. ***What did God create when He made the world? How can we enjoy those things as part of our Sabbath celebration?*** (Take a picnic to a forest or park and enjoy the trees and plants God made. Go to a garden and look at the growing things. Go to the zoo and look at all the different types of animals God made. Look at nature books.)

3. ***What are some other ways we can worship God on the Sabbath?*** (Worship God at church. Sing praise songs to God. Pray and read God's Word. Show our love for God by obeying Him.)

"Remember the Sabbath day by keeping it holy." Exodus 20:8

WHAT A WEEK!

Genesis 1—2:3

The Challenge

When God created the universe, He was busy! Use the letter and number under each line to find a picture of something God made. Write what's in the picture on the line.

Day 1 = _____ _____
         2-D   1-A

Day 2 = _____
         2-A

Day 3 = _____ _____ _____
         3-A   1-B   3-C

Day 4 = _____ _____
         3-B   2-C

Day 5 = _____ _____
         1-D   1-C

Day 6 = _____ _____
         3-D   2-B

Day 7 = REST!

	A	B	C	D
1	gives	me	and	rest
2	you	Him.	to	God
3	and	day	a	worship

The Super Challenge

Write the words from each picture on the blank lines in the order of the days of creation. You'll find a gift from God.

_____ _____ _____ _____

_____ _____ _____ _____ _____

TAKE NOTE!

Exodus 15:2

The Challenge → Make a joyful noise to the Lord! For this puzzle, you have to be able to read music(sort of!). Use the music-note code to write out the verse that will be music to your ears!

"THE LORD IS MY STRENGTH AND MY SONG, HE HAS BECOME MY SALVA- TION. HE IS MY GOD, AND I WILL PRAISE HIM."

PROPHET-SHARING

Isaiah 9:1-7; Micah 5:2-5

Ready or not, here He comes!

The Challenge → God chose men called prophets to tell people about Jesus before He was even born! Can you trace this prophet's journey to Bethlehem to see Jesus?

The Super Challenge → Use the map to write down a special message from God for you. The first clue is done for you. Follow the clues to finish your message.

4-F	5-A	2-B	1-D	2-E	3-A	4-D	3-E	3-C	5-F
Cele brate	the	birth	of	the	prom	ised	Sav	ior.	

GOING AROUND IN CIRCLES!

Luke 1:26-56

The Challenge → You might get dizzy doing this puzzle! Starting at the letter F in the balloon, go clockwise around the circle, skipping a letter each time. Write the letters you land on and you'll discover God's secret message to you, the same message the angel told Mary! Go around the circle twice until every letter is used.

FOR WITH GOD NOTHING WILL BE IMPOSSIBLE.

See Luke 1:37.

The Super Challenge → Find 10 things in the picture that aren't in the original story of Mary and the angel.

BALLOON   SODA CAN   SUITCASE   EYEGLASSES   UMBRELLA
FLAG   CELL PHONE   WATCH   AIRPLANE   SNEAKERS

SUPER STARS!

Luke 2:1-20

The Challenge → The birth of Jesus was heralded in the night sky by the star of Bethlehem. Unscramble the letters in each star cluster to read this celestial message.

REJOICE THE SAVIOR IS BORN

The Super Challenge → Circle at least 15 things that are different between each scene.
20 THINGS ARE DIFFERENT ON THE SECOND SCENE.

GO FLY A KITE!

Proverbs 2:6

The Challenge → Follow Ann's kite string to the end, picking up the words you pass as you go. Write down each word in order. Then follow Sam's string and finally Hadiki's string, doing the same. You will find an awesome verse!

" The Lord gives wisdom, and from his mouth come knowledge and understanding ."

LOST AND FOUND

Luke 15:3-7

The Challenge → The shepherd has lost a sheep, and like the Good Shepherd, he will search high and low for it. In the blanks, write the letters you find on the sheep. Read the hints for help. It's a word that tells what God feels for us.

C O M P A S S I O N

(Hints: The first letter is a curve. The sixth and seventh letters are the same consonant. The fourth letter has a straight line and a curve in it. The last letter is a consonant made of three straight lines.)

The Super Challenge → The shepherd is looking for one specific sheep. It looks just like the one in his picture. Can you find it? When you do, circle it.

ANSWER KEY
ANSWER KEY

UP CLOSE AND PERSONAL!

Matthew 26:17-30

The Challenge → Number Jesus' disciples alphabetically, and then write the word below each disciple in the matching blank. Read the words in order to discover some good news about Jesus. (Hint: Save the two disciples with the same name for last.)

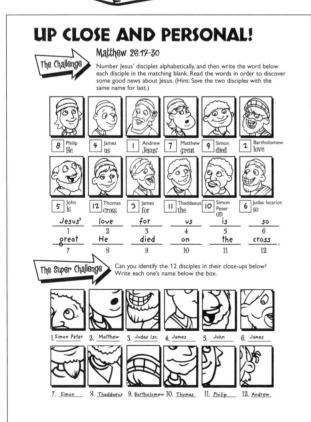

8 Philip **He**	4 James **us**	1 Andrew **Jesus'**	7 Matthew **great**	9 Simon **died**	2 Bartholomew **love**
5 John **is**	12 Thomas **cross**	3 James **for**	11 Thaddaeus **the**	10 Simon Peter **on**	6 Judas Iscariot **so**

Jesus'	love	for	us	is	so
1	2	3	4	5	6
great	He	died	on	the	cross
7	8	9	10	11	12

The Super Challenge → Can you identify the 12 disciples in their close-ups below? Write each one's name below the box.

1. Simon Peter 2. Matthew 3. Judas Isc. 4. James 5. John 6. James

7. Simon 8. Thaddaeus 9. Bartholomew 10. Thomas 11. Philip 12. Andrew

HOSANNA!

Mark 11:1-11

The Challenge → Can you solve the rebus? It's going to echo the shouts of joy that followers of Jesus made when He entered Jerusalem on a donkey.

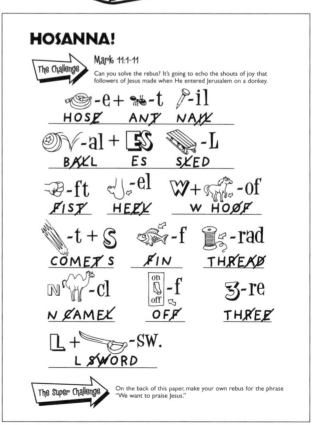

HOSE ANY NAIL

BALL ES SLED

FIST HEEL W HOOF

COMETS FIN THREAD

N CAMEL OFF THREE

L SWORD

The Super Challenge → On the back of this paper, make your own rebus for the phrase "We want to praise Jesus."

LIFE SUPPORT SYSTEM

1 John 5:11

 The Challenge — Solve this rebus telling about God's incredible gift to us.

"GOLD   HATS   G+5-F+N
         GIVEN

-B   -M+ /-I
BUS   METER NAIL

L + /-KN   -H   3rd -RD+S
L KNIFE,   HAND   THIRD S

L + /-KN   -FH
L KNIFE   FISH

-CH   -VE+S   -PGE
CHIN   HIVE S   SPONGE"

DIZZY SPELLS!

John 3:16

 The Challenge — These kids are getting dizzy trying to solve this puzzle! Start at the center of the spiral and fill in the missing vowels. After you do, memorize the verse. (Hint: Read the verse in your Bible for help.)

COMPUTER VIRUS!

Proverbs 3:5,6

 The Challenge — The computer has some sort of a glitch. When the verse was input, the words ran together in places and became difficult to read. Can you separate the words and write out the verse correctly?

"Trus tint he Lordwithal lyour
"Trust in the Lord with all your
hea rtand leanno ton youro wn
heart and lean not on your own
understa nding, inallyour
understanding; in all your
waysack nowle dgehi m,and
ways acknowledge him, and
hewi flma keyou r
he will make your
pat hsstr aight."
paths straight."

A-MAZE-ING LOVE

1 John 4:11

 The Challenge — "Dear friends, since God so loved us, we also ought to love one another."

Find your way through the maze by finding the words of 1 John 4:11 in order and then try to memorize the verse!

SHARD SEARCH

The Challenge > Cross off all the pieces of pottery with Y, T, K, S, A or L written on them.

How do you remember something? Write yourself a note? Tie a ribbon around your trowel? Put the date on a calendar? Ask your mom to remind you?

The Super Challenge > Unscramble the remaining letters to find a word:

REMEMBER

MADE IN THE SHADE!

Genesis 1:26-31

The Challenge > God created Adam and Eve and gave them the Garden of Eden to live in. Unscramble the words on each insect, and then write the word from each one below the matching insect at the bottom of the page. You'll find out why God created Adam and Eve and you!

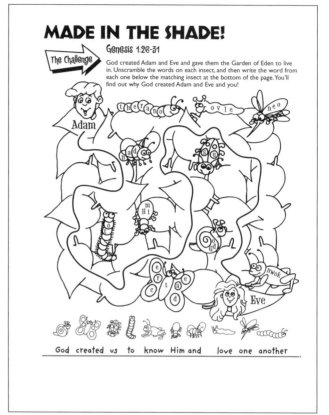

God created us to know Him and love one another

IN STEP WITH JESUS

Acts 10:43

"Everyone who believes in him receives forgiveness of sins through his name."

The Challenge > Start at the stone the boy is standing on and trace each letter of the verse until you reach Jesus at the end of the maze.

BUTTERFLY KISSES!

2 Corinthians 5:17

The Challenge > As you know, some caterpillars change into butterflies, just as if they were new creations. The caterpillars below are changing into butterflies. Find the hidden number on each butterfly and caterpillar and then write the words of the verse in order. Just for fun, circle the one caterpillar who hasn't changed into a matching butterfly!

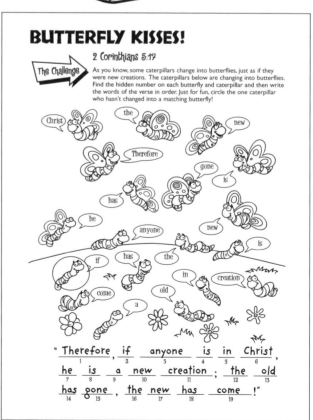

"Therefore, if anyone is in Christ,
he is a new creation; the old
has gone, the new has come!"

GOD'S GOT YOUR NUMBER!

The Challenge
Ephesians 4:32

Use the number code below to discover the words of the verse.

A=1	B=2	C=3	D=4	E=5	F=6
G=7	H=8	I=9	J=10	K=11	L=12
M=13	N=14	O=15	P=16	Q=17	
R=18	S=19	T=20	U=21	V=22	
W=23	X=24	Y=25	Z=26		

2.5 / 11.9.14.4 / 1.14.4 /
"Be Kind and

3.15.13.16.1.19.19.9.15.14.1.20.5
compassionate

20.15 / 15.14.5 / 1.14.15.20.8.5.18
to one another,

6.15.18.7.9.22.9.14.7
forgiving

5.1.3.8 / 15.20.8.5.18,
each other,

10.21.19.20 / 1.19 / 9.14
just as in

3.8.18.9.19.20 / 7.15.4
Christ God

6.15.18.7.1.22.5 / 25.15.21
forgave you."

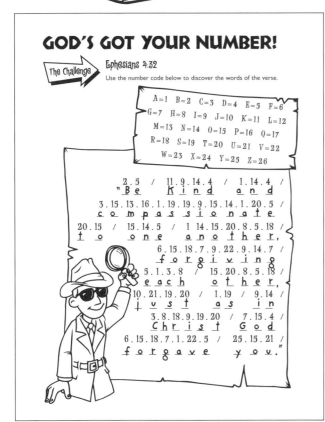

JONAH'S ALL WASHED UP!

The Challenge
Jonah

Break the code to discover what Jonah said in Jonah 1:9 about God.

I worship the Lord, the God of heaven.

The Super Challenge
You know what happened to Jonah. There's something fishy about all the stuff washed up on the beach. Eyeball the picture for a minute; then turn over the page to see how many items from the picture you can write down.

THE UNFORGIVING SERVANT

The Challenge
Matthew 18:21-35

When Peter asked Jesus how many times he should forgive someone, Jesus answered "seventy-seven times" (Matthew 18:22).* What did Jesus mean? Find out by writing on each blank line the letter that comes between the two letters below each line.

FORGIVE
EG NP QS FH HJ UW DF

OTHERS MORE
NP SU GI DF QS RT   LN NP QS DF

TIMES THAN
SU HJ LN DF RT   SU GI ZB MO

YOU CAN
XZ NP TV   BD ZB MO

COUNT!
BD NP TV MO SU

The Super Challenge
*Some Bible translations say "seventy times seven."
How many times would that be?   490
In order to forgive someone that many times in a year, how many times a week would you need to forgive? almost 10 times!

GOD FEEDS NEEDS!

The Challenge
Philippians 4:19

These papers have gotten all mixed up, but if you write the words from each paper in order on the numbered lines below, you will find the Bible verse.

"My God will meet all your needs according to his glorious riches in Christ Jesus."

FEAST ON THIS!

Nehemiah 8

The Challenge → God commanded the children of Israel to take some special time off to celebrate! Cool, huh? Unscramble the letters on the flags to find out what the Israelites said about God's command to feast and rest.

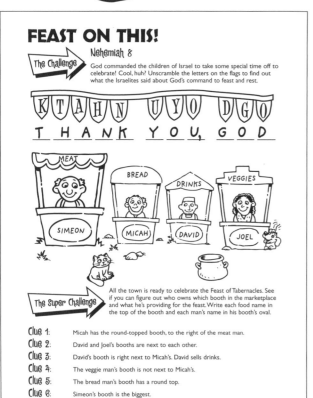

KTAHN UYO DGO

T H A N K   Y O U,   G O D

The Super Challenge → All the town is ready to celebrate the Feast of Tabernacles. See if you can figure out who owns which booth in the marketplace and what he's providing for the feast. Write each food name in the top of the booth and each man's name in his booth's oval.

Clue 1: Micah has the round-topped booth, to the right of the meat man.

Clue 2: David and Joel's booths are next to each other.

Clue 3: David's booth is right next to Micah's. David sells drinks.

Clue 4: The veggie man's booth is not next to Micah's.

Clue 5: The bread man's booth has a round top.

Clue 6: Simeon's booth is the biggest.

PINBALL PARLOR!

1 Chronicles 16:29

The Challenge → "Ascribe to the Lord the glory due his name. Bring an offering and come before him; worship the Lord."

Follow the arrows to find the path that goes through all the words of the verse.

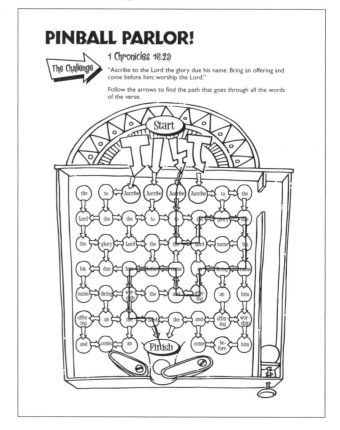

PICK-UP STICKS!

1 Kings 5—8

The Challenge → The builders of the Temple used a lot of logs to build the Temple. To solve this puzzle, pretend you're playing Pick-up Sticks. "Pick" up the log that's on top of the pile. Write the word on it in the first blank below. If you pick up the logs in the correct order, you'll spell out why we can worship God.

God will
always be
a protector
in your time
of trouble or
of need.

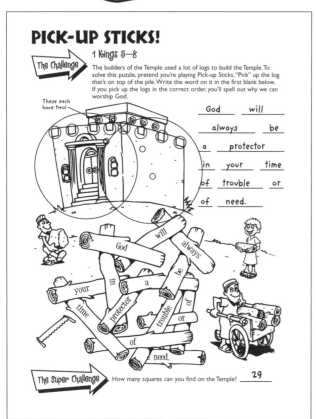

These each have two!

The Super Challenge → How many squares can you find on the Temple? ___29___

MUSIC TO YOUR EARS!

Psalm 33:11

The Challenge → The word of God is music to your ears. If you follow the instructions, you'll have something to sing about.

Step 1: Cross off the jobs.

Step 2: Cross out all the words with a double z in them.

Step 3: Everyone loves animals, but we don't need them here.

Step 4: You didn't eat your vegetables, so cross off all the desserts!

Step 5: Cross off the places to go.

Step 6: Finally, lose all the round things.

Step 7: Write the remaining words on the blank lines.

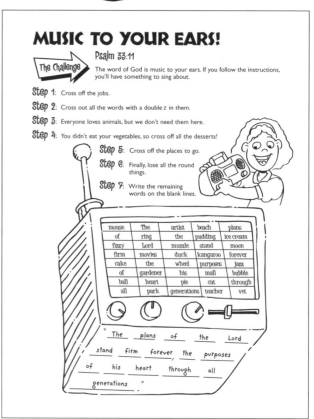

mouse	The	artist	beach	plans
of	ring	the	pudding	ice cream
fizzy	Lord	muzzle	stand	moon
firm	movies	duck	kangaroo	forever
cake	the	wheel	purposes	jazz
of	gardener	his	mall	bubble
ball	heart	pie	cat	through
all	park	generations	teacher	vet

" The plans of the Lord
stand firm forever the purposes
of his heart through all
generations "

I'LL PASS ON THAT!

Exodus 12

The Challenge

Lead Moses to the Hebrew family. Make sure you pass by all the sheep. Avoid the homes of the Egyptians marked by the pharaoh.

The Super Challenge

Write down the words as you pass them, and find what Moses wanted to tell the Hebrew family about God.

Whenever we need help, we can depend on God's power.

STORY TIME!

2 Chronicles 34—35

The Challenge

The kids have written the story of their time at the Passover feast, but they mixed up some of the words. Figure it out to read the story.

I [remember] when we went to the verPasso feast near the pleTem. [What] a day! The estpri
           Passover   _Temple_   _priest_
was excited about the goodness of [God]. He wore long elegant esrob of plepur and ldgo.
                       robes   _purple_   _gold_
After ingpray at the taral, he [has] tily came out and proclaimed the tionbracele. When he was
   praying   _altar_   _celebration_
[done], everyone chedeer and started to isepra God. At the feast, I ate lots of tableveges.
        cheered   _praise_   _vegetables_
After eating, we ceddan be [for] e the Lord. Later we ate the Passover mbla. My father was one
       danced   _lamb_
of the erssing. It was a eatgr day. It was the rstfi time the Passover had been celebrated since
   singers   _great_   _first_
Samuel the phetpro was alive. [You] should have seen it! I still had vense days of fun [and] the
   prophet   _seven_
astFe of Unleavened eadBr to enjoy. [Praise] God. I love [Him] !
Feast   _Bread_

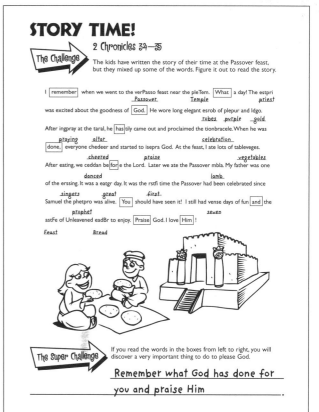

The Super Challenge

If you read the words in the boxes from left to right, you will discover a very important thing to do to please God.

Remember what God has done for you and praise Him.

BOOK 'EM

Psalm 119:66

The Challenge

"Teach me knowledge and good judgment, for I believe in your commands."

Use the words of the verse to get from start to finish. Don't jump over any book or cross over any book. It can be tricky because the words are repeated on more than one book.

LIBRARY LOONIES!

Psalm 119:11

The Challenge

There are some very loony books at the library these days. Put the books in alphabetical order. (Hint: Number them in the circles on the spines.) Take the middle word from each title and write the words in order below to read the verse.

" _I_ _have_ _hidden_ _your_ _word_ _in_ _my_
heart _that_ _I_ _might_ _not_ _sin_ _against_ _you_ ."

THE TALK OF THE TOWN!

The Challenge

Acts 28:31

"Boldly and without hindrance he preached the kingdom of God and taught about the Lord Jesus Christ."

All the words from the verse can be filled in the crossword grid. Are you up to the challenge?

2 Letters
he
of

3 Letters
and
and
God
the
the

4 Letters
Lord

5 Letters
about
Jesus

6 Letters
Boldly
Christ
taught

7 Letters
kingdom
without

8 Letters
preached

9 Letters
hindrance

WHAT A WEEK!

The Challenge

Genesis 1—2:3

When God created the universe, He was busy! Use the letter and number under each line to find a picture of something God made. Write what's in the picture on the line.

Day 1 = <u>light</u> <u>day/night</u>
         2-D   1-A

Day 2 = <u>clouds/water</u>
         2-A

Day 3 = <u>trees</u> <u>fruit/veggies</u> <u>flowers</u>
       3-A   1-B   3-C

Day 4 = <u>sun</u> <u>moon/stars</u>
       3-B   2-C

Day 5 = <u>fish</u> <u>birds</u>
        1-D   1-C

Day 6 = <u>animals</u> <u>people</u>
        3-D   2-B

Day 7 = REST!

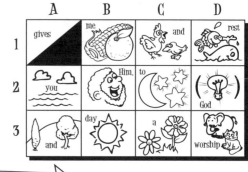

The Super Challenge

Write the words from each picture on the blank lines in the order of the days of creation. You'll find a gift from God.

<u>God</u> <u>gives</u> <u>you</u> <u>and</u> <u>me</u>
<u>a</u> <u>day</u> <u>to</u> <u>rest</u> <u>and</u> <u>worship</u> <u>Him.</u>

Leading a Child to Christ

One of the greatest privileges of serving in Sunday School is to help children become members of God's family. Some children, especially those from Christian homes, may be ready to believe in Jesus Christ as their Savior earlier than others. Ask God to prepare the children in your class to receive the good news about Jesus and prepare you to communicate effectively with them.

Talk individually with children. Something as important as a child's personal relationship with Jesus Christ can be handled more effectively one-on-one than in a group. A child needs to respond individually to the call of God's love. This response needs to be a genuine response to God—not because the child wants to please peers, parents or you, the teacher.

Follow these basic steps in talking simply with children about how to become members of God's family. The evangelism booklet *God Loves You!* (available from Gospel Light) is an effective guide to follow. Show the child what God says in His Word. Ask the questions suggested to encourage thinking and comprehension.

1. God wants you to become His child. (See John 1:12.) **Do you know why God wants you in His family?** (See 1 John 4:8.)

2. You and all the people in the world have done wrong things. (See Romans 3:23.) **The Bible word for doing wrong is "sin." What do you think should happen to us when we sin?** (See Romans 6:23.)

3. God loves you so much He sent His Son to die on the cross for your sins. Because Jesus never sinned, He is the only One who can take the punishment for your sins. (See 1 Corinthians 15:3; 1 John 4:14.) **The Bible tells us that God raised Jesus from the dead and that He is alive forever.**

4. Are you sorry for your sins? Do you believe Jesus died to be your Savior? If you do believe and you are sorry for your sins, God forgives all your sins. (See 1 John 1:9.)

When you talk to God, tell Him that you believe He gave His Son, Jesus Christ, to take your punishment. Also tell God you are sorry for your sins. Tell Him that He is a great and wonderful God. It is easy to talk to God. He is ready to listen. What you are going to tell Him is something He has been waiting to hear.

5. The Bible says that when you believe in Jesus, God's Son, you receive God's gift of eternal life. This gift makes you a child of God. This means God is with you now and forever. (See John 3:16.)

Give your pastor the names of those who make decisions to become members of God's family. Encourage the child to tell his or her family about the decision. Children who make decisions need follow-up to help them grow in Christ.

NOTE: The Bible uses many terms and images to express the concept of salvation. Children often do not understand or may develop misconceptions about these terms, especially terms that are highly symbolic. (Remember the trouble Nicodemus, a respected teacher, had in trying to understand the meaning of being "born again"?) Many people talk with children about "asking Jesus into your heart." The literal-minded child is likely to develop strange ideas from the imagery of those words. The idea of being a child of God (see John 1:12) is perhaps the simplest portrayal the New Testament provides.

Bible Story Index and Bible Verse Index

Honor Your
Sunday School Teachers

**On Sunday School Teacher Appreciation Day
the Third Sunday in October**

**SUNDAY SCHOOL
TEACHER
APPRECIATION DAY**
Third Sunday in October

Churches across America are invited to set aside the third Sunday in October as a day to honor Sunday School teachers for their dedication, hard work and life-changing impact on their students. That's why Gospel Light launched **Sunday School Teacher Appreciation Day** in 1993, with the goal of honoring the 15 million Sunday School teachers nationwide who dedicate themselves to teaching the Word of God to children, youth and adults.

Visit **www.mysundayschoolteacher.com** to learn great ways to honor your teachers on Sunday School Teacher Appreciation Day and throughout the year.

NOMINATE YOUR TEACHERS
FOR SUNDAY SCHOOL TEACHER
OF THE YEAR!
**Winner Receives a Dream Vacation
to Hawaii!**

An integral part of Sunday School Teacher Appreciation Day is the national search for the **Sunday School Teacher of the Year.** This award was established in honor of Dr. Henrietta Mears— a famous Christian educator who influenced the lives of such well-known and respected Christian leaders as Dr. Billy Graham, Bill and Vonette Bright, Dr. Richard Halverson and many more.

You can honor your Sunday School teachers by nominating them for this award.
If one of your teachers is selected, he or she will receive **a dream vacation for two to Hawaii,** plus free curriculum, resources and more for your church!

Nominate your teachers online at **www.mysundayschoolteacher.com** or call the Sunday School Teacher Appreciation Day hotline—**1-800-354-4224**—to receive more information.

Sponsored by

Gospel Light

*Helping you honor Sunday School teachers,
the unsung heroes of the faith.*

Partners

More Great Resources from Gospel Light

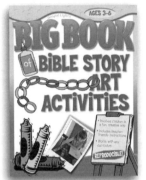

The Big Book of Bible Story Art Activities for Ages 3 to 6
Young children will love hearing favorite Bible stories as they enjoy creative art activities. Instructions for making puppets, collages, chalk art, friendship bracelets and more are provided to help children create Bible story art. Reproducible, perforated pages.
ISBN 08307.33086

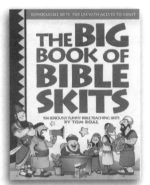

The Big Book of Bible Skits
Tom Boal

104 seriously funny Bible-teaching skits. Each skit comes with Bible background, performance tips, prop suggestions, discussion questions and more. Ages 10 to adult. Reproducible.
ISBN 08307.19164

The Really Big Book of Kids' Sermons and Object Talks with CD-ROM
This reproducible resource for children's pastors is packed with 156 sermons (one a week for three years) that are organized by topics such as friendship, prayer, salvation and more. Each sermon includes an object talk using a household object, discussion questions, prayer and optional information for older children. Reproducible.
ISBN 08307.36573

The Big Book of Volunteer Appreciation Ideas
Joyce Tepfer

This reproducible book is packed with 100 great thank-you ideas for teachers, volunteers and helpers in any children's ministry program. An invaluable resource for showing your gratitude!
ISBN 08307.33094

The Big Book of Christian Growth
Discipling made easy! 306 discussion cards based on Bible passages, and 75 games and activities for preteens. Reproducible.
ISBN 08307.25865

The Big Book of Bible Skills
Active games that teach a variety of Bible skills (book order, major divisions of the Bible, location references, key themes). Ages 8 to 12. Reproducible.
ISBN 08307.23463

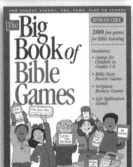

The Big Book of Bible Games
200 fun, active games to review Bible stories and verses and to apply Bible truths to everyday life. For ages 6 to 12. Reproducible.
ISBN 08307.18214

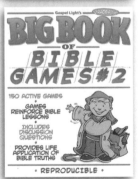

The Big Book of Bible Games #2
150 active games—balloon games, creative team relays, human bowling, and more—that combine physical activity with Bible learning. Games are arranged by Bible theme and include discussion questions. For grades 1 to 6. Reproducible.
ISBN 08307.30532

Gospel Light
God's Word for a Kid's World!

To order, visit your local Christian bookstore or www.gospellight.com